Reading Strategies and Practices

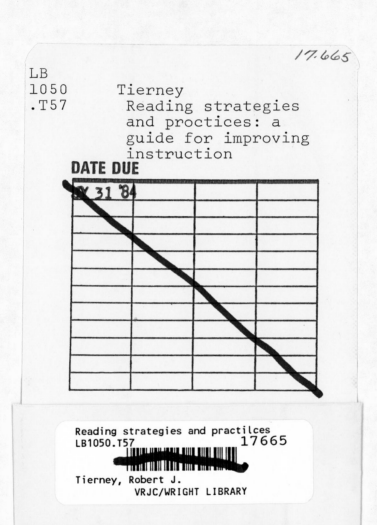

Reading Strategies and Practices

A Guide for Improving Instruction

Robert J. Tierney
University of Arizona

John E. Readence
University of Georgia

Ernest K. Dishner
University of Northern Iowa

Allyn and Bacon, Inc.
BOSTON LONDON SYDNEY TORONTO

[redacted]

Library of Congress Cataloging in Publication Data
Tierney, Robert J.
Reading strategies and practices.

Bibliography: p.
Includes index.
1. Reading—Textbooks. I. Readence, John E., 1947- joint author. II. Dishner, Ernest K., 1943- joint author. III. Title.
LB1050.T57 428'.4'07 79-19569
ISBN 0-205-06717-4

Managing Editor: Robert Roen
Preparation Buyer: Linda Card

Printed in the United States of America.

[redacted]

Robert J. Tierney is currently Associate Professor of Reading at the University of Arizona. He received his M.Ed. and Ph.D. in Reading from the University of Georgia. A teacher, consultant, and researcher in both the United States and Australia, Dr. Tierney has authored numerous articles dealing with theory, research, and practice. In 1979–1980 he was a visiting research professor at the Center for the Study of Reading at the University of Illinois, Urbana-Champaign. Over the past few years, his major interest has focused upon theory and practice related to teaching reading comprehension.

John E. Readence received his M.A. at Ohio State University and his Ph.D. in reading education at Arizona State University. A teacher at both the secondary and college levels, and a consultant for numerous school districts, Dr. Readence has published many articles in the education field. He has held the positions of Assistant Professor at Ohio University, Coordinator of Reading/Language Arts at Kansas State University and currently serves as Assistant Professor of Education at the University of Georgia.

Ernest K. Dishner received his M.A. at East Tennessee State University and his Ed.D. in reading education at the University of Georgia. Having taught at the elementary, high school, and college levels, Dr. Dishner has also authored a variety of articles and acted as a consultant for a number of school districts. He has held the positions of Assistant Professor at Arizona University, Associate Professor, Director of the Reading Center and Chairman of the Division of Educational Services at Delta State University, and is currently Professor and Chair of the Department of Curriculum and Instruction, University of Northern Iowa.

Contents

Preface

Reading Strategies and Practices: A Guide for Improving Instruction presents the reader with a reference work of strategies and practices designed to meet the reading needs and abilities of students. Thus this text has not been conceived of as a traditional reading methods textbook. Instead, it is a compendium of instructional techniques presenting as honestly as possible several common and significant strategies and practices.

As designed, the compendium affords an examination and evaluation of selected instructional strategies and practices. To this end the text is intended to be read selectively and critically. The reader is meant to select from among the units and strategies those they wish to review, and their review is meant to entail critical evaluation. The purpose, rationale, limitations, and steps for implementation are presented; and answers are forthcoming to such questions as: With whom and when are the strategies and practices most appropriate? What are some of the problems with the strategies and practices? Where can I learn more about these strategies? How can I use these strategies diagnostically? How can I improve my effectiveness as a teacher?

Reading Strategies and Practices is expected to stimulate reflection, discussion, evaluation, and intelligent selection of instructional procedures. To this end, then, *Reading Strategies and Practices* should prove an invaluable resource for all persons connected with reading improvement—teachers, teacher aides, tutors, volunteers, supervisors, principals, and university personnel.

Here are some remarks by the authors . . .

With the completion of this book, I, as an author, reflect and wonder how it will be received. Will the reader recognize that, as a compendium, strategies and practices were included regardless of biases? Will the reader recognize that an attempt was made to represent strategies and practices honestly and accurately? Will the reader reflect on the questions raised within the cautions and comments section? Will the reader realize that the cautions and comments sections afforded my co-authors and me an opportunity to express a point of view?

Among the readers of this book will be many friends and colleagues who have nurtured me through this and other endeavors. Thank you for your influence. I appreciate our shared faiths and hopes. To my co-authors, thank you for the fellowship this project provided.

RJT

Working on this text with my co-authors has provided me the rare opportunity to grow both as a professional and as a person. Though my thoughts may have changed since the completion of this text, the work which has been put into it has been well worthwhile and an experience I wish my fellow reading professionals may be lucky enough to have. I sincerely hope that the reading of this text inspires teachers to pause and reflect about their students and the teaching of reading as its writing has done me.

I wish to express my sincere thanks to Rob and Ernie, my co-authors, for the opportunity they have given me. Special mention goes to my wife, Jo; my daughter, Dawn; my father; and the rest of my family for the love and support they have given me.

JER

Anyone involved in the writing of a professional text cannot avoid learning a tremendous amount from the experience. As my own professional career continues to move in the direction of administration in higher education, my opportunities to participate in writing projects of this type will become fewer; therefore, I am especially pleased to have shared this writing experience with two very competent friends. It is my hope that you will find this work a valuable addition to your professional library. We invite your reactions, both general and specific, as we now begin work on what, hopefully, will be the next edition of this text.

I would like to take this opportunity to thank countless teachers, administrators, colleagues, secretaries, and students with whom I have worked over the years. My very special thanks go to Allie Lou Silbreath, a master teacher, who introduced me to the world of reading education, and to Ira Aaron, a master organizer and administrator, who provided me with numerous opportunities to develop and refine my own professional skills. Finally, I am indebted to the Georgia Bulldogs, the Arizona State Sun Devils, and the Lady Statesmen of Delta State University for occasional but very entertaining R and R, a must for all professional workaholics.

EKD

Finally, we, the authors, would like to extend our appreciation to the Allyn and Bacon staff who worked with us on this manuscript. To Bob Roen, especially, we express our thanks for his faith in us and this book.

RJT
JER
EKD

Reading Strategies and Practices

Introduction

How to Use This Book

INTENDED PURPOSES

There are certain purposes that the authors do not intend in this volume, namely, to suggest that users of this text change strategies or practices as they might change clothes. Likewise, the authors do not expect our readers to become familiar with all of the strategies or practices presented in the text, nor do the authors even advocate reading the text from cover to cover.

Rather, the purpose of this volume is to afford the reader an active role in examining and evaluating instructional techniques. To this end, the text should be read selectively and reflectively. Readers should select from the units and strategies those they wish to review and to critically evaluate.

HOW IS THIS BOOK ORGANIZED?

For organizational purposes the text is divided into an Introduction and three parts. The Introduction is designed to aid the reader in using the text book. The authors delineate their intent, and provide recommendations for using various strategies and practices. Part One comprises the major portion of the book. It consists of eight units under which the various strategies and practices have been classified. The eight units are as follows:

Unit One: Lesson Frameworks and Strategies for Improving Comprehension

Unit Two: Strategies for Content Area Reading and the Improvement of Study Skills

Unit Three: Strategies and Practices for Teaching Reading as a Language Experience

Unit Four: Recreational Reading Strategy

Unit Five: Oral Reading Strategies and Practices

Unit Six: Strategies for Improving Word Identification
Unit Seven: Multisensory Strategies for Teaching Reading
Unit Eight: Practices for Individualizing Reading

Some readers may disagree with the separation of teaching strategies and practices into these strands. This breakdown is intended as a viable method of organization and not suggested as a "divinely inspired" division of reading instruction or curriculum.

In addition to the teaching strategies and practices enumerated in Part One, the authors present two unique parts. Part Two explains and illustrates how teachers might use teaching strategies for various diagnostic purposes. The authors also provide a description of the diagnostic use of selected strategies, illustrated with examples of diagnostic analyses of actual student responses to these strategies. Part Three deals with the topic of examining teacher effectiveness. Examples of observational methods, self-appraisal methods, and needs assessment methods are presented.

USING THE PARTS

Using Part One

Part One is the core and bulk of the text. It includes eight units detailing over thirty strategies and practices. As an aid to examining and evaluating these techniques, Part One provides the reader with an overview for each unit and with a consistent organizational pattern. The following describes how these aids might be used.

Unit Overview

At the beginning of each unit in Part One, as well in the beginning of the last two parts of the book, an overview provides an introduction to the various strategies and practices presented in that section. This overview serves three essential purposes:

1. Since selected strategies only have been included within the various units, the overview will provide information on the basis for selecting strategies
2. Since several strategies could be classified in more than one unit, the overview will provide information on the basis for the present classification
3. The overview will provide the reader with a brief orientation, which will enable purposeful reading of each section and thus will facilitate the evaluation, comparison, and intelligent selection of strategies and practices or their adaptations

Strategies and Practices

In an attempt to detail the major features of the various strategies and practices, the discussion of each adopts the following framework:

Purpose
Rationale
Intended Audience
Description of Procedures
Cautions and Comments

Where further information might be desired, each unit provides an annotated list of references to guide readers in their research.

Using Part Two

Part Two includes various teaching strategies suggested as means of directing learning in various settings. Part Two selects from among the teaching strategies described in Part One and details their use diagnostically. Accordingly, there is a shift in emphasis and format. Namely, Part Two provides the reader an opportunity to examine the potential utility of selected strategies within the framework of analyzing the actual responses of students. The section begins with an overview, a discussion of the general diagnostic purposes teaching strategies might serve, and proceeds with a description of the specific use of selected strategies. In other words, Part Two provides an opportunity to review the potential utility of selected teaching strategies within the framework of diagnostic teaching. As such it gives the reader a capsulated view of both diagnostic teaching and the possible use of selected strategies.

Using Part Three

Part Three is different in format, content, and intent from either Part One or Part Two. It goes beyond teaching strategies to an examination of teacher appraisal strategies. This part is rather restricted in scope, but it does afford a description of strategies for improving teacher effectiveness. The reader interested in teacher self-appraisal should find this chapter interesting and unique. It provides a brief overview of teacher appraisal and gives observation methods, self-appraisal devices, and needs assessment.

PART 1

Strategies and Practices

1

Lesson Frameworks and Strategies for Improving Comprehension

UNIT OVERVIEW

The Unit and Its Theme

The basic goals of reading are to enable children to gain an understanding of the world and of themselves, to develop appreciations and interests, and to find solutions to their personal and group problems. Logically, comprehension should be considered the heart of reading instruction, and the major goal of that instruction should be the provision of learning activities that will enable students to think about and react to what they read—in short, read for meaning.

The Strategies

The present unit describes six strategies for the improvement of reading comprehension. Four of them deal exclusively with this goal. Two of the six strategies, the Directed Reading Activity and the Directed Reading-Thinking Activity, may serve as lesson frameworks. These strategies also deal with reading comprehension, but not exclusively. Combined with related activities (for example, word-recognition skill building), the Directed Reading Activity and the Directed Reading-Thinking Activity assume more of the character of "total" reading lessons.

ReQuest Procedure

The ReQuest Procedure uses a reciprocal questioning technique in an attempt to encourage students to formulate their *own* questions about material and thereby learn purposeful, thoughtful reading. The ReQuest Procedure can be applied to either a reading passage or a picture, and it is suggested for use with students at all levels.

Cloze Techniques

Involving the systematic replacement of words deleted from a passage, the cloze technique, now in widespread use as a teaching and a testing tool, is suggested for use with students at various levels. This unit discusses various adaptations of this technique for the improvement of reading comprehension.

REAP Technique

Designed to improve students' analytical reading skills, REAP also results in improved writing and study skills. The strategy consists of four basic steps: *R*ead, *E*ncode, *A*nnotate, *P*onder; thus, the resulting acronym—REAP.

Guided Reading Procedure

Incorporating the techniques of unaided recall of facts, self-correction, recognition of implicit questions, organization of ideas, and brief quizzes, the Guided Reading Procedure attempts to improve attitudinal and skill aspects of reading comprehension. While the Guided Reading Procedure can be used with children at various levels, it seems best suited for grades three and above.

Directed Reading Activity (DRA)

Found extensively in the guides accompanying most basal readers, the Directed Reading Activity is probably the most widely used framework for a "total" reading lesson. There are five basic steps that constitute a DRA. These steps provide the structure for the improvement of a wide spectrum of reading skills—the most important of which is comprehension. This strategy may be applied to reading selections varying in both length and readability and is suggested for use with students at all grade levels.

Directed Reading-Thinking Activity (DR-TA)

Assuming critical reading performance requires the reader to become skilled at determining purposes for reading, the Directed Reading-Thinking Activity emphasizes that the reader declares his or her own purposes for reading. As with the DRA, the Directed Reading-Thinking Activity may be applied to reading selections varying in both length and readability and is suggested for use with students at all grade levels.

Utilization

These comprehension strategies are not ends in themselves. The success or failure of a strategy remains contingent upon:

1. A thorough understanding of the intent and procedures of a strategy
2. A teacher's ability to select and adapt a strategy to the needs of students and to the material at hand

The following descriptions of strategies can help meet the needs of the first contingency.

THE REQUEST PROCEDURE

Purpose

The ReQuest Procedure (Manzo, 1968) is designed to encourage students to:

1. Formulate their own questions about the material they are reading and develop questioning behavior
2. Adopt an active inquiring attitude to reading
3. Acquire reasonable purposes for reading
4. Improve their independent reading comprehension skills

Rationale

Manzo, the originator of the ReQuest procedure, suggests that while teacher questioning and purpose setting are important to reading comprehension, of greater importance is the development of the students' abilities to ask their own questions and to set their own purposes for reading. He suggests that these skills facilitate the students' acquisition of an active, inquiring attitude and their ability to examine alternatives and originate information. These things he considers essential if students are to transfer problem-solving involvement to different contexts.

Intended Audience

ReQuest is suitable for use with students at levels ranging from kindergarten to college. While originally devised for use on a one-to-one basis, it can also work with groups of up to approximately eight persons.

Description of Procedures

In the ReQuest procedure an individual student and teacher silently read sections of a selection and then take turns asking and answering each other's questions about that selection. The teacher's function is to model good questioning behavior, to provide feedback to the student about his or her questions, and to assess whether the students have established reasonable purposes for independently completing the passage.

There are six steps teachers should follow in using the ReQuest procedure. These are:

1. Preparation of material
2. Development of readiness for the strategy
3. Development of student questioning behaviors
4. Development of student predictive behaviors
5. Silent reading activity
6. Follow-up activities

1. Preparation of Material

Preparation of the material entails previewing the selection for the purpose of:

a. Selecting material at an appropriate level for the student
b. Selecting material appropriate for making predictions
c. Identifying appropriate points within the selection where the student could plausibly make predictions

2. Development of Readiness for the Strategy

Manzo suggests the following protocol and guidelines as those appropriate for beginning a ReQuest session.

> The purpose of this lesson is to improve your understanding of what you read. We will each read silently the first sentence. Then we will take turns asking questions about the sentence and what it means. You will ask questions first, then I will ask questions. Try to ask the kinds of questions a teacher might ask in the way a teacher might ask them.
>
> You may ask me as many questions as you wish. When you are asking me questions, I will close my book (or pass the book to you if there is only one between us). When I ask questions, you close your book. (Manzo, 1969, p.124)

The teacher might also explain these points during or prior to the session: each question deserves to be answered fully; "I don't know" as an answer is unacceptable; unclear questions are to be rephrased; and uncertain answers should be justified by reference to the text. In addition, it may be necessary at times to introduce some of the vocabulary contained in the selection and/or develop some background for understanding the passage. For example, the teacher may need to give the student oral familiarity with some of the more difficult words in the selection. Also, in order to develop some background for understanding the passage, the teacher might alert the student to the basic concepts involved by a brief and general discussion of the title.

Therefore in introducing the ReQuest procedure, the teacher should be aware of the need to:

a. Build student interest in the procedure
b. Introduce selected vocabulary
c. Develop some background for understanding the passage
d. Provide the student with an understanding of the rules of ReQuest

3. Development of Student Questioning Behaviors

At this point, both the teacher and the student participate in the reciprocal questioning procedure. As Manzo's protocol suggests, this procedure entails:

a. *Joint silent reading.* Both the student and teacher read the first sentence of the selection
b. *Student questioning.* The teacher closes his or her book, and the student questions the teacher. The teacher responds as well as possible, reinforces appropriate questioning behavior and, if necessary, requests rephrasing of unclear questions
c. *Exchange of roles.* The student finishes questioning and removes his or her copy of the material. Then the teacher questions the student

Throughout this phase, the teacher exhibits good questioning behavior and provides feedback to the student about the student's questions. When taking the role of questioner, the teacher should endeavor to extend the student's thinking. To this end, the teacher might use various types of questions, including questions that build upon prior questions and require the student to integrate information. When responding to the student's questions, the teacher could use both verbal and nonverbal reinforcement. For example, a student's question might be reinforced with a pat on the back and a statement such as "That's a great question. I really have to . . . " or, "I hope I can ask questions that tough which will make you . . . "

4. Development of Student Predictive Behaviors

At an appropriate point in the procedure (i.e., when the student has read enough to make a prediction about the rest of the material), the exchange of questions is terminated. Assuming the role of agitator, the teacher attempts to elicit predictions and validations from the student. At this point, the teacher might ask, "What do you think will happen? . . . Why do you think so? . . . Read the line that proves it." It may prove helpful to develop a list of suggested predictions and a ranking from most likely to least likely.

If the predictions and verifications are reasonable, the teacher and student can move to the next step–silent reading activity. If the predictions are unreasonable, the teacher and student may continue reading and exchanging questions until another opportunity to elicit predictions arises. However, if the student is unable to make a reasonable prediction after having read three paragraphs, the teacher should terminate the activity. As Manzo suggests, "It may be self-defeating to continue beyond this point" (Manzo, 1969, p. 125).

5. Silent Reading Activity

The teacher now directs the student to read the remainder of the selection. At this point, the teacher might say, "Read to the end of the selection to see if you are right." During this period, the teacher can either read along with the student or stand by to assist. It is suggested that an important aspect here is to give aid in a manner which does not disrupt the student's comprehension. That is, do not destroy the student's train of thought.

6. Follow-up Activities

Numerous worthwhile tasks are suitable for follow-up activities. Manzo suggests that readers might engage in activities that verify or apply the information gained from reading. Other useful activities may emanate from a reconsideration and discussion of student predictions. For example, the teacher could encourage the student to consider manipulation of the story.

Cautions and Comments

For those teachers using ReQuest for the first time, Manzo offers a number of suggestions. He advises working with individuals rather than with groups, and, for the first encounter, he suggests the use of specific question types: immediate reference, common knowledge, related information, open-ended discussion, personalized discussion, further reference, and translation. More recently, Dishner and Searfoss (1974) offer an evaluation form that can be used in conjunction with a teacher's use of the procedure. A copy of this form appears at the end of this section.

With children for whom ReQuest is a new experience, a questioning game or activity is often essential for their readiness. Students may wish to underline those ideas about which they want to ask questions; students' confidence in their ability to formulate questions can be vital to their successful involvement in the ReQuest Procedure.

At certain times, modifications of the ReQuest procedure may be desirable. For example, in order to provide more varied interactions between questioner and respondent, it may be desirable to alternate the role of questioner after each question. Also, greater flexibility seems desirable in the selection of sections of the passage to be read at one time. Rather than proceed sentence by sentence, one might look for natural breaks within the passage. In a group situation, there are numerous possibilities. One example is ReQuest, whereby the roles of questioner and respondent either alternate around a circle or proceed at random within the circle. Often a group, as a whole, enjoys challenging the teacher. With kindergarten children, Legenza (1974) has successfully applied a modification of the ReQuest using pictures. The suggested protocol in this situation runs as follows:

> Let's ask each other questions about this picture to see if we can learn all the things we can about it. In order to help us to learn all we can, let's both look at the picture first and ask me any questions you can think of about this picture and I'll see if I can answer them—then I'll ask you some questions and you see if you can answer them. (Manzo and Legenza, 1975, p. 482)

With advanced students, another possible modification is an incomplete questioning technique. This technique requires the student or teacher to initiate an incomplete question, for example, "Why did John . . . ?" The other party completes the question and directs it at the initiator.

With or without these modifications, the ReQuest procedure appears to be a very effective strategy. The various permutations of the ReQuest procedure provide a viable tool for exploring, extending, and encouraging student hypothesizing. ReQuest facilitates student involvement in problem solving and necessitates teacher awareness of the student's level of involvement. Studies by Manzo, the originator of ReQuest, and Legenza, provide empirical support for these claims. In the hands of a sensitive teacher, ReQuest can indeed be an effective means of improving comprehension.

REQUEST EVALUATION FORM

Observer________________________

Name________________________

Date______________ Grade Level _______

INTERVIEW Before lesson begins: ask these questions; record responses; check the boxes.

	Information Accurate Yes	No
a) What is the instructional level of students?		
b) What is the reading level of the selected story?		
c) Where will first prediction be elicited?		
d) At what point will eliciting predictions stop?		
e) How long is the story?		
f) Does the story have setting, characters, and an unfamiliar plot?		

	Yes	No
1. Was appropriate material selected?		

OBSERVATION When the lesson begins: answer the questions on the left first.

Record: Time lesson begins

	Yes	No
a. Were the rules accurate?		
b. Were the rules complete?		
c. Were the rules received?		
d. Were the rules understood?		

	Yes	No
2. Was rule given?		

Did teacher

	Yes	No
a. Direct joint silent reading?		
b. Give the correct amount to be read?		
c. Close the book?		
d. Direct students to keep books open?		
e. Direct students to ask questions?		
f. Answer students' questions?		

	Yes	No
3. Was student questioning directed?		

Did teacher

	Yes	No
a. Open books?		
b. Direct students to close books?		
c. Ask students questions?		

	Yes	No
4. Was teacher questioning conducted?		

RECORD During the lesson: record the number of questions from each category.

	Student	Teacher
LITERAL: "What in the story tells . . . ?"		
INTERPRETIVE: "From these clues, why . . . ?"		
APPLIED: "How do you think . . . ?" or "In your opinion, what . . . ?"		

	Yes	No
5. Were all question categories sampled?		

Did teacher	Yes	No	N/A
a. Ask questions different from students' questions?			
b. Integrate information from previous sentences?			
c. Request rephrasing of unclear questions?			
d. Employ problem-solving strategies when needed?			
e. Select effective strategies?			

	Yes	No
6. Did questions meet specifications?		

Did teacher attempt to	Yes	No
a. Elicit prediction at earliest point?		
b. Elicit prediction of another story *content?*		
c. Elicit more than one prediction?		

	Yes	No
7. Were predictions elicited?		

Did teacher	Yes	No
a. Ask students to support other students' predictions?		
b. Request ranking of predictions according to likelihood?		
c. Refrain from making value judgments about students' predictions?		

Record: Time-predicting ends

	Yes	No
8. Were evaluations of predictions elicited?		

Did teacher	Yes	No
a. Direct students to read to end of story?		
b. Ask students to compare *actual* with *predicted* story *content?*		

	Yes	No
9. Were predictions compared to story content?		

	Time	Time Estimate for Grade Level	Well Timed? Yes	Well Timed? No
Lesson began:				
Predictions ended:				
Lesson ended:				

10. Was lesson well paced? Yes ☐ No ☐

SUMMARY After lesson ends: Go back and check 1–10. If all questions were answered Yes, ReQuest was performed.

Was ReQuest Performed? Yes ☐ No ☐

REFERENCES

Dishner, E. K., and Searfoss, L. W. "Improving Comprehension through the ReQuest Procedure." *Reading Education: A Journal for Australian Teachers* 2 (Autumn, 1977): 22–25.
Presents an expanded and more specific set of directions for the ReQuest procedure.

Dishner, E. K., and Searfoss, L. W. "ReQuest Evaluation Form." Unpublished paper, Arizona State University, 1974.
Evaluation form that provides step-by step implementation.

Legenza, A. "Questioning Behavior of Kindergarten Children." Paper presented at Nineteenth Annual Convention, International Reading Association, 1974.
Describes the use and effectiveness of the ReQuest Picture Treatment with kindergarten children.

Manzo, A. V. "Improving Reading Comprehension through Reciprocal Questioning." Unpublished doctoral dissertation, Syracuse University, 1968.
Primary reference. Describes the original development of the ReQuest procedure, rationale, piloting, and empirical support of its effectiveness.

Manzo, A. V. "The ReQuest Procedure." Journal of Reading 2 (1979): 123–126.
Manzo's first article based upon the ReQuest Procedure. Describes the rational, procedures, and suggestions for use.

Manzo, A. V., and Legenza, A. "Inquiry Training for Kindergarten Children." *Educational Leadership* 32 (1975): 479–483.
Presents the procedures and empirical support for use of the ReQuest procedure with kindergarten children.

CLOZE PROCEDURE

Purpose

When used as a teaching strategy the cloze technique is to improve the comprehension skills of students. More specifically, the technique forces students to use the context of a passage or sentence to suggest replacements for deleted words.

Rationale

Taylor (1953) describes the cloze procedure as

> . . . a method of intercepting a message from a 'transmitter' (writer or speaker), mutilating its language patterns by deleting parts, and so administering it to 'receivers' (readers and listeners) that their attempts to make the patterns whole again potentially yield a considerable number of cloze units. (p. 416)

As readers attempt to discover a writer's message, they rely on three major strategies or clues to unlock the meaning. Goodman (1967) describes these clues: (1) syntactic or grammatical word order clues; (2) semantic or meaning clues; and (3) graphophonic or sound-symbol clues. A teacher may adopt cloze exercises to emphasize readers' use of these strategies concurrently and interchangeably and thus may discourage readers' over-reliance on any one strategy.

Intended Audience

The cloze technique as a comprehension-building strategy has been recommended for use with readers at all levels. Its use has been referenced at the first grade level (Gove, 1975) through college level (Bloomer, 1962; Friedman, 1964; Blumenfield and Miller, 1966; Martin, 1968; and Guice, 1969).

Description of the Procedure

For those individuals who have used the cloze procedure as a measure of the comprehensibility of printed material, perhaps it would be best to note some differences between the use of the technique in those settings and the use of the strategy as an instructional device. We will mention these essential differences later in this section; we have summarized them in the following table:

CLOZE PROCEDURE

Characteristic	*As a measuring device*	*As a teaching tool*
Length	(1) 250–350 word selections	(1) Initially, may use single sentences. Later, passages of no more than 150 words
Deletions	(2) Delete every *n*th word with approximately 50 for the total word passage	(2) Make deletions selectively and systematically in accordance with proposed use
Evaluation	(3) With this procedure, only exact word replacement is correct. Sometimes a teacher may analyze student responses in terms of their syntactic and semantic characteristics	(3) Synonyms or other replacements are appropriate
Follow-ups	(4) Usually none	(4) Student and teacher discussion of the exercise helps comprehension

Several individuals have attempted to outline systematic procedures for using the cloze technique as a comprehension-building strategy (Bloomer, 1962; Schell, 1972; Bortnick and Lopardo, 1973; and Gove, 1975). The following procedural outline incorporates the thoughts of each of those individuals. As with many of the strategies within this volume, discussion of the procedure will follow a two-step sequence: (1) teacher preparation and (2) instruction.

1. Teacher Preparation

a. *Selecting materials.* Schell (1972) suggests that, in the early stages, materials should be at the students' independent reading level. Teachers can extract written selections from stories and poems in basal readers, from selections in subject matter texts, or from language experience stories the students themselves generate. There are some cloze-type materials available through several publishers. It is important to note that teachers themselves produce some of the most effective materials.

As we mentioned earlier, passages should be shorter that those passages generally used when cloze is a testing device. For example, teachers may use single sentences initially with first graders, gradually moving to selections in which ten to fifteen deletions have been made (Gove, 1975).

b. *Designing the cloze exercise.* There appears to be a logical progression in the format for presenting cloze exercises. Consider the examples that follow only as a guideline for developing cloze exercises. We present them in order of difficulty and suggest that the teacher follow this order in using the exercises with students.

1. Sentences in which the teacher deletes one word; a multiple choice format with two choices. Notice in the following example that the two choices include the correct item and a foil, or an incorrect item, that is quite different graphically and is a different part of speech.

   1. monkey
   "We saw a at the zoo."
   2. soon

2. The same format as above, but with the foil somewhat graphically similar to the correct item and a different part of speech.

   1. mostly
   "We saw a at the zoo."
   2. monkey

3. Two choices, both the same part of speech.

   1. monkey
   "We saw a at the zoo."
   2. money

4. Three choices that include the correct item, a word of the same part of speech, and a word that represents a different part of speech.[1]

   1. money
   "We saw a 2. mostly at the zoo."
   3. monkey

From these highly structured examples, one can move to less structured items. Again, in terms of difficulty, one could progress with exercises of this type:

1. A single graphophonic clue in a sentence where only one word could reasonably fit.

   "I think the square t________ will look better in the dining room than the round one you considered buying."

2. A single graphophonic clue in a sentence where several choices are possible.

   "We bought a bag of p________ at the grocery store."

1. This example is similar to a testing strategy, the maze technique, described by Guthrie et al. (1974).

Finally, the teacher could use sentences and passages similar to these, but without the graphophonic clue.

Again, we suggest this sequence simply to provide a guideline for the development of cloze activities. Obviously, the teacher must consider the difficulty of the printed materials and the reading sophistication of the students when developing exercises of this type.

The reader may have noticed that each of the examples above contains a noun deletion. Schell (1972) suggests that in the early stages of instruction, the teacher should delete only nouns and verbs. Later, he or she may emphasize categories such as adjectives or adverbs.

2. Instruction

In many kindergartens and first grade classrooms, the instructional program might include oral cloze activities. The following is an example of one such activity:

> I am going to say some sentences, but I will leave off the last word of each sentence. See if you can tell me what word I left out. Let's try this one: "At Joe's birthday party on Saturday, we had some ice cream and ________." What word(s) make(s) sense there?

Discussion then could center on why students have various answers. This type of activity provides a logical introduction to the use of written cloze activities.

When initiating written cloze activities, the teacher might begin with a whole class activity focused on material presented on an overhead projector. The teacher should direct students to read through the entire sentence or passage before attempting to supply the deleted word(s). A student volunteer could read the material and supply the missing word(s). One other student who has responded differently could read and provide his responses. Class discussion would center on such questions as:

> Why did you choose this word? What word or group of words indicate to you "building" should be placed in the blank? How does your word contribute to the meaning of the passage? When your word is in the sentence, what does the sentence (or passage) mean? How does your word contribute to the meaning in a different way? When your word is in the sentence, does the sentence (or passage) have a different meaning? (Gove, 1975, p. 38)

Other students could add their suggestions with continued discussion centered on these questions.

Later, the teacher could give the mimeographed cloze passages to complete individually. In small group discussions the teacher asks each student to explain why he or she used a particular word. The small group discussions would then lead to large group discussion of some of the more interesting or controversial items.

An exercise such as the following might be used with a group of intermediate level readers. Obviously, the teacher would not type the deleted words on the students' mimeographed copies, but we include the words here for discussion purposes.

> Would you like to find a rich (*gold*) mine? There's one in the Superstition Mountains of Arizona. Jacob Walz, an (*old*) prospector from Germany, was one of the last known persons to (*visit*) the mine. Before Walz died in 1891, he gave (*simple*) directions to the mine. There is also supposed to be a map. But no one has ever been able to find what is now (*called*) "The Lost Dutchman Mine."[2]

Each of the words in parentheses offers students the opportunity to supply a variety of other words. For example, in place of the word "old," students might offer replacements such as "elderly," "adventurous," "interesting," "ugly," or "eccentric." Discussion then could center on why these choices are feasible, and why words like "young," "robust," and so on are not acceptable.

Jongsma (1971) and others have suggested that this discussion procedure may be the key to the successful use of cloze as a teaching strategy. There is very little evidence to suggest that cloze exercises alone will produce better comprehenders.

Cautions and Comments

There appear to be an endless number of ways that teachers can use the cloze procedure to improve the comprehension skills of readers. For example, Rankin (1959) proposed the use of cloze exercises to assist readers who have difficulty with text in their content classrooms. More recently, Blachowicz (1977) proposed using the cloze technique with primary grade students.

Furthermore, there seem to be a number of alternative cloze formats. Two additional cloze formats have appeared in recent research studies and may present possibilities for use in teaching. A limited cloze technique (Cunningham and Cunningham, 1978) employs the traditional deletion pattern of every fifth word with the deleted words randomly ordered and placed in columns on a separate sheet.

EXAMPLE OF LIMITED CLOZE

> Money that people choose to save rather than spend is very important. Here is the reason. The ________ and machinery a worker ________ have a great deal ________ to do with how much ________ can get done. You ________ know this. But tools ________ machinery cost money. Someone ________ get together enough money ________ build the factory and ________ machinery to help workers ________ more.

2. R. G. Smith and Robert Tierney, *Fins and Tales*, Scott, Foresman Basics in Reading. (Glenview, Ill.: Scott, Foresman, 1978) p. 72.

List of Deletions for Limited Cloze:

to	tools
he	must
has	already
and	to
buy	produce

Another format, the least-major-constituent limited-cloze (Cunningham and Tierney, 1977), deletes every fifth least-major-constituent (syntactic unit sometimes larger than words) and randomly orders them in columns on a separate sheet. The following example provides the same selection as above, but deletes syntactic units.

EXAMPLE OF LEAST-MAJOR-CONSTITUENT LIMITED-CLOZE

Money that people choose to save rather than spend is very important. _________ is the reason. The tools and machinery a worker _________ have a great deal to do with_______ he can get done. You already know _________. But tools and machinery cost money. _________ must get together enough money to build________ and buy machinery to help __________ produce more.

Deleted Units:

how much	has
the factory	workers
here	someone
this	

(Cunningham and Tierney, 1977)

With the widespread use of cloze, however, comes the need for caution. Indeed, it seems that some people are using cloze haphazardly. The reader should note that merely completing cloze activities will not result in students' improved comprehension. Rather, comprehension improvement using cloze depends upon the reader's purpose, the text's demands and the teacher's follow-up during and after a cloze activity. To this end teachers should use cloze selectively with passages and purposes where students' ability to produce replacement words or phrases is a worthwhile activity. For example, cloze might be inappropriate with text for which a more reader-based understanding is appropriate.

REFERENCES

Blachowicz, C. L. Z. "Cloze Activities for Primary Readers." *The Reading Teacher* 31, no. (1977): 300–302.

Describes how teachers can use variations of cloze successfully with primary readers.

Bloomer, R. H. "The Cloze Procedure as a Remedial Reading Exercise." *Journal of Developmental Reading* 5 (Spring, 1962): 173–181.
Describes the use of the cloze procedure as a remedial technique for college students.

Blumenfield, J. P., and Miller, G. R. "Improving Reading through Teaching Grammatical Constraints." *Elementary English* 43 (November, 1966): 752–755.
Presents a description of a study in which twenty college English students completed a variety of cloze exercises.

Bortnick, R., and Lopardo, G. S. "An Instructional Application of the Cloze Procedure." *Journal of Reading* 16 (January, 1973): 296–300.
Provides specific direction for using cloze procedure to improve comprehension. Emphasis is placed on the importance of teacher direction.

Cunningham, J. W., and Cunningham, P. M. "Validating a Limited-Cloze Procedure." *Journal of Reading Behavior,* 10, 2 (1978): 211–213.
Presents a variation of the traditional cloze format.

Cunningham, J. W., and Tierney, R. J. "Comparative Analysis of Cloze and Modified Cloze Procedures." Paper presented at National Reading Conference, New Orleans, 1977.
Provides a comparison of the traditional cloze format with two modified versions.

Friedman, M. "The Use of the Cloze Procedure for Improving the Reading of Foreign Students at the University of Florida." Unpublished doctoral dissertation, University of Florida, 1964.
Describes an experimental study in which one group received cloze passages constructed from *McCall-Crabbs Standard Test Lessons in Reading.*

Goodman, K. S. "Reading: A Psycholinguistic Guessing Game." *Journal of the Reading Specialist* 4 (May, 1967): 126–35.
Describes the syntactic, semantic, and graphophonic clues a reader uses to obtain meaning from print.

Gove, M. K. "Using the Cloze Procedure in a First Grade Classroom." *The Reading Teacher* 29 (October, 1975): 36–38.
Describes how the teacher can use cloze procedure in conjunction with basal readers and with the language experience approach.

Guice, B. M. "The Use of the Cloze Procedure for Improving Reading Comprehension of College Students." *Jounal of Reading Behavior* 1 (Summer, 1969): 81–92.
Provides a description of four groups of college students who received instruction using cloze passages.

Guthrie, J. T., Burnham, N. A., Caplan, R. I., and Seifert, M. "The Maze Technique to Assess, Monitor Reading Comprehension." *The Reading Teacher* 28 (November, 1974): 161–168.
Presents a multiple-choice-type variation of the cloze procedure.

Jongsma, E. *The Cloze Procedure as a Teaching Technique.* Newark, Del.: International Reading Association, 1971.
Presents descriptions of past research which used cloze procedure as a teaching tool; offers suggestions for future cloze research.

Martin, R. W. "Transformational Grammar, Cloze, and Performance in College Freshman." Unpublished doctoral dissertation, Syracuse University, 1968.
Describes a study in which researchers gave three groups of college students passages to improve their reading comprehension.

Rankin, E. "Uses of the Cloze Procedure in the Reading Clinic." *Proceedings of the International Reading Association* 4 (1959): 228-232.
Suggests ways of using cloze procedure to bridge the gap between clinical instruction and instruction in the content classrooms.

Schell, L. M. "Promising Possibilities for Improving Comprehension." *Journal of Reading* 5 (March, 1972): 415-24.
Presents detailed information on the use of cloze as a teaching technique.

Taylor, W. L. "Cloze Procedure: A New Tool for Measuring Readability." *Journalism Quarterly* 30 (Fall, 1953): 415-33.
Provides the first description of the cloze technique.

Weaver, G. C. "Using the Cloze Procedure as a Teaching Technique." *The Reading Teacher* 32, no. 5 (1979): 632-636.
Presents a comprehensive review of the use of cloze as an instructional tool.

REAP TECHNIQUE

Purpose

The REAP technique (Eanet and Manzo, 1976) is to:

1. Improve the comprehension skills of readers by helping them synthesize an author's ideas into their own words
2. Develop students' writing ability as an aid for future study and recall of ideas they acquire through reading

Rationale

The REAP (*R*ead, *E*ncode, *A*nnotate, *P*onder) techinque starts from the premise that readers comprehend best when asked to communicate the ideas gleaned from a passage they have read. REAP is conceived as an alternative to the Directed Reading Activity and the Guided Reading Procedure, described in this unit.

Specifically, the REAP technique actively involves readers in processing the ideas an author has set down in print. The purpose is for readers to communicate in their own words a text-based understanding and discuss those ideas with others. In this way the readers internalize a text-based understanding. It is perceived that this internalization enhances the meaningful processing of those ideas, thus crystallizing the readers' own thinking concerning the author's message.

REAP uses writing as a vehicle to translate an author's ideas into the readers' own words, so this strategy also serves to enhance the writing skills of students. Additionally, these written translations may serve as the basis for continued study or for review of an author's ideas. Thus REAP, requiring active involvement with print, can encourage students' maturity and independence in reading.

Intended Audience

The REAP technique is intended for use with secondary level readers, junior high through college. It may provide the basis for group instruction or may be adapted for individual use as a study method.

Description of the Procedure

The REAP technique consists of four stages:

R–*Reading* to discover the author's ideas;
E–*Encoding* the author's ideas into one's own language;
A–*Annotating* those ideas in writing for oneself or for sharing with others;
P–*Pondering* the significance of the annotation.

Central to the REAP technique is developing students' ability to write annotations. Therefore, the discussion of the REAP strategy follows these steps:

1. Writing annotations
2. Teaching students to write annotations
3. Pondering the annotations

1. Writing Annotations

Writing annotations requires readers to interact with the ideas of the author, to synthesize them into their own language, and to set them down in writing. Eanet and Manzo (1976) and Manzo (1973) have described several different types of annotations that students might use. Types include the heuristic annotation, summary annotation, thesis annotation, question annotation, critical annotation, intention annotation, and motivation annotation.

To serve as examples, annotations have been constructed for the following selection:

> We encourage children to act stupidly, not only by scaring and confusing them, but by boring them, by filling up their days with dull, repetitive tasks that make little or no claim on their attention or demands on their intelligence. Our hearts leap for joy at the sight of a roomful of children all slogging away at some imposed task, and we are all the more pleased and satisfied if someone tells us that the children don't really like what they are doing. We tell ourselves that this drudgery is good preparation for life, and we fear that without it children would be hard to "control." But why must this busywork be so dull? Why not give tasks that are interesting and demanding? Because, in schools where every task must be completed and every answer must be right, if we give children more demanding tasks they will be fearful and will

> instantly insist that we show them how to do the job. When you have acres of paper to fill up with pencil marks, you have no time to waste on the luxury of thinking. By such means children are firmly established in the habit of using only a small part of their thinking capacity. They feel that school is a place where they must spend most of their time doing dull tasks in a dull way.[3]

a. *Heuristic Annotation*

> We encourage children to act stupidly, not only by scaring and confusing them, but by boring them. . .

The heuristic annotation depicts the essence of the author's message through the selection of the author's words. Like the above quotation, it should stimulate a reaction.

b. *Summary Annotation*

> Schools may become more interesting places for children if they are provided with meaningful activities designed to promote thinking rather than dull, repetitive busywork.

The above annotation provides a summary of the selection by condensing the author's ideas on the type of activities children should face in school. The summary annotation omits examples, descriptions of presently used activities, and explanations of recommended school tasks. It presents only a synopsis of the author's main ideas.

c. *Thesis Annotation*

> If schools became places to think they would challenge and threaten the status quo.

A thesis annotation is a precise statement of the selection's theme, the author's point of view. Use of this type entails detailing what the author is saying. The above statement attempts to do this briefly and incisively.

d. *Question Annotation*

> What do teachers consider good preparation for life? Why is there no time to work on "the luxury of thinking"? How do students react to school?

A question annotation involves addressing the germane ideas of a selection in question form. In the above annotation, the questions address the points in the passage by Holt.

e. *Intention Annotation*

> As Holt tries in his other writing, he attempts to convince his reader of his thesis by painting a negative picture of the status quo.

An intention annotation entails specifying the author's reasons for writing. The annotator considers what is given by the author and what is known of the author. It is obvious that the annotator of the above annotation has read other material of Holt.

3. J. Holt, *How Children Fail.* (New York: Pitman, 1964) pp. 210–211.

f. *Motivation Annotation*

Holt is trying to suggest what is wrong with schools and a solution to the problem. It is his argument that schools are monotonous when they should be challenging students to think.

A motivation annotation is a statement in which the author's motives, biases, and perceptions are addressed. The above annotation speculates as to Holt's motives for writing the selection.

g. *Critical Annotation*

Holt is right. Schools may become more interesting places for children if they provide experiences which challenge them to think. Clearly, school is more learning the system than learning to solve problems. Clearly, schooling is largely irrelevant.

The critical annotation details the author's point of view, the annotator's reaction to this position, and the basis for the annotator's reaction. In the above annotation, the annotator reacts positively to Holt and defines some reasons.

The different annotations may or may not be suitable for different selections. As Eanet and Manzo suggest ". . . some annotations are more suitable to some types of writing than are others" (p. 648). The teacher or annotator will need to address this possibility prior to proceeding with annotations.

2. Teaching Strategies to Write Annotations

It is suggested that students cannot be expected to cogently write annotations without prior exposure to the process. That is, students must learn this skill and practice it before a teacher can expect them to use it successfully.

To this end, Eanet and Manzo (1976) recommend the following paradigm in teaching students to write annotations:

Step One: Recognizing and Defining
Step Two: Discriminating
Step Three: Modeling the Process
Step Four: Practicing

A Summary Annotation will illustrate the paradigm.

a. Step One: *Recognizing and Defining.* The teacher asks students to read a short selection and then furnishes them with a Summary Annotation. Using questioning techniques and discussion, the teacher should elicit from the students how the furnished annotation relates to the selection read. In lieu of whole-group instruction, the teacher may choose to have small groups of students attempting jointly to work at this task. In either case, the goal of the teacher is to aid students in formulating the concept of the Summary Annotation.

b. Step Two: *Discriminating.* As in the previous step, the teacher asks the students to read another short selection. However, the teacher now presents them with multiple annotations. The recommended number is three annotations, one of which constitutes a good Summary Annotation. The other two should be erroneous in some fashion—either too broad, too narrow, or too divergent from the ideas in the selection. Again through class discussion, students should choose the best annotation. They should justify their choice and explain why the other choices are unsatisfactory. Small groups are also a recommended alternative to the whole-group instructional situation. The task of discriminating between good and poor annotations will further refine students' skill with annotations.

c. Step Three: *Modeling the Process.* Students now read a third selection. The teacher demonstrates to the students how to write the Summary Annotation effectively. It is most crucial that the teacher "walk" the students through this step by telling them the thought processes undertaken in writing the annotation. The teacher should demonstrate to the students the relationships between the major ideas so students will be able to write a cogent annotation, or rewrite it as necessary. This modeling process is essential in communicating what a good Summary Annotation is, and what students should do to arrive at a good one.

d. Step Four: *Practicing.* The practicing step has two parts. First, the students read a new passage and individually write an annotation. Then, forming groups of three or four, students develop the best Summary Annotation possible, using their individual attempts as the basis for this interaction. Students also may refer to the passage, if necessary. The total group then compares, discusses, and evaluates the final group products.

By the second part, the procedure for writing annotations should be well enough established that students can write a Summary Annotation on their own. Students read a new selection, write an annotation, and hand this in to the teacher. At this point, the teacher can identify those students needing additional reinforcement with the annotation process or with the skills prerequisite to annotation writing.

3. Pondering the Annotations

This part of the annotation process corresponds to the "ponder" stage of the REAP strategy. The students "ponder", or process it, for personal study or for classroom activities. The annotation has now become a powerful tool for comprehension and study, limited only by teachers' imagination and students' needs.

Specifically, Eanet and Manzo (1976) recommend four uses of annotations. First, this technique may be useful in a reading class, either developmental or remedial, which uses individualized instruction. As the teacher works with individuals, the other students read individually from materials of their choice. Before the end of class, each student writes a Summary Annotation on the material read that day. This process serves the students as a short review when they begin reading the next day. It also provides the basis for both an individual conference with the teacher and a progress check. When the students have read the whole book, they write a new, more comprehensive annotation that includes a critical evaluation and attach it to the book. This annotation will serve as an aid for other readers who choose to read the book.

Second, the instructor may adapt this annotation procedure for the school library. As students finish reading a book, they write an annotation, and the library keeps it on file. When new readers are selecting a book, they can consult the annotations file in making their decision. The annotations can provide other students with information about a book before they read it.

Third, annotations may be used to prepare secondary or college English students in classes for writing projects. The annotations can serve as a foundation for more extensive critique writing. For example, students may read and annotate two or three articles that offer varied opinions on a topic of interest. Next, students would write a comparative essay or research paper on the topic, using the annotations as the basis.

Finally, the teacher may use the annotations as required readings to enhance students' study efforts on materials of importance in the curricula. This assignment promotes in-depth study and provides the basis for classroom discussion and review. These required annotations may also serve to improve the writing skills of students.

Cautions and Comments

The REAP technique affords a systematic procedure by which teachers can guide their students' interactions with authors' ideas. Specifically, this technique can serve to direct and record purposeful interactions between a reader and a text. REAP can guide the reader to use alternative annotations as a way to select appropriate procedures for gleaning, recording and using textual information.

The strategy appears to have some major shortcomings. Specifically, many students may find the task of writing annotations both difficult and painstaking. Students who lack the ability to adequately derive main ideas from reading selections may find the task of writing annotations particularly arduous. Teachers desiring to use the REAP technique may wish to teach main idea skills to such students before proceeding. To this end, Dishner and Readence (1977) and Putnam (1974) provide systematic procedures which may be useful for teaching students main idea skills. Obviously the teacher should use the strategy selectively, with students for whom it is appropriate and with text for which it is relevant. If teachers use REAP in a lock-step fashion with all students, they may find the strategy either inappropriate or more difficult than the task they intended to teach.

REFERENCES

Dishner, E. K., and Readence, J. E. "A Systematic Procedure for Teaching Main Idea." *Reading World* 16 (1977): 292–298.
Prescribes a teaching strategy to aid students in determining the main idea.

Eanet, M. "An Investigation of the REAP Reading/Study Procedure: Its Rationale and Efficacy." In P. D. Pearson and J. Hansen, eds., *Reading: Discipline Inquiry in Process and Practice.* Twenty-seventh Yearbook of the National Reading Conference, Clemson: National Reading Conference, 1978, pp. 229–232.
Reports a study in which the efficacy of REAP is explored.

Eanet, M. G., and Manzo, A. V. "REAP—A Strategy for Improving Reading/Writing/Study skills." *Journal of Reading* 19 (1976): 647-652.
Presents a detailed discussion of how to use the REAP technique in the classroom.

Manzo, A. V. "CONPASS: English—A Demonstration Project." *Journal of Reading* 16 (1973): 539-545.
Describes the use of annotations as an aid to improving reading comprehension.

Putnam, L. R. "Don't Tell Them to Do It . . . Show Them How." *Journal of Reading* 18 (1974): 41-43.
Advocates a procedure to help students identify the main idea.

GUIDED READING PROCEDURE

Purpose

As developed by Manzo (1975), the Guided Reading Procedure is designed to:

1. Assist students' unaided recall of specific information read
2. Improve the students' abilities to generate their own (implicit) questions as they read
3. Develop the students' understanding of the importance of self-correction
4. Improve the students' abilities to organize information

Rationale

Many teachers expect their students to remember the facts in a story or in a chapter from a content textbook. The Guided Reading Procedure (GRP) is intended to provide the teacher with a logical series of instructional steps that can lead to the majority of the students in a given classroom addressing the content. The group or whole class recalls orally the information they have just read silently. The teacher then asks them to confirm, organize, and note relationships. These, Manzo argues, are essential factors in advancing an attitude of comprehension accuracy and, ultimately, reading comprehension ability. As Manzo (1975) contends:

> . . . the GRP enriches skills by having the teacher allow students to see implicit questions, by strengthening determination to concentrate during reading, and by encouraging self-correction and organization of information with minimal teacher direction. (p. 288)

Intended Audience

Teachers can use the Guided Reading Procedure at the primary level, although it appears most appropriate for students in the middle grades through college level.

It also is important to note that GRP is a group activity and may not be effective as a one-on-one strategy.

Description of the Procedure

The Guided Reading Procedure may use narrative selections or informational material. The selection should be short enough so that the majority of the students can complete the reading comfortably in one sitting. Manzo (1975) provides a rule of thumb to use in deciding appropriate length. His suggestions on number of words and amount of reading time for average readers follow. For primary students, allow three minutes or approxiamtely 90 words; for intermediate students, three minutes or approximately 500 words; for junior high students, seven minutes or approximately 900 words; for senior high students, ten minutes or approximately 2,000 words; and for college students, twelve minutes or approximately 2,500 words.

Manzo (1975) outlines six basic steps to be followed for the GRP and presents a seventh step as an optional phase.

1. Prepare the Student for the Reading Assignment

As with any good teaching lesson, students should work through some form of readiness task before they plunge into the actual reading assignment. This preparation may take the form described under the Directed Reading Activity (Unit One), the Instructional Framework (Unit Two), the Survey Technique (Unit Two), or the ReQuest Procedure (Unit One). Regardless of which strategy the teacher employs, it is vitally important that the students understand why they are reading the printed material before them. The general purpose, at least for this particular lesson, is for them to remember as much of the details as possible. Teacher/student agreement on this purpose is of vital importance to the strategy's success.

2. Students Read and Recall Information

With their purpose clearly in mind, the students read the material silently while the teacher stands by to assist those students who may have difficulty with the reading. Students are advised that, upon completion of their reading, they are to turn the material face down on their desks and wait until their classmates have finished the assignment.

When the large majority of the students have finished the reading, the instructor asks the students to tell what they remember. The emphasis at this point is on unaided recall of the material read. The teacher serves as the recorder and notes on the chalkboard each bit of information suggested by the students. In order to speed the process and avoid extensive writing, an abbreviated form of recording is suggested.

3. Return to Article for Additional Facts and Corrections

When the students are no longer able to recall information from memory, the teacher allows them to return to the selection in order to add additional information and to correct inaccurately recalled details. The teacher adds the new information to the board and corrects inaccuracies noted by the students.

4. Organize the Remembered Material

The teacher now asks the students to organize the material into a modified outline form. Sometimes the instructor may ask questions to lead the students to an outline highlighting the main ideas and supporting details through the locating of more general statements and their supporting details. Sometimes the teacher may have the students organize the information and the sequence in which the information was presented. Questions such as the following may be useful: "What happened first in this selection?" "What came next?" "Where does this information appear to fit best?" At other times, the teacher or the student may suggest alternative outline forms.

5. Provide Students with Thought-Provoking Questions

The teacher should direct his or her efforts at this point toward helping the students understand how this new information relates to material they previously learned. Initially, the questions may need to be fairly specific. For example, "How does this new information about Jackson support what we learned about him last week?" As the students become more familiar with this segment of the technique, the teacher may turn to less specific questions that place more responsibility upon the students during this transfer-of-learning stage. Questions of a more general type might include: "Do you see any relation between this information and the material we studied last week?" or "Give me some examples of how this material supports last week's unit." During this step, the teacher serves as a model by asking thoughtful questions that require students to synthesize new information with previously learned information.

6. Test Students on Their Knowledge of the Information

Following this rather intense reading/reacting activity, the teacher should take time to check the students' short-term memory of the ideas they presented. A short quiz will provide the students an opportunity to reveal how much information they have learned as a result of the procedure. Although Manzo suggests no specific test format, the teacher could use either matching, multiple-choice, short answer, essay items, or some appropriate combination of question types.

The teacher may provide students additional opportunities to ". . . . manipulate and deliberate" (Manzo, 1975, p. 291) over the material read. The teacher may also wish to check recall over longer periods of time.

Cautions and Comments

The GRP strategy is a rather intense activity which used selectively, may prove beneficial. For example, with selected "meaty" reading material (i.e., material containing much important information), the GRP affords students an opportunity to read that information, to interact with others' interpretations of the material in the classroom, and to organize the material. The GRP is a teacher-directed but student-dominated activity which can lead to improvements in readers' understandings. Cunningham, Arthur, and Cunningham (1977) describe an interesting variation of the Guided Reading Procedure. They label it simply the Guided Listening Procedure. After sufficiently preparing them for the listening activity, the teacher asks the students to remember as much as they can from the selection. The teacher then reads a short selection orally, taping it at the same time. The remaining steps are similar to those we described earlier, with one obvious exception. Rather than returning to the printed material to confirm student recall, the teacher plays the tape recording and asks the students to raise their hands to stop the tape when they wish to discuss specific pieces of information.

Due to the nature of this particular strategy, Manzo (1975) recommends that the teacher use the Guided Reading Procedure no more than once a week. With appropriate reading selections, a logical variation might be to use the GRP every other week, with the Guided Listening Procedure employed on the off-week (Cunningham, Arthur, and Cunningham, 1977).

REFERENCES

Cunningham, P. M., Arthur, S. V., and Cunningham, J. W. *Classroom Reading Instruction k-5: Alternative Approaches.* Lexington, Mass.: D. C. Heath, 1977, p. 241.

Presents a brief description of a variation of the GRP—the Guided Listening Procedure.

Manzo, A. V. "Guided Reading Procedure." *Journal of Reading* 18 (1975): 287–291.

Provides the rationale and specific steps that make up GRP strategy.

DIRECTED READING ACTIVITY

Purpose

The purpose of the Directed Reading Activity (DRA) (Betts, 1946) is to:

1. Give teachers a basic format from which to provide systematic instruction on a group basis
2. Improve students' word recognition and comprehension skills
3. Successfully guide students through a reading selection

Rationale

The DRA is synonymous with the basal reader lesson. Betts (1946) compiled the guidelines that various authors of basal readers generally recommended for teaching their reading selections. Betts described a plan to follow when there was general agreement among the authors:

> First, the group should be prepared, oriented, or made ready, for the reading of a story or selection. Second, the first reading should be guided silent reading. Third, word-recognition skills and comprehension should be developed during the silent reading. Fourth, the reading—silent or oral, depending upon the needs of the pupil—should be done for purposes different from those served by the first, or silent, reading. Fifth, the follow-up on the "reading lesson" should be differentiated in terms of pupil needs. (p. 492)

Thus, the general plan of instruction in basal readers, what became known as the Directed Reading Activity, originated as a comprehensive means to provide reading instruction to children through a reading selection.

Intended Audience

The DRA is normally associated with basal reader instruction in the elementary grades, but the teacher may adapt it for any reading selection. For example, Shepherd (1973) has illustrated the use of DRA with content area textbooks from the middle school level through high school.

Description of the Procedure

Although there may be minor differences as to what constitutes the DRA, it usually contains the following components, all of which the teacher may modify to fit a student's needs:

1. Readiness
2. Directed silent reading
3. Comprehension check and discussion

4. Oral rereading
5. Follow up activities

1. Readiness

The readiness, or preparation, stage of the DRA involves getting students ready to enter the story by relating the story selection to their past experiences, developing their interest in reading it, and setting their purposes for reading. Four components comprise the readiness stage of the DRA.

a. *Develop concept background.* Here it is suggested that the teacher connect the new concepts the students will be exposed to in the reading selection with students' previous experiences or readings. Any misconceptions or hazy understandings by the students are expected to be clarified before they read the story.

The teacher may build background through various means, including discussions centering around the story title and illustrations within it, personal experiences of the students related to the story content, films, pictures, maps, or other audiovisual displays.

b. *Create interest.* Starting with the notion that children must be interested, or motivated, to read a selection in order to maximize their comprehension and enjoyment of its contents, the teacher attempts also to create interest in the early stages. The mechanical side of the selection alone, its title and the various illustrations, many times may serve to arouse students' interest; however, the teacher may also have to keep creating enthusiasm for students to read the story effectively. In this case, a thorough job by teachers in developing conceptual background (the previously discussed section) may suffice. If not, the teacher may choose to read a short, introductory portion of the selection and thus inspire the students to want to read the rest. At other times, the teacher may wish to use multimedia material and/or experiences to stimulate interest.

c. *Introduce new vocabulary.* Here the teacher's task is to prepare students for any words they will encounter that are outside the students' reading vocabularies and word recognition abilities. To emphasize word meanings and not just word pronunciations, the teacher may introduce new vocabulary in context, both orally and visually. For example, the teacher might first use the word *orally* in a sentence, followed by a visual presentation on the chalkboard using meaningful phrases or sentences. The introduction of new vocabulary is not a time for drill or for emphasizing word attack skills. Instead, it is the time to give students oral familiarity with selected words. Typically, a teacher introduces no more than five words at once.

d. *Establish purpose.* Based upon the notion that the establishment of clear, concise purpose for reading a selection determines the quality of the readers' comprehension, at this point the teacher should pose questions for the students to answer in their silent reading. The overall question the teacher should consider is, "What are the students reading for?" For example, the teacher must decide whether to set a general purpose for the entire selection, such as "Read to find out the series of events which led to the downfall of the dictator," *or,* if the teacher decides to set more specific purposes for each part of a selection, another example is "Read to find out how the dictator came to power before going on to other parts of the selection."

The presentation of the readiness stage of the DRA should take approximately five to fifteen minutes but will vary in length and emphasis according to the ability of the students and the complexity of the selections. For less advanced students, it may be necessary to spend a longer time preparing them to read the selection than for preparing more advanced students. Depending upon how the teacher approaches the readiness stage, one component may encompass other aspects of this step. For instance, introducing new vocabulary may create interest and develop concept background simultaneously. With the exception of establishing purpose, which should conclude the readiness stage, the teacher need not present the other components in any established order.

2. Directed Silent Reading

Following the readiness stage of the DRA, the students should read the selection silently to seek answers to the purpose-questions that the teacher has set. It is emphasized that the teacher have students read the selection silently, and not orally. This way is more rapid, it is more characteristic of everyday reading needs, and it gives the students an opportunity to use their word attack skills without expressed effort.

If readiness activities have been thorough, many students will work efficiently with very little, if any, teacher help. The teacher should encourage students to work out word recognition problems independently; however, he or she might also be available in the event a student requests help with confirmation or analysis. Since silent reading is not a time for word attack drills, it is suggested that teachers guide students requiring help to clues which will aid them in unlocking the meaning of unknown words. If students seem unable to decode certain words, the teacher usually will provide these words so that reading may proceed. The teacher can make note of words giving students particular difficulty and/or specific skill needs of students as they attempt to decode words. Later, teachers can plan appropriate individual and/or group activities to counteract those difficulties.

3. Comprehension Check and Discussion

Discussion activities ordinarily develop spontaneously following silent reading. An obvious start of the discussion can be answering the purpose-questions set during the readiness stage, although discussion may begin naturally on other aspects of the selection.

During the discussion it is appropriate to stress and develop comprehension abilities. For example, teachers might formulate discussion questions on the interpretive or critical levels (thinking questions) to extend the ideas students glean from reading to set purposes.

4. Oral Rereading

This stage of the DRA may occur in conjuction with the previous stage (comprehension check and discussion) or the teacher may use it to set new purposes for reading. The teacher may set these purposes independently, or new purposes may develop out of the discussion or serve as a preparation for a follow-up activity. Rereading may also occur if students are confused about one of the discussion questions. If such is the case, the new purpose is for students to read to solve problems which have resulted from the discussion. Students reread rapidly to locate information under question and orally reread to the group to alleviate the confusion or to verify a point.

5. Follow-up Activities

Follow-up activities include those experiences that build and extend skill development, and activities that add to, or enrich, students' understanding of the concepts in the story. Activities that extend skill development include introducing new word attack skills, establishing the new terms of the story firmly in students' vocabulary, and further developing the students' comprehension abilities. This is also an appropriate time for the teacher to review any skills he or she noted during the silent reading that produced difficulty. Such activities are suitable on an individual basis, in a small group, or in a whole class situation.

The rationale behind this type of follow-up activity is that practice with, and opportunities to use, those skills presenting difficulty to students will provide them the reinforcement necessary to master those skills. As such, the use of basal reader workbooks, teacher-made worksheets, or commercially available material is often suggested to strengthen those specific skills that the DRA showed to be of concern.

Activities that can enrich or extend students' understanding of the story's concepts start with the premise that the application of newly learned concepts to other types of activities will further enhance and broaden new learning. Such extension activities may involve creative work, study activities, or extended reading. Creative work may include writing about personal experiences related to the story, dramatization, and making illustrations for the story. Study activities may include workbook exercises and teacher-made practice material. Students may also do research into the information they gain from the selection in order to organize it into a chart or table format. Examples of extended reading might include selected readings in other texts or library books on related topics, or reading to find answers to questions that arise in the discussion of the story.

Cautions and Comments

The effective use of the DRA requires teacher sensitivity to the students' needs, to the differential demands of text and to the adequacy of the DRA as a lesson framework. In this respect, the DRA seems to have one shortcoming; namely, it seems to be too teacher-dominated. Teacher-pupil interactions flow mainly from the questions and other activities the teacher prescribes. As a result, the DRA has the potential to develop students who are overly dependent upon teacher direction rather than upon their own reading-thinking processes. For this reason, the teacher might use alternate strategies to vary the approach to teaching a reading selection. In particular, aspects of the DR-TA, the ReQuest or the Guided Reading Procedure may serve as supplements to the Directed Reading Activity and also involve students more fully. For example, teachers can effectively utilize ReQuest as a replacement for the readiness stage of the DRA.

Another concern about the use of the DRA involves skills development, including oral reading, word recognition, comprehension and study skills. If implemented properly, skills instruction relates to the actual reading assignment; it can be purposeful and relevant. Isolated skills instruction or the practice of rotating turns of reading aloud or oral reading can become quite meaningless.

Despite these limitations, the DRA has adaptive potential to teach almost any reading selection. Indeed, teachers have used the DRA extensively in conjunction with both basal reading material and with content area reading material. For example, often within classrooms using basal reading programs, teachers use the DRA for a week with various ability groups. An example of such a schedule is included in this section.

A WEEK-LONG SCHEDULE FOR A DIRECTED READING ACTIVITY

Day One

Minutes	*Group I*	*Group II*	*Group III*
3–5	Teacher briefs students he or she does not work with directly. Students working directly with teacher organize themselves.		
25–30	*Stage I—Introducing the Selection* (Teacher present) Teacher introduces new story. *Stage II—Directed Silent Reading* (Teacher present) Students read story silently. *Stage III & IV—Comprehension Check and Oral Reading* (Teacher present) *Stage V—Follow-up* Students reread and write an alternative ending.	*Independent Reading* (Students independently) or *Bookmaking*	*Phase V—Follow-up Activities* (Students independently) Students work through activities reviewing outline. Students check own work. *Independent Work* (Students independently) Students begin work on a research problem.

Minutes	Group I	Group II	Group III
5–10	Teacher checks those students working independently, giving individuals help if needed.		
20–25	*Stage V—Follow up* (Students independently) Workbook activities. *Independent Reading* (Students independently)	*Stage I—Introducing the Selection* (Teacher present) *Stage II—Directed Silent Reading* (Teacher present) *Stage III—Comprehension Check* (Teacher present) *Stage IV—Oral Rereading* (Teacher present)	*Stage V—Follow-up* Students skim story to locate answers to questions. They create questions and ask them of each other. *Independent Reading*

Day Two

Minutes	Group I	Group II	Group III
3–5	Teacher organizes for instruction and briefs students.		
	Stage V—Follow-up (Teacher present) Teacher goes over work exercises. *Stage IV—Oral Rereading* (Teacher present) Oral rereading of selected conversations in story. *Stage V—Follow-up* (Teacher present) Word identification instruction.	*Independent Reading* (Students independently)	*Independent Reading* (Students independently)
3–5	Teacher organizes for instruction and briefing.		

Minutes	*Group I*	*Group II*	*Group III*
15–20	*Stage V—Follow-up Activities* (Students independently) Workbook activities. *Independent Reading* (Students independently)	*Stage V—Follow-up Activities* (Students independently) Students complete master dealing with context clues. *Independent Work* Research project.	*Stage V—Follow-up* (Teacher present) Review work from previous day. Students classify information from story and summarize.
5–10	Teacher checks work of groups, organizes for instruction, and briefs students.		
15–20	*Independent Reading* (Students independently)	*Stage V—Follow-up* (Teacher present) Teacher reviews use of context and other word identification skills.	*Stage V—Follow-up* (Students independently) Students continue work. *Independent Reading of Work*

Day Three

Minutes	*Group I*	*Group II*	*Group III*
3–5	Teacher organizes for instruction and briefs students.		
15–20	*Independent Reading* or *Independent Work* (Students independently) Dictated story; Bookmaking.	*Stage V—Follow-up* (Students independently) Students reread story silently to answer thought questions. Students prepare dramatization.	*Stage V—Follow-up* (Teacher present) Review classifying and summarizing. Reread parts of story for a radio show.
5–10	Group III shares reading experiences with Group I and II (radio play).		

Minutes	Group I	Group II	Group III
20–25	*Stage V—Follow-up* (Teacher present) Teacher checks work-book exercises. *Stage I—Introduces the Story* (Teacher present) *Stage II—Directed Silent Reading* (Teacher present) Stage III & Stage IV *Comprehension Check & Oral Rereading* (Teacher present)	*Stage V—Follow-up* (Students indepen-dently) Continue on previous activities. *Independent Reading* *or* *Independent Work* (Students indepen-dently) Research project.	*Stage V—Follow-up* (Students indepen-dently) Read related stories. Students use reference books to look for answers to ques-tions related to stories.
3–5	Teacher checks with other two groups and organizes class.		
10–15	Group II presents dramatization of story.		

Day Four

Minutes	Group I	Group II	Group III
3–5	Teacher organizes for instruction and briefs students.		
20–25	*Stage V—Follow-up* (Students indepen-dently) Students skim story to locate answers to specific questions. Students organize events from story into the correct sequence. *Independent Reading* (Students indepen-dently)	*Independent Reading* (Students indepen-dently) *Independent Work* (Students indepen-dently) Research project.	*Stage V—Follow-up* (Teacher present) Discussion of previous work. *Stage I—Introduces the Selection* (Teacher present) *Stage II—Directed Silent Reading* (Teacher present) *Stage III—Comprehen-sion Check & Stage IV—Oral Rereading* (Teacher present)
3–5	Teacher checks work of groups, organizes for instruction, and briefs groups.		

20–25	*Independent Reading* (Students independently) *Independent Work* Students move to learning center for research work.	*Stage VI—Follow-up* (Teacher present) Teacher discusses students' answers to thought questions from previous day. *Stage I—Introduces Selection* (Teacher present) *Stage II—Directed Silent Reading* (Teacher present) *Stage III—Comprehension Check* *Stage IV—Oral Rereading* (Teacher present)	*Stage V—Follow-up* (Students independently) Students organize information they recall from story into an outline. *Independent Reading* (Students independently)
3–5	Teacher introduces several new books for independent reading. Children share books they have read and enjoyed.		

Day Five

Minutes	*Group I*	*Group II*	*Group III*
3–5	Teacher briefs class and organizes for instruction.		
15–20	All three groups participate in independent reading. This may be through the use of U.S.S.R.		
3–5	Children terminate reading. Organize for class activity.		
15–20	Selected students may elect to continue reading for a few minutes. Remainder of class shares personal reading through book reports, posters, dramatizations, or displays. Teacher and children list five favorite magazine or newspaper articles.		
15–20	*Stage V—Follow-up Activities* (Teacher present) Students discuss and develop a mural based upon story.	*Independent Reading or Work* (Students independently)	*Independent Reading or Work* (Students independently)
Note:	The above pattern is suggestive rather than prescriptive. For each group the sequence would vary from week to week. Depending upon the nature of activities and the students' needs, the teacher might alter group structure in terms of size, membership, and number.		

REFERENCES

Betts, E. A. *Foundations of Reading Instruction.* New York: American Book, 1946.
Presents one of the original descriptions of the general principles and assumptions behind the DRA.

Karlin, R. *Teaching Elementary Reading: Principles and Strategies*, 2nd ed. New York: Harcourt, Brace, Jovanovich, 1975, pp. 146–151.
Describes the steps involved in the DRA when used with a basal reader.

Miller, W. H. *The First R: Elementary Reading Today*, 2nd ed. New York: Holt, Rinehart and Winston, 1977, pp. 59–78.
Provides general guidelines for using the DRA in the guise of a basal reader lesson.

Sheperd, D. L. *Comprehensive High School Reading Methods.* Columbus, Ohio: Charles E. Merrill, l973, pp. 132–138.
Outlines steps to adapt the DRA for use in the content fields.

Spache, G. D., and Spache, E. B. *Reading in the Elementary School,* 4th ed. Boston: Allyn and Bacon, 1977, pp. 46–53.
Provides an outlined procedure for teaching a typical basal reader lesson.

Stauffer, R. G. *Directing Reading Maturity as a Cognitive Process.* New York: Harper & Row, 1969, pp. 35–86.
Describes an alternative procedure to the DRA—The Directed Reading-Thinking Activity. Using the same fundamental steps as the DRA, this strategy promotes more student involvement.

DIRECTED READING-THINKING ACTIVITY

Purpose

The Directed Reading-Thinking Activity (DR-TA) is intended to develop students' ability to read critically and reflectively. Broadly speaking, it attempts to equip readers with:

1. The ability to determine purposes for reading
2. The ability to extract, comprehend, and assimilate information
3. The ability to examine reading material based upon purposes for reading
4. The ability to suspend judgments
5. The ability to make decisions based upon information gleaned from reading

Rationale

Russell Stauffer (1969) developed the DR-TA to provide conditions that would produce readers who could think, learn, and test. Stauffer suggests these readers

> . . . will learn to have the strength of their convictions and the courage to deal with ideas. They will not be fearful but courageous; not blind, but discerning; not hasty, but deliberate; not deceitful, but honest; not muddled, but articulate; not acquiescent, but militant; not conceited, but modest; not imitative, but original. (Stauffer, 1969, p. 84)

Stauffer based his notions upon the belief that reading is a thinking process that involves the reader in using his or her own experiences to reconstruct the author's ideas. The reconstruction begins with the generation of hypotheses based upon the reader's doubts and desires. It continues with the reader's acquisition of information and the generation of further hypotheses during reading. The reconstruction terminates with the resolution of the reader's doubts and desires. Stauffer puts this into practice with the DR-TA as follows:

> . . . either the reader declares his own purposes or if he adopts the purposes of others, he makes certain how and why he is doing so. He also speculates about the nature and complexity of the answers he is seeking by using to the fullest his experience and knowledge relevant to the circumstances. Then he reads to test his purposes and his assumptions. As a result, he may: one, find the answer he is seeking literally and completely stated; two, find only partial answers or implied answers and face the need to either restate his purposes in light of the new information gained or to suspend judgment until more reading has been done; three, need to declare completely new purposes. (Stauffer, 1969, p. 40)

Intended Audience

As with the Directed Reading Activity, the teacher can easily adapt the DR-TA for any selection at any level of difficulty. Toward a balanced reading program, Stauffer suggests the extension and differentiation of the DR-TA for both group and individual use. With groups, he suggests using it with from eight to twelve students. Shepherd (1978) has also suggested using the DR-TA with content fields.

Description of the Procedure

The DR-TA has two parts—a process cycle and a product. The process cycle involves the reader in the following: setting purposes for reading, adjusting the rate from these purposes and the material, reading to verify purposes, pausing to evaluate understanding, then proceeding to read with the same or with different purposes. The product of the DR-TA is the extension and refinement of students' ideas and thinking.

In describing the DR-TA Stauffer suggests procedures for a group DR-TA, which the teacher can extend and adapt into an individualized version.

1. Group DR-TA

There are certain essential phases in the implementation of a group DR-TA. The first phase involves directing reading-thinking processes. The second phase involves fundamental skill training.

a. *Phase One: Directing the reading-thinking process.* Directing the reading-thinking process involves the reader in three steps: predicting, reading, and proving. As students proceed through a selection, they predict or define purposes for reading, they read and select relevant data, and they evaluate and revise predictions using the information they acquire.

The teacher, the material and the group are all essential to the success of this activity. The teacher has to create an environment which will arouse students' curiosities and meet their reading needs. The group serves to audit and extend the thinking of its members. The material provides, Stauffer states, "the substance for cognition" (1969, p. 46). To this end, he suggests the material should be well-written, appealing in content, and of an appropriate difficulty level. For the purpose of directing the reading-thinking processes, the teacher may treat the selection in segments. Here is an example of how teachers might implement this phase with a selection divided into segments.

1. Each student would either receive or locate a copy of the selection; the teacher would direct the student to study either the title or the pictures on the first page.

    - What do you think a story with this title might be about?
    - What do you think might happen in this story?
    - Which of these predictions do you agree with?

    The teacher would encourage students to make several different suggestions and to discuss agreement or disagreement with one another's suggestions. The teacher serves to promote this interaction.
2. When the teacher introduces the DR-TA, he or she would first familiarize students with the strategy for dealing with unknown words. That is, if students encounter unknown words, the teacher would expect the students to implement the following steps in the specified order:

    a. Read to the end of the sentence
    b. Use picture clues, if available
    c. Sound out the word
    d. Ask the teacher for help

    Before asking for teacher assistance, the student would have to try to figure out the word and, according to Stauffer, the teacher should give the student the opportunity to do so.
3. The teacher would direct the students to read a segment of the story silently to check their predictions. The teacher would be

responsible for ensuring students read for meaning, observing reading performance, and helping students who request help with words. When the latter occurs, the teacher might have the student suggest a word it might be, explain what the student did to figure out the word, and, if the word is still unknown, the teacher would provide the word. Note that the teacher introduced no vocabulary prior to reading the story. Stauffer suggests this is unnecessary, given the vocabulary controls and systematic word identification programs found in basal readers.

4. After students have read the first segment, the teacher would ask them to close their books and the comprehension check would begin.

   Questions would serve to guide the students' examination of the evidence, their evaluation of their previous predictions, and their generation of new predictions.

   "Were you correct?" or *"What do you think now?"* would force students to examine the proof of their predictions. Oral reading of a particular sentence would direct students to share their evidence with other group members.

   "What do you think now?" or *"What do you think will happen?"* would encourage students to screen their ideas and to make predictions about events to come.

5. The students would read the next segment of text and with each new segment of reading material, would continue the predicting, reading, and proving cycle. As students proceed, they come upon more and more information, and divergent conjectures would begin to converge. At the beginning of the selection, predictions would tend to be divergent. Toward the end of the reading, predictions would tend to converge.

b. *Phase Two: Fundamental Skill Training.* After the students have read the selection, the teacher has completed first phase of the DR-TA—directing the reading-thinking of the selection. Now the second phase begins. Stauffer refers to this phase as the phase when "skill training of a different kind is accomplished" (1969, p. 64). The second phase entails re-examining the story, re-examining selected words or phrases, and pictures or diagrams, for the purpose of developing systematically and concurrently the students' reading-thinking abilities and other reading-related skills. These might include word attack, the use of semantic analysis, concept clarification and development, power of observation, and reflective abilities. The format of these activities would vary, but, in many cases, would also be similar to the suggested exercises in the teacher's edition, the workbooks or the skillbooks accompanying most basal reading systems.

2. Individualized DR-TA

Individualized DR-TAs apply, extend, and refine the skills and abilities students acquire in group DR-TAs. Stauffer claims that individualized DR-TAs afford a systematic method by which students can learn about themselves in terms of their own interests, tasks, judgments, and thinking abilities.

Teachers can introduce individualized DR-TAs after group DR-TAs or for use in conjunction with them. Familiarity with group DR-TA procedures is a prerequisite for introducing an individualized DR-TA.

There are several features which distinguish an individualized DR-TA:

a. It does not use traditional grouping; instead, each student is free to work with a minimum of interruption, in pursuit of his or her interests. If interests coincide, students may occasionally work together.
b. The teacher expects students to know why they are to select materials, what materials they might select, and how they should select them. To this end, the teacher schedules time for selection of material and for discussion of selection techniques. The teacher may help students either individually or in groups to formulate interests, needs, and methods for selection.
c. Students should generate their own reading purposes and be familiar with the predicting, reading, proving cycle of the DR-TA. Either worksheet or student record cards might direct these processes.
d. At scheduled times, students should share their work or what they have read with others. This process might involve the use of posters, bulletin boards, dramatizations, reports, and the like.
e. As the need arises, students receive incidental or systematic skills instruction, individually or in groups.
f. Students should abide by class rules established to ensure individual rights and efficient learning.
g. Students should keep meaningful records on a daily or weekly basis. These records might track students' activities, the stories they read, or their skill needs.
h. Students can develop other language-related skills (oral expression, written expression, listening) through presentations, reports, verbal sharing, and other activities.
i. Throughout the individualized DR-TAs, the teacher should serve various functions, including the following:
    1. Organizing groups for projects and skill training
    2. Organizing the schedule to ensure flexibility and efficiency
    3. Pacing the various activities to afford maximum success and a mininum of frustration
    4. Establishing operating rules to facilitate learning and thinking
    5. Maintaining meaningful records to map individual progress and planning future activities
    6. Guiding, directing, and assisting students

Cautions and Comments

As lesson frameworks, the Directed Reading Activity and the DR-TA are suitable for use with almost any reading selection. But the DR-TA has certain features which distinguish it from the Directed Reading Activity. First, the DR-TA places a heavy emphasis upon the relationship between reading and thinking. It encourages students to be aware of and to develop their own reading-thinking processes through initiating their own purposes for reading. Second, the DR-TA material governs teacher-pupil interactions and students' purposes for reading; the teacher's questioning does not prescribe this interaction. Third, the teacher does not assume the role of either questioner or judge. Instead, the teacher becomes a moderator, and a facilitator. Fourth, the student does not meet words prior to reading but as they occur in context. To see some of these differences more clearly, consider the use of both the DRA and DR-TA with a single selection (see the sample lesson plan in this section).

For teachers familiar with traditional reading materials, the DR-TA affords a useful alternative, but one that they should not use repeatedly. For example, teachers might need to vary both the treatment of the reading-thinking phase and the format of activities within the fundamental skill phase. With repeated use, children can become "programmed" to the strategy rather than involved in reading-thinking interactions. If teachers find their students unable or unwilling to make predictions, they may need to supplement the approach with games and activities which encourage predictive behaviors. Teachers may find the presentation of either incomplete pictures, jigsaw pieces, or cartoons useful devices for generating predictions. Teachers may sometimes read a story to students for the purpose of either introducing or supplementing the predicting, reading, proving cycle.

SAMPLE LESSON PLAN FOR A DIRECTED READING ACTIVITY AND A DIRECTED READING-THINKING ACTIVITY

To compare the use of a Directed Reading Activity and a Directed Reading-Thinking Activity, here are two lesson plans for the same selection. One lesson plan represents what a teacher might typically do using a Directed Reading Activity Approach. The other lesson plan represents what a user might typically do with a Directed Reading-Thinking Activity.

The Selection

The selection we have chosen for this purpose is a story entitled "The Surprise," suitable for use in a second grade classroom. "The Surprise" tells what happened to a child's box of cookies. The child had made the cookies for his or her teacher. The teacher inadvertently sits on the box, crumbling the child's cookies. The story ends happily, with the children and the teacher having a party.

Directed Reading Activity

I. *Introducing the Selection*

In the Directed Reading Activity, the teacher introduces the selection by attempting to do four things: build an interest in the story, build concept background, introduce new vocabulary, set purposes.

Show children a white box. Ask them what they think the box is (create interest). Explain to students that what you have is a surprise. Have them relate surprises they have received (concept background). Write the words *surprise* and *children* on the chalkboard. Have the students say the words and use them in a sentence (introduce vocabulary). Direct children to the story entitled "The Surprise" and have them read the first page to learn who is getting the surprise (setting purpose).

II. *Directed Silent Reading*

As the students silently read the designated section, the teacher stands by to help. If the student has difficulty with a word, the authors suggest the teacher provide it immediately. Once the students have located the answer to the question, the teacher directs them either to mark with their finger, or to remember the word, sentence, or section that told them the answer.

III. *Comprehension Check and Skill Building*

Directed Reading-Thinking Activity

I. *Introducing the Selection*

In the Directed Reading-Thinking Activity, the teacher encourages the students to make their own predictions concerning what they are about to read. The teacher neither introduces vocabulary nor sets purpose.

Show children a white box. Ask them what they think the box is. Explain to students that what you have is a surprise. Have them turn to the story entitled "The Surprise" and have them make predictions about the surprise. Ask questions like:

What do you think a story like this is about?

What do you think will happen in this story?

(The teacher might refer them to the picture clues.) Direct students to read the first page to learn about their predictions.

II. *Directed Silent Reading*

As the students silently read the designated section, the teacher stands by to help. If the student has difficulty with a word, there is a set procedure to follow. This procedure involves:

1. Reading to the end of the sentence
2. Using picture clues, if available
3. Sounding out the word
4. (If the students still do not recognize the word) asking the teacher

Once the students have finished the designated page, they turn over their books and await the teacher.

III. *Comprehension Check and Skill Building*

IV. *Oral Rereading*
The teacher asks the students to answer this previous question:

Who was the surprise for?

The students share their answers and verify them by orally rereading the sentences or sentence that yielded the answer. The teacher asks other related questions:

Who is Miss Day?

Who is Jay?

Repetition of Phases I, II, III & IV
As the students progress through the rest of the selection in segments, the teacher sets further purposes for their reading, the teacher checks their comprehension, and the students orally reread to verify answers.

IV. *Oral Rereading*
The teacher asks the students how accurate their predictions were. The students produce the proof they used to verify their predictions by orally rereading the sentences or sentence that yielded the answer. The teacher asks students to share what else they now know.

Repetition of Phases I, II, III & IV
As the students progress through the rest of the selection in segments, the teacher asks them to make further predictions, to silently read to verify them, to revise, and to evaluate these predictions. The students refine the predictions with more information, as in the phases described under *Introducing the Selection.* Students repeat Directed Silent Reading, Comprehension Check, Skill Building, and Oral Rereading.

A teacher may use the patterns exemplified here for teaching a story or article at any level; however, there may be some differences. The teacher may or may not break the selection into segments. What the teacher actually does within each phase will vary. These variations will depend upon the selection, the students themselves, and their purposes for reading.

Follow-up Activities

In the Directed Reading Activity, various and sundry follow-up activities usually occur. In the main, they center upon developing the following skills:

1. Comprehension
2. Word identification
3. Study skills
4. Literary appreciation and understanding
5. Vocabulary
6. Oral reading

In addition, typical follow-up activities would afford opportunities for enrichment.

Follow-up Activities

In the Directed Reading-Thinking Activities, the follow-up activities would be virtually the same as those we propose for a Directed Reading Activity. Indeed, a teacher might use the examples here across both strategies. To follow-up the Directed Reading-Thinking Activity, Stauffer suggests Fundamental Skill Activities which would be similar to the follow-up activities suggested in most basal programs.

Here are some examples:

1. *Oral rereading.* Explain to students that the story they have read has plenty of conversation; have them take parts and reread the story.

2. *Comprehension.* Write several sentences which describe events that either did or did not happen in the story. Have the students decide which events did happen and then arrange the order.

   The children did not like the cookies.
   The children had a party.
   Jay made little cookies.
   Jay dropped the box.
   They went to the zoo.

3. *Word identification.* Have students locate the following words in the story: looked, carried, hurried, parties. Have students locate the ending and root words.

4. *Enrichment.*

   (a) Present the students with a recipe they might follow to make cookies. Make some as a group project.
   (b) Have students make a surprise for a friend.
   (c) Dramatize the story.

REFERENCES

Shephard, D. L. *Comprehensive High School Reading Methods,* 2nd ed. Columbus, Ohio: Charles Merrill, 1978.
Presents a discussion of how the Directed Reading-Thinking Activities might be used in the content areas.

Stauffer, R. G. *Directing Reading Maturity as a Cognitive Process.* New York: Harper & Row, 1969.
Intended for the graduate or advanced student, this text presents a detailed description of the procedure and its rationale.

Stauffer, R. G. *The Language-Experience Approach to the Teaching of Reading.* New York: Harper & Row, 1970, pp. 132–176.
Presents a readable description of the strategy and its use.

Stauffer, R. G. "Productive Reading-Thinking at the First Grade Level." *Reading Teacher* 13 (1960): 183–187.
Presents a brief description of the use of reading-thinking strategies with first graders.

Stauffer, R. G. *Teaching Reading as a Thinking P.ocess.* New York: Harper & Row, 1976.
Intended for the less advanced student, this text presents the procedure in detail, but with less theory.

Stauffer, R. G., and Harrel, M. M. "Individualized Reading-Thinking Activities." *The Reading Teacher* 28, no. 8 (1975): 765–769.
Describes a program for individualizing Directed Reading-Thinking Activities.

2

Strategies for Content Area Reading and the Improvement of Study Skills

UNIT OVERVIEW

Content teachers are aware of numerous students who have difficulty understanding content area reading material despite their having received either so-called basic reading skills instruction or corrective training in separate reading classes. To overcome these shortcomings, attention has recently focused on providing content area teachers and their reading teacher colleagues with tools to guide students in reading content area material. In other words, the emphasis has shifted from indirect to direct instruction in content area reading material and in content classrooms. Few would disagree that the work of Harold Herber (1970, 1978) has been instrumental in this change and in initiating new techniques.

The Strategies

Obviously there are countless strategies which are suitable for guiding and improving content area reading. This unit, however, will limit its presentation to some of the more common strategies that content area reading advocates suggest. In all, the unit presents eight teaching techniques a teacher may use specifically in content classrooms. All but one of these are very specific in nature. The more general strategy, the instructional framework, provides a total lesson design for the subject matter teacher. The remaining seven techniques could function as important components of the framework or as substitutes for the framework design. The reader who is interested in going beyond this unit to other suitable strategies may want to review Unit One: Lesson Frameworks and Strategies for Improving Comprehension.

The unit begins with a brief description of each of the instructional strategies for content reading.

Instructional Framework

The three major phases of the instructional framework—preparation, guidance, independence—provide the content teacher with a viable design for presenting a unit of study. The framework provides a means for teaching both the important reading skills (process) the students need, as well as the important concepts (product) of the unit. Thus, process and product merge in the development of independent learners. The strategy is appropriate for both fictional and expository materials and would appear most suitable for students in grades four and above.

Study Guides

The backbone of the instructional framework is the study guide, which students use in dealing with the content. Study guides can guide students through their content area textbook reading by focusing their attention on the major ideas presented.

Selective Reading Guide-O-Rama

The Selective Reading Guide-O-Rama provides the content teacher an opportunity to guide the students to the relevant information within the content unit. This helps the student to see the significant information within the chapter. Suited for students in grades six and above, the technique appears to offer more assistance to those readers who may experience difficulty with the material.

Structured Overviews

Numerous techniques exist for introducing the new technical vocabulary of a content unit to a class. Based upon the concept of advanced organizers, the structured overview provides the content teacher an opportunity not only to present the new terms prior to assigning the unit, but also to indicate through a visual schema how these new words relate to each other.

Notetaking System for Learning

Much of what students learn in secondary and college classrooms comes from the instructor via the lecture method. Effective notetaking procedures can do much to aid students in learning and retaining a vast amount of information. Although the literature describes several notetaking methods, the authors have selected one successful technique for inclusion in this unit.

Herringbone

A strategy best suited for the history classroom, the herringbone technique can provide the students a logical means of outlining and thus remembering the events of history. Appropriate for students in the middle grades and above, the technique would be useful to all students initially, but it appears most beneficial to students who experience difficulty with organizing material.

SQ3R Method of Study

The reading literature describes a variety of study methods. Some techniques appear to be useful across all subject areas; others are specifically for individual content subjects. This unit discusses the SQ3R procedure and refers to several other study techniques.

Survey Technique

Designed as a spinoff of the SQ3R method of study, the survey technique is a strategy which could be a substitute for the preparation stage of the instructional framework or for the readiness stage of a Directed Reading Activity. The technique offers the teacher and students an opportunity to "walk through" the chapter together. Most useful with students who might find the material especially difficult, the survey technique also furnishes the teacher an opportunity to show the students a model of good study techniques.

Utilization

Either through in-service or pre-service training, the reading field has much to offer the subject matter instructors at all levels in the form of practical teaching suggestions. The present unit should assist the content teacher, or the reading specialist who works with subject matter instructors, by providing a discussion of strategies for helping students to cope with content material.

INSTRUCTIONAL FRAMEWORK

Purpose

The purpose of the instructional framework (Herber, 1970) is to:

1. Provide content area teachers with a structure for presenting a content lesson
2. Teach not only the content (product) of the unit, but also the skills (process) necessary to understand the content

Rationale

Most content reading materials are written at a relatively high level of sophistication. The introduction of new concepts can be confounded by technical vocabulary and complex explanations.

It would seem students need a structure that will help them cope with the process of learning in order that they meet the product expectancies of learning. Herber's instructional framework is designed to do just that. Specifically, the instructional framework provides a structure for lessons that is intended to guide students' reading processes and products. The eventual aim is to enable students to apply these structures independently in their own reading.

Intended Audience

The technique may be used at all levels with students whose learning demands understanding content reading material. The study guide component allows for individual instruction or for instruction with the entire class.

Description of the Procedure

Before the classroom teacher can implement the instructional framework, decisions are necessary regarding: (1) the major concepts to be emphasized within a given selection; (2) each concept's relative importance to the unit and to the subject as a whole; (3) the major technical vocabulary terms that appear to be important in understanding and communicating the major concepts; and (4) the specific skills the students need in order to learn the concepts. After he or she has made these decisions (Herber, 1970), the content instructor is ready to prepare the content lesson.

The basic structure of the instructional framework has three major components:

1. Preparation
2. Guidance
3. Independence

A sample lesson plan for an instructional framework follows the description of these three components.

1. Preparation

Before students are assigned to read the new chapter, the teacher should "prepare" them for the assignment. The amount of time spent on the preparation stage of the lesson will depend upon the students' reading and study skills and their background experiences with the topic. The order may vary from one unit to the next, but the specific stages of the preparation phase are:

a. *Motivation.* Although sometimes difficult to attain, the goal should be to complete the preparation stage of the lesson with each student *wanting* to learn more about the topic. This can be accomplished by involving the students as much as possible in the learning act itself. Field trips, films, filmstrips, records, tapes, study prints, and demonstrations are just a few of the motivational techniques the classroom teacher might use. The remaining steps within the preparation phase of the instructional framework are designed to provide the students with further motivation.

b. *Background Information and Review.* Authors of content material assume that students have a certain amount of knowledge related to the particular content unit. If this background information is not present, it is the responsibility of the content teacher to "fill the gaps." Otherwise, a review of information already known by the students also is suggested. This segment of the strategy provides the important "mind set" for learning the new information.

c. *Anticipation and Purpose.* At the conclusion of the preparation stage, students should anticipate certain new understandings to be gained. Establishing purposes in two very specific areas—the product (ideas to be discovered) and the process (skills to be applied in order to gain that information)—can heighten students' anticipation.

d. *Direction.* After students understand what skills will be necessary to learn the new information, the instructor gives the students specific assistance in ways to use the identified skills. If the students are already accomplished in the specific skill, a brief review may be all that is necessary; however, if the teacher is aware of student skill deficiencies, this would be the time when skills teaching takes place. For example, suppose that the author of the unit under consideration has consistently used the organizational pattern of cause-effect (Niles, 1965). An understanding of cause-effect patterns might then be appropriate for students as it will aid their text understanding.

e. *Vocabulary Development.* A major hurdle for students in content material is the technical language of the particular subject under study. To assist the student in the acquisition of the important concepts, the major vocabulary in any given unit is pretaught. One specific method of preteaching vocabulary, the structured overview, appears later in this unit.

2. Guidance

As a logical follow-up to this purpose setting and direction, the teacher should now provide guidance in two important areas—the development of skills (the process), and the development of concepts (the product). This structured form of support is determined by the nature of the material and the abilities of the students. The two components of the guidance phase of the instructional framework are:

a. *Development of Skills.* Here, Herber (1970) suggests the use of reading guides, a special type of study guide "designed to show students how to apply skills as they read" (p. 36). A detailed explanation of the development and use of reading guides, including numerous examples, is available in Herber's *Teaching Reading in Content Areas* (1978).

Using the example from Niles (1965), during the direction portion of the preparation stage the instructor would teach the students how to recognize and how to glean information from the organizational pattern of cause-effect. A reading guide could then be used to develop the new skill further, while, at the same time, the teacher guides the student to the important information within the unit. For example, the teacher might list in a study guide some possible causes and require the students to supply the effects they gleaned from the selection.

b. *Development of Concepts.* Another type of study guide, designed to improve students' understanding of the major concepts of the unit, is the reasoning guide (Heber, 1970). The reasoning guide involves the development and use of a study guide for postreading extensions. This form of guidance allows the content instructor to lead the student to the major concepts within the selection and to extend the student's understanding both critically and creatively.

3. Independence

Finally, the teacher must provide opportunities for students in the

a. Application of Skills
b. Application of Concepts

In both instances, it is important that students have occasions to use these newly acquired skills and concepts in other settings. As Herber (1978) suggests, this may entail coaching by the teacher. (For example, indirect questioning by the teacher may implicitly alert the student to the use of the framework in the student's own reading. This may entail recalling prior uses of the framework and a discussion of its possible use with other material.)

Cautions and Comments

The instructional framework provides teachers with a structure for presenting a content lesson; it provides students with a procedure for acquiring understandings from content reading. But the strategy is teacher-dominated rather than student-centered. Indeed, the constant use of the lesson plan format along with study guides and structured overviews may impose on rather than develop students' own reading-learning abilities and strategies. Toward the goal of increasing student independence, the teacher will need to vary the instructional framework with the differential needs of students across texts.

The constant use of this lesson plan format along with the teacher-developed study guides may result in less than exciting lessons. The creative teacher should seek ways to vary the strategy in order to insure total student involvement and eventual student independence.

An individual content teacher may find it extremely difficult and time consuming to develop a program centered around the concept of the instructional framework. For that reason, teacher teams might be formed to develop such a program. Personnel involved in pre- and in-service training sessions could set aside sufficient amounts of time so that teachers could take part in meaningful activities designed to "pay off" in the classroom. Finally, an increasingly large number of school districts are reassigning their more experienced reading teachers to positions as resource teachers. One of the major functions of these individuals could well be to assist the content teachers in the development and use of the instructional framework.

For an extended discussion of this strategy, the reader is directed to the description of study guides, and to the structured overview given in this unit.

SAMPLE LESSON PLAN FOR AN INSTRUCTIONAL FRAMEWORK[1]

Example of Instructional Framework

I. PREPARATION

A. Motivation

1. Could discuss possible results of "suburban sprawl." What happens each time a new subdivision is built in our community?
2. Refer to picture on page 232 of a portion of a marketplace in Guadalajara, Mexico. "What do you see? What basic need of man could be filled by the items pictured?" (Kimble, Teachers Edition, p. 233)

B. Background Information and Review

1. If available, show film, "Foods around the World." (Coronet Instructional Films, 11 min., color)
2. Following specific discussion of film, ask, "What is needed in order to use land for growing crops or raising animals?" (Kimble, T. E., p. 233) List these points on board. List might include: sunlight, soil, water, proper temperature, seed, methods of planting, methods for insuring proper growth, methods for harvesting, food for animals, shelter for animals.

1. Developed for "Trailblazers in the Search for Food," in G. H. T. Kimble, *Man and His World*. Morristown, N.J.: Silver Burdett, 1972, ch. 12, pp. 232–251.

3. "Can we raise crops or animals in an area that does not have all these things? If so, what is needed to do so?" (Kimble, T. E., p. 233)
4. "Can you see how we can relate what we learned in the last chapter on the haves and the have-nots to this chapter on food?"

C. Anticipation and Purpose
1. As a result of the above discussion, students should have some notion of the type of information we will be learning in this chapter.
2. Set purposes in terms of
   a. Content. Ex: "In our study of this chapter, we will want to note
      (1) How increased population effects the available land and the actual food supply
      (2) Ways in which dependence on other nations is good and bad
      (3) How improved technology might overcome some of our problems"
   b. Process. Ex: "You will learn much of this information if you can
      (1) Accurately interpret the wealth of information displayed on the six maps in this short chapter
      (2) Recognize the two writing patterns that the author uses throughout this chapter—cause-effect and comparison-contrast"

D. Direction

If students do not possess sufficient map reading skills or if they have not been taught the two organizational patterns mentioned above, provide appropriate instruction for one or both of these skills. This teaching can be done by using the material within this chapter or by using supplemental material. If students already possess these skills, instruction will not be necessary.

E. Language Development

This particular chapter is divided into three segments by the text author. The following terms may be pretaught as an introduction to each lesson

Lesson 1 Arable land, cultivation, tillage, polder
Lesson 2 Strains, steppes, plant breeder, animal breeding, mixed farming
Lesson 3 Custom, tradition, agricultural specialists

II. GUIDANCE

Guide(s) may be developed to provide students with an opportunity to use the newly acquired skill(s) taught in Direction phase mentioned above and, at the same time, to learn the important chapter content.

The following guide could be used with the first portion of this chapter.

Cause-Effect Relationships

Cause	*Effect*
1. "In England and Wales, . . . more than 100,000 acres of land are needed yearly for new homes, factories, airfields, highways, parking lots, and playing fields. Nearly all of this land is first-rate farming land." (Kimble, p. 233)	1.

The following actions resulted in specific changes to land previously thought of as nonproductive (p. 235):

2. In the Netherlands, they turned the Zuider Zee into land called *polders.*	2.
3. The Egyptians built the High Dam across the Nile at Aswan.	3.
4. The Soviet Union built dams and irrigation canals.	4.

Additional guides may be developed to provide students with the necessary structure for learning both the process of learning the material and the material itself.

Students may use the guides individually, followed by small group discussion, then large group discussion.

III. INDEPENDENCE

The teacher should provide opportunities in which students might use their newly learned skills and concepts in new settings.

Here are some of the possibilities with this chapter:

- Establish research groups to explore more specifically the Netherlands *polder* plan, the Aswan Dam, and other land-reclamation projects.
- Invite a local agricultural specialist to class ". . . to discuss new strains of plants or animals that are being developed in your own area." (Kimble, T. E., p. 242)
- "Divide the class into groups and assign each one a vegetable—rutabaga, broccoli, brussels sprouts, etc. Each group is to plan a campaign that will 'sell' the vegetable to the rest of the class." (Kimble, T. E., p. 250)

REFERENCES

Herber, H. L. *Teaching Reading in Content Areas.* Englewood Cliffs, N.J.: Prentice-Hall, 1970.
The original source of information on the instuctional framework.

Herber, H. L. *Teaching Reading in Content Areas,* 2nd ed. Englewood Cliffs, N.J.: Prentice-Hall, 1978.
The primary and updated source of information on the instructional framework.

Niles, O. S. "Organization Perceived." In H. L. Herber, ed., *Developing Study Skills in Secondary Schools.* Newark, Del.: International Reading Association, 1965.
Describes the various organizational patterns in factual writing and provides numerous examples of the four major writing patterns—enumerative order, time order, cause-effect, and comparison-contrast.

STUDY GUIDES

Purpose

Study guides (Earle, 1969; Herber, 1978) are designed to:

1. Guide a student through reading assignments in content area textbooks
2. Focus a reader's attention on the major ideas presented in a textbook

Rationale

Reading in a content area textbook may demand a relatively high level of skill development. As Herber argues, this kind of reading entails the student's acquiring an awareness of levels of comprehension and of how to function at each level. Then, once secure in these levels, the student should acquire the ability to consider and deal with the organizational patterns of the different reading materials. Toward this end, study guides can be useful in developing the ability of students to learn how to read. Specifically, study guides purport to develop the *student's* understanding of, and ability to deal with, levels of comprehension, the organizational patterns of different texts, and the specific skills these might require. Study guides do this by structuring and guiding the reading of textbook material or students' post-reading reasoning.

Intended Audience

Study guides are used mainly in conjunction with content area subjects. They may be used in both individual and group instructional situations and can be adapted to aid students regardless of the students' ability level in reading.

Description of the Procedure

Discussion of study guides as an integral part of a well-planned lesson will include the following three components:

1. Development of Study Guides
2. Construction of Study Guides
3. Use of Study Guides

1. Development of Study Guides

Before they can construct a study guide for use with their students, teachers must analyze the content material to be read by the students for both content and process (Earle, 1969). By analyzing the materials, teachers are assured that the study guide material used by students will be in keeping with the content objectives teachers have in mind.

In analyzing the material for both content and process, teachers themselves should first thoroughly read the material they plan to assign to students. Teachers are then better able to select the content to be emphasized during the lesson. In this way, portions of the assigned material fitting the overall objectives of the subject will be emphasized, and those portions not doing so can be deleted, leaving students the opportunity to concentrate on the portions deemed important.

For example, with a reading assignment from a social studies course involving "the Black Revolution," a teacher might decide that the concepts *black, nationalism, non-violence, black power, separatism,* and the *advocates* of these courses of action, are important for students to master.

Once the content to be emphasized has been decided, teachers then must decide the processes (skills) that students must use in acquiring that content. Earle (1969) and Herber (1978) suggested the decisions made regarding the skills to be used in mastering the material concern an understanding of levels of comprehension and patterns of organization.

Herber (1978) described three levels of comprehension: literal, interpretive, and applied. Literal understanding involves identifying factual material and knowing what the author said. Interpretive understanding involves inferring relationships among the details and knowing what the author meant. Finally, applied understanding involves developing generalizations which extend beyond the assigned material. Herber suggests that it is necessary to master understanding at one level before proceeding to the next. With the content to be emphasized, the teacher must decide what levels of understanding students will need.

Earle (1969) described four patterns of organization in which textual information is frequently found: cause and effect, comparison and contrast, sequence or time order, and simple listing. Dealing with the particular way in which information is organized in a text aids students in mastering the content. Therefore, the teacher must ascertain the pattern of organization for the information in a given text. Together with levels of comprehension, the identification of patterns of organization provides students with the necessary structure to study the assigned material.

Continuing with our example of "the Black Revolution," the teacher might determine that all three levels of understanding are necessary to deal successfully with the portions of the text to be emphasized. In addition, the comparison-and-contrast pattern of organization may be found to be used by the text authors in organizing their information.

One last step must be accomplished before the study guide is constructed. The teacher must consider the students' abilities in relation to the content and processes to be emphasized. By doing this, the teacher can provide differing amounts of assistance to insure that all students complete the assignment successfully.

In this step the teacher must consider two points: the students' competencies and the difficulty of the material itself (Earle, 1969). Keeping these two factors in mind, the teacher decides how much structure should be provided each student to address the content. For instance, the teacher can provide aids to locate the desired material in the form of page and/or paragraph numbers. Also, the teacher must decide whether guides should be constructed for only a single level of comprehension or for differential levels, so particular students may be assigned only to deal with those levels commensurate with their abilities. Teachers, knowing the individual needs and abilities of their students, will have to make these kinds of judgments and to vary the structure of study guides to insure the success of their students.

2. Construction of Study Guides

Once decisions have been made regarding the content and process and the types of assistance to be provided, teachers are ready to construct their study guides. Although there is no standard form which a study guide must take, Earle (1969) recommends the following guidelines:

a. Avoid overcrowding print on the study guide as it may overwhelm some students
b. Make the guide interesting enough so students will be motivated to deal with the information
c. Be sure the guide reflects the instructional decisions made with regard to content and process

Continuing with our previous example, study guides can be constructed to aid students in mastering the concepts and in acquiring the skills needed to do so.

Here are two examples of study guides, one concerning levels of comprehension and the other involving the comparison-and-contrast pattern of organization.[2]

READING GUIDE #1: LEVELS OF COMPREHENSION

* Literal level
** Interpretive level
*** Applied level

* 1) What are the basic steps of a nonviolent campaign? (p. 634, par. 4)

*** 2) Why did the political leaders of Birmingham refuse to engage in good faith?

** 3) Why does Stokely Carmichael think "integration is a joke"? (p. 636)

*** 4) Why do you think the authors say that the SNCC has become more militant since the early 1960s?

** 5) Why did SNCC choose the black panther as its symbol? (p. 637)

* 6) What is black nationalism? (p. 639, par. 1)

** 7) Why did the man in the tavern say the extremists would end up in concentration camps? (p. 640)

*** 8) Why do so many people think the racial problem has to be solved in our generation? (p. 640)

* 9) What does the term "black Jim Crow" mean? (p. 641, par. 4)

* 10) Who is Thurgood Marshall? (p. 642, par. 3)

** 11) Why does Thurgood Marshall fear the black militants? (p. 643, par. 2)

*** 12) Why do black people think black studies programs are essential?

READING GUIDE #2: PATTERNS OF ORGANIZATION

Directions:
1.) Match the name of a black leader in Column A with his strategy in Column B. Put the number of that name in the blank provided in Column B.
2.) Match the name of a black leader in Column A with the ideas in Column C. Put the number in the blank provided in Column C.

2. Based on material from M. Sandler, E. Rozwenc, and E. Martin, Strategies of the 'Black' Revolution," in *The People Make a Nation.* Boston: Allyn and Bacon, 1971, pp. 634–644.

A. *Names*

1) Martin Luther King
2) Stokely Carmichael
3) Roy Innis
4) Roy Wilkins
5) Thurgood Marshall

B. *Strategies*

______black nationalism
______anti-separatism
______non-violence
______leadership through education
______black power

C. *Ideas*

______Our philosophy is one of self-determination.
______White power has been scaring black people for 400 years.
______Direct action is the only way to force the issue. (p. 635)
______You can't use color for an excuse for not doing what you should be doing. (p. 643)
______Current black studies programs represent another form of segregated education. (p. 641)
______Nothing will be settled with guns or rocks.
______You must be able to accept blows without retaliation.
______We must rehabilitate blacks as people. (p. 639)
______Black history is significant only if taught in the context of world history.
______Our idea is to put men in office who will work for the people they represent. (p. 638)

It should be noted that these sample guides have been constructed with varying amounts of assistance (page and paragraph numbers) and level of comprehension designated. Teachers may decide to use only one or all of the levels, depending on what decisions have been made with regard to individual students.

3. Use of the Study Guides

Study guides should be used in the context of a well-planned lesson. Students should be prepared for the reading assignment through background development and a purpose-setting discussion. A follow-up discussion also might be provided after the guides have been used. The instructional framework (described in this unit) or the Directed Reading Activity (described in Unit 1) may provide the lesson framework needed to incorporate the study guides as one element in that lesson.

When first using study guides, teachers may need to "walk" students through a portion of a guide so that they will become acquainted with the procedure and will be better able to use the guides. Specifically, this step may aid students in seeing how the relationship between content and process can be fostered.

Groups of students can work on study guides cooperatively in lieu of using them individually. In this way, students can collaboratively arrive at responses to the guide. The activity promotes students' active involvement in the reading/learning process.

Finally, as students develop sensitivity to study guides and begin to transfer their new learning to other situations, the varying structure included in the initial guides may be progressively withdrawn. In this way, students are encouraged toward independence in their reading.

Cautions and Comments

Study guides can provide the means by which to encourage students to become active participants in the learning process rather than passive observers. Additionally, study guides aid teachers in insuring that the important concepts present in text material are communicated to students. Particularly in group situations, study guides represent a unique opportunity to explore ideas and do not tie students directly to recall-type learning. They are versatile, and their judicious use may provide the kind of instuctional environment necessary to develop students' independence in reading and thinking.

Two cautions should be mentioned with regard to study guides. First, it does take time and effort on the part of the teacher to develop, construct, and use them effectively. This caution, however, should be put into perspective alongside the benefits to students' understanding.

Second, although study guides are designed to move readers toward eventual independence, they are essentially teacher-directed activities. Teachers, not readers, decide what is important in reading the texts. Decision making, therefore, in this learning situation rests almost entirely with teachers. Those educators concerned with creating a learning environment involving students as much as possible must bear this factor in mind when using study guides. In partial response to this point, Herber (1970) remarked:

> How much better for students to expend energy using skills to explore content rather than discovering the skills by which the content will eventually be explored. Although we should fear too much structure, we should also fear the lack of it. (p. 131)

Check appendix for the following:
Examples of Study Guides

REFERENCES

Dishner, E. K., and Readance, J. E. "Getting Started: Using the Textbook Diagnostically." *Reading World* 17 (1977): 36–49.
Recommends the use of study guides as diagnostic tools for the content area teacher.

Earle, R. A. "Developing and Using Study Guides." In H. L. Herber and P. L. Sanders, eds., *Research in Reading in the Content Areas: First Year Report.* Syracuse, N.Y.: Reading and Language Arts Center, Syracuse University, 1960, pp. 71–92.
Provides directions for the content area teacher in how to develop and use study guides as an instructional tool.

Estes, T., and Vaughan, J. L. *Reading and Learning in the Content Classroom.* Boston: Allyn and Bacon, 1978, pp. 157–176.
Discusses the uses of study guides with examples.

Herber, H. L. *Teaching Reading in the Content Areas.* Englewood Cliffs, N.J.: Prentice-Hall, 1970.
Original source for the rationale and use of study guides.

Herber, H. L. *Teaching Reading in Content Areas*, 2nd ed. Englewood Cliffs, N.J.: Prentic-Hall, 1978.
Discusses the use of study guides in conjunction with the instructional framework, a teaching strategy for content area teachers.

SELECTIVE READING GUIDE-O-RAMA

Purpose

The major objectives of the Selective Reading Guide-O-Rama (Cunningham and Shablak, 1975) are:

1. To lead students to the major ideas and supporting details within a content text chapter
2. To teach students flexibility in their reading

Rationale

The Selective Reading Guide-O-Rama assumes that since most students are not "experts" in the subject, they are not able to select with ease the important textual information. That is, it assumes most students read the material as if everything within the chapter were of equal importance. The subject matter instructor is in a position to guide students through the reading assignment by providing them with clues as to which information is important and which can be skimmed lightly.

Intended Audience

The Selective Reading Guide-O-Rama can be used with students in grades six and above. It would appear to be better suited for use with those students who need additional guidance in their reading.

Description of the Procedure

Before an instructor can design any type of guidance tool for students, several important decisions must be made during the planning stage of the lesson. Of primary importance is the identification of the major concepts and understandings to be derived from the chapter. Subject matter instructors should be asking themselves the following questions:

1. What should students know when they finish this chapter?
   a. What are the major concepts that the students should understand?
   b. What supporting information or details should they remember on a long-term basis?
2. What should students be able *to do* when they finish the chapter?
   a. What background information is essential to perform the required tasks?

By making a brief list of the answers to the above questions, content teachers can identify the essential information within the text chapter that they want their students to understand. The next step is to move through the book chapter and identify those portions of the text that provide students with the previously identified important information. After lightly noting the margins of their teacher's edition the letters "M" for main ideas and "D" for important details, content instructors are ready to design the Guide-O-Rama.

Perhaps the easiest way to approach this task is to imagine a group of three or four students. It is assumed that content teachers have already completed the preparation stage of the lesson (see description of the instructional framework in this unit). Students will have their texts open to the first page of the chapter to be studied and are now ready to read the chapter. What information should the teacher provide so that the students will key in on the important ideas that have been identified? The response to this question is the type of information that will be written down in guide form.

Several examples might be in order to illustrate the preceding discussion. The teacher might note important information in the following manner:

- p. 93, paragraphs 3–6. Pay special attention to this section. Why do you think Hunter acted in this manner? We will discuss your ideas later in class.

- p. 94, subtopic in boldface print at top of page. See if you can rewrite the topic to form a question. Now read the information under the subtopic just to answer the question. You should pick up the five ideas very quickly. Jot down your answers in the space provided below.
- p. 94, picture. What appears to be the reaction of the crowd? Now read the fifth paragraph on this page to find out why they are reacting as they are.
- p. 95, paragraphs 5–8. Read this section very carefully. The order of the events is very important and you will want to remember this information for our quiz.

The same approach is used when noting information within the chapter which, based upon the content teacher's analysis, is of little or no importance. The following example illustrates this situation:

- p. 179, all of column 1. The author has provided us with some interesting information here, but it is not important for us to remember. You may want just to skim over it and move on to the second column.
- pp. 180 and 181. These pages describe a fictitious family who lived during the Civil War. You may skip this section because we will learn about the lifestyles of the time through films, other readings, and class discussions.
- pp. 221–222. Recent discoveries in science have disproved the information contained on these pages. I will discuss this information with you in class. Now move on to page 223.

By pointing out unimportant information as well as important ideas in the text, content teachers are purported to be effectively communicating to their students that they must be flexible in their reading. Teachers may even wish to communicate literally to their students the notion that all words in print are not necessarily of equal value for the reader attempting to ascertain the author's important ideas.

The completed guide should appear in a logical order and should move the student from the beginning of the chapter through the end of the unit. Thus, through the use of the Selective Reading Guide-O-Rama content teachers are saying to the youngsters (1) pay close attention to this, (2) skim over this material, (3) read this section carefully, and (4) you can read this section rather quickly, but see if you can find out why, and so on.

Cautions and Comments

Like most guidance tools, it should be used sensitively. The Selective Reading Guide-O-Rama might work best with those students who need the assistance and who could profit from structured approaches to developing selected skills. A conscious effort should be made by the teacher to remove this assistance as the students learn the mechanics of reading and studying text material. This weaning process might begin following the use of the Guide-O-Rama for a two- or three-month period. The students should be told when this is taking place and occasionally reminded that, for example, they should continue to pay particular attention to the pictorial information within the unit.

For those students who have difficulty handling the written version of a Guide-O-Rama, the instructor can just as easily design a cassette tape version. Oral direction will now lead the students through the selection. The instructor might advise the student to ". . . turn off the recorder now and read very carefully these first two paragraphs on page 96. When you have finished, turn the recorder on again and I will discuss the material you read." By providing approximately five seconds of dead space on the tape, the student is allowed sufficient time to handle the mechanics of turning off and on a cassette tape recorder. Of course, the student will have all the time necessary to read and study once the recorder is off.

Check the appendix for the following:
Example of a Guide-O-Rama

REFERENCES

Cunningham, D., and Shablak, S. L. "Selective Reading Guide-O-Rama: The Content Teacher's Best Friend." *Journal of Reading* 18 (1975): 380–382.
Introduces the concept of the Guide-O-Rama and provides examples for its construction.

STRUCTURED OVERVIEWS

Purpose

The structured overview (Earle, 1969a) is intended to:

1. Provide a logical means of pre-teaching the technical vocabulary of a content chapter
2. Present the students an "idea framework" designed to show important relationships between content vocabulary
3. Help content teachers clarify teaching goals

Rationale

The technical vocabulary of a content subject often proves quite difficult for the secondary or college student. It is Earle's argument that the content teachers must be ever mindful of this fact and should seek ways of making the task less complicated for the students. The structured overview provides a systematic approach for doing just that. The subject matter instructor presents a picture, or schematic diagram, of the important words within the chapter and discusses with the students how these words relate one to another. Barron (1969) stated that "words assume the form of 'advance organizers' and provide the students with the cues to the 'structure' of subjects" (p. 29). Thus, the overview serves as a point of reference as the students begin reading and studying the chapter in more detail.

Intended Audience

Earle (1969b) reports the use of the structured overview with students in grades seven and above. It is further suggested that teachers in grades four, five, and six could profit from the use of the technique. On occasion, the procedure might be used by the teacher alone in the preparation of a particularly difficult unit.

Description of the Procedure

In order to describe the use of the structured overview by the content teacher, the following three stages will be discussed:

1. Preparation
2. Presentation
3. Follow-up

1. Preparation

Perhaps the most critical stage in the development and use of structured overviews is this very first step. It is at this point that the instructor, by working through this rather simple process, makes some key decisions regarding the major ideas to be stressed during the unit. Four components of the preparation stage appear to summarize the desired sequence.

a. *Select words.* Rather than moving through the chapter in search of "difficult" words, the teacher is advised to proceed in a more systematic manner (Herber, 1978). The first step in this preparation stage, then, is for the instructor to select the major concepts or understandings that are important for the students to know at the conclusion of their study of the topic. By working through the chapter in this manner, the teacher is actually establishing instructional objectives for that particular chapter.

Word selection logically follows selection of major concepts. The teacher can now deal with one major idea at a time and ask the question, "What important words in this chapter help to describe, explain, and/or communicate this idea?" By asking this question for each of the major concepts, the content teacher has identified those technical terms that the students will need to know. Often a number of difficult words within the chapter will be eliminated because they do not tie directly to the major concepts.

To give an example, a social studies teacher may be introducing a chapter on organization of the United States government. The concepts chosen for instruction are: (1) the United States government consists of three governing branches; and (2) a system of checks and balances maintains the powers of each branch of government. The words that might be selected by the teacher as important for understanding these concepts are as follows: checks and balances; Senate; legislative; United States government; executive; judiciary; House of Representatives; President; veto; override; judicial review.

b. *Arrange words.* The task now is to arrange these words into a diagram form that will help students see the terms and how they interrelate. There is not necessarily a right or a wrong diagram for a given set of terms, but it would appear that some arrangements are better than others. With several pieces of scratch paper available, the teacher might try out several possibilities, then select the one that appears to be the most appropriate.

Continuing the example of the words chosen by the social studies teacher, the words might be arranged in numerous ways. Here is one example:

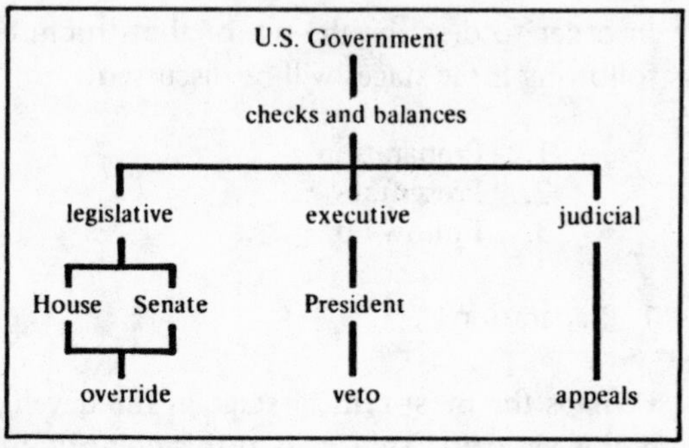

Structured overviews may be designed for the total chapter. For longer, more complicated chapters, the subject matter instructor may wish to design several structured overviews, each tied to a major concept. Whatever the decision, the overriding question to be answered is, "Will this overview assist students in better understanding the major concepts and major words of the chapter?" If the answer is "yes," then the teacher has developed a valuable teaching tool.

c. *Add previously learned key words and ideas.* Learning new information is generally easier for students if they can relate the new ideas to previously learned information; therefore, the content instructor is advised to select several important words that the students mastered in previous units and insert these in this new overview. By completing this step, the teacher is saying to the students that the subject is more than a set of isolated units with little or no relationship to each other.

In the example of the words dealing with the United States government, the teacher may decide to add previously learned vocabulary if that would enhance understanding of the structured overview.

d. *Evaluate overview.* Content instructors by their very training, interest, and experience are experts in their chosen fields; therefore, they may have forgotten what it was like when they first began to pursue information in their major subject. A structured overview may be easily interpretable by the content specialist but still be too difficult for a group of high school juniors. This final step in the preparation stage, therefore, is critical. It is advised to try out the overview on someone who is not an expert in the field. One could do this with a student or with a fellow teacher in another discipline. Explain the overview and then ask appropriate questions that tell you whether the person grasps the relationships among the terms in the overview. Often people will answer questions in such a manner that they provide the kind of information necessary to suggest some minor revisions which will result in a more appropriately constructed design. Once satisfied with the appropriateness of the overview, the teacher should use it in the context of a total lesson in a regular classroom.

2. Presentation

As a pre-teaching tool, the overview is presented on the chalkboard or with an overhead transparency. The instructor actually "talks" the students through the overview and adds new pieces to it. Students are encouraged to participate. They may add information with which they are already familiar or ask questions regarding the overview. The teacher may pose questions to better judge students' understanding of the overview. The important thing is that the teacher and the students use the language of the subject matter and simultaneously explore the relationships of these words to each other. The word "overview" is important; one should not anticipate mastery of terms and relationships at this time.

The entire procedure may take anywhere from five to ten minutes, depending upon the ability and achievement level of the students and upon the complexity of the overview. At the conclusion of this segment of the preparation stage, the students should have an "idea framework" which should make more detailed learning easier.

3. Follow-up

The structured overview may also be used as the students move further into the chapter itself. A student's reaction to an especially difficult idea encountered in the reading might result in the teacher responding, "Do you remember how this idea tied to . . ." as a portion of the overview is recreated on the chalkboard. Thus, the overview becomes a major point of reference throughout the teaching of a particular chapter. New information may be added when the instructor suggests, "Let's see how this new information fits into the overview that we have been using." For some classes, the overview might be placed on a large piece of poster paper and placed on the bulletin board. In this way, students may refer to it at any time.

Cautions and Comments

The structured overview alone may not teach the technical vocabulary of a chapter as thoroughly as the content instructor may desire. The term "overview" does suggest that this will be the case. A support system designed to teach more thoroughly the language of the subject is suggested. Earle and Barron (1973) outline a strategy that includes three components: (1) structured overview, (2) skills teaching and (3) extension activities. Structured overviews are designed and utilized in the manner just described. The skills teaching phase of the strategy occurs in the preparation stage of the instructional framework (see discussion of the instructional framework in this unit) and involves the detailed teaching of several of the more important terms used in the overview. Extension activities give students opportunities to use the words during and/or following the reading of the chapter. Extension activities are generally paper-and-pencil exercises designed to reinforce the students' understandings of the terms. Matching exercises, word puzzles, and categorizing activities may be used for this purpose. A good source book of such exercises is a book by Herber entitled *Success with Words* (1973). Small group and/or whole class discussion may follow the completion of the activities.

Several studies cited in the reference section indicate the value of this procedure. However, one wonders whether a strategy that imposes upon students a structure for thinking and reading would be as beneficial as a strategy which might activate students' own ideas. To this end, an overview might be developed from the student's own ideas prior to, during, or after reading. In this way, the overview may become more personalized and less abstract.

Check appendix for the following:
Examples of Structured Overviews

REFERENCES

Barron, R. F. "The Use of Vocabulary as an Advance Organizer." In H. L. Herber and P. L. Sanders, eds., *Research in Reading in the Content Areas: First Year Report.* Syracuse, N.Y.: Reading and Language Arts Center, Syracuse University, 1969, pp. 29–39.
Presents the basis for the use of structured overviews within the content classroom. Describes how structured overviews may be used in relation to a total vocabulary teaching strategy utilizing pre-teaching and extension activities.

Earle, R. A. "Reading and Mathematics: Research in the Classroom." In H. A. Robinson and E. L. Thomas, eds., *Fusing Reading Skills and Content.* Newark, Del.: International Reading Assoc., 1969a, pp. 164–170.
Discusses the use of the structured overview as a tool to introduce new vocabulary in the content classroom.

Earle, R. A. "Use of the Structured Overview in Mathematics Classes." In H. L. Herber and P. L. Sanders, eds., *Research in Reading in the Content Areas: First Year Report.* Syracuse, N.Y.: Reading and Language Arts Center, Syracuse University, 1969b, pp. 49–58.
Describes a study in which structured overviews were used in both seventh and ninth grade mathematics classes. Significant differences in favor of the use of structured overviews versus no pre-teaching were observed when a delayed-relationship test was administered.

Earle, R. A. "The Use of Vocabulary as a Stuctured Overview in Seventh Grade Mathematics." In H. L. Herber and R. F. Barron, eds., *Research in Reading in the Content Areas: Second Year Report.* Syracuse, N.Y.: Reading and Language Arts Center, Syracuse University, 1973, pp. 36–39.
Reports a second study using structured overviews and a conventional means of introducing mathematics units. Significant differences in favor of the structured overview approach were discovered when students were asked to complete a vocabulary relationships test. No significant differences were found when students were administered a teacher-constructed content test and a standardized test of mathematics achievement.

Earle, R. A., and Barron, R. F. "An Approach for Teaching Vocabulary in Content Subjects." In H. L. Herber and R. F. Barron, eds., *Research in Reading in the Content Areas: Second Year Report.* Syracuse, N.Y.: Reading and Langauge Arts Center, Syracuse University, 1973, pp. 84–100.
Describes a total vocabulary teaching strategy designed for content teachers. Strategy components include: (1) structured overviews, (2) skills teaching, and (3) extension activities.

Estes, T. H., Mills, D. C., and Barron, R. F. "Three Methods of Introducing Students to a Reading-Learning Task in Two Content Subjects." In H. L. Herber and P. L. Sanders, eds., *Research in Reading in the Content Areas: First Year Report.* Syracuse, N.Y.: Reading and Language Arts Center, Syracuse University, 1969, pp. 40–47.
Describes two studies using advance organizers, structured overviews, and purpose questions in an English and in a biology classroom. Results of the English class experiment indicated no significant differences in the three

pre-teaching approaches. The structured overview proved superior in the biology class experiment.

Estes, T. H., and Vaughan, J. L., Jr. *Reading and Learning in the Content Classroom.* Boston: Allyn and Bacon, 1978, pp. 138–152; 177–184.
Discusses the use of the structured overview for purposes of pre-reading anticipation and reflective reaction.

Herber, H. L. *Success with Words.* New York: Scholastic Book Services, 1973.
Presents a sourcebook of ideas for dealing with technical vocabulary in social studies, English, science, and math.

Herber, H. L. *Teaching Reading in Content Areas.* Englewood Cliffs, N.J.: Prentice-Hall, 1970, pp. 150–198.
Presents a rationale and practical suggestions for dealing with vocabulary development in subject areas.

Herber, H. L. *Teaching Reading in Content Areas,* 2nd ed. Englewood Cliffs, N.J.: Prentice-Hall, 1978, pp. 47–158.
Discusses the use of the structured overview with examples.

A NOTETAKING SYSTEM FOR LEARNING

Purpose

The Notetaking System for Learning (Palmatier, 1973) is designed to:

1. Provide students with a systematic means of organizing class notes
2. Provide a sound means for reviewing content information

Rationale

Although there are certainly exceptions, many content classrooms at the secondary and college levels are structured around class lectures, supplemented by textbook assignments. Most traditional notetaking techniques consider only one portion of the class at a time; that is, they deal with taking notes in lectures *or* with notetaking procedures for specific reading assignments. Palmatier's Notetaking System for Learning (NSL) is a flexible system that encourages the student to combine the two approaches.

Intended Audience

Although it is believed that some simplified notetaking procedures should be taught at an earlier point, the Notetaking System for Learning appears best suited for students in the ninth grade through college. It also would seem appropriate for above-average students in grades seven and eight.

Description of the Procedure

Obviously, in order for students to use any type of notetaking procedure, they need to have available the basic notetaking materials—paper and pencils. As many classroom teachers know, this is the point at which many notetaking strategies can and do break down.

It is suggested that students use only one side of 8½X11-inch loose-leaf notebook paper with a three-inch margin on the left side of the page. If this legal-line paper cannot be purchased, students can add their own margins to standard notebook paper. The following discussion of procedure will focus on these three major components of the system:

1. Recording
2. Organizing
3. Studying

1. Recording

Notes generally are first recorded from the lecture, with reading notes added at a later time. The lecture notes are placed to the right of the three-inch marginal line. The specific format is best left to the individual student, but Palmatier (1973) does suggest the use of a format which utilizes both (a) subordination—a modified outlining procedure—and (b) space. Space will vary depending upon the degree of change between items presented. If the lecture information appears to flow easily from one idea to another, then little space is left between the noted ideas; however, at the point when the topic obviously changes course or when there is some confusion as to how the ideas tie together, the student would be advised to leave a larger space so that more information may be added later.

Again, the student should not use the back of the notebook paper. This will only cause confusion when the student later tries to organize or study the notes. The completed notetaking procedure should result in a format similar to the one shown in Figure 2-1. Note that each page should be numbered as the notes are recorded. This will avoid some confusion during the study portion of the procedure.

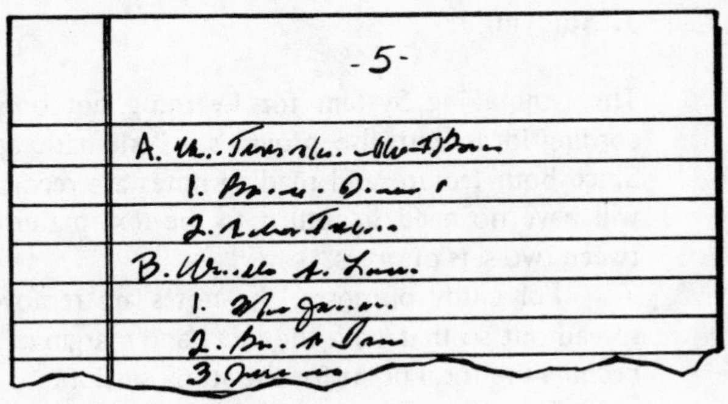

Figure 2-1.

2. Organizing

If time is available, immediately following the lecture session the student should organize his or her notes while the ideas and details are fresh. The student has two tasks during this portion of the NSL procedure:

a. *Labeling.* By examining separately each informational unit within the recorded notes, the student should be able to provide labels that briefly describe the information presented. Labels should be placed to the left side of the marginal line and directly in line with the appropriate recorded notes.
b. *Adding.* Following the labeling process, Palmatier (1973) suggests that the student now insert important information from the text directly into the lecture notes. If adequate space has been provided between important ideas, the reading notes may be easily added to the lecture note page; if more space is needed, the back of the notebook paper can now be used in this integration process.

Following the above procedure, a page of notes now could resemble the example in Figure 2-2.

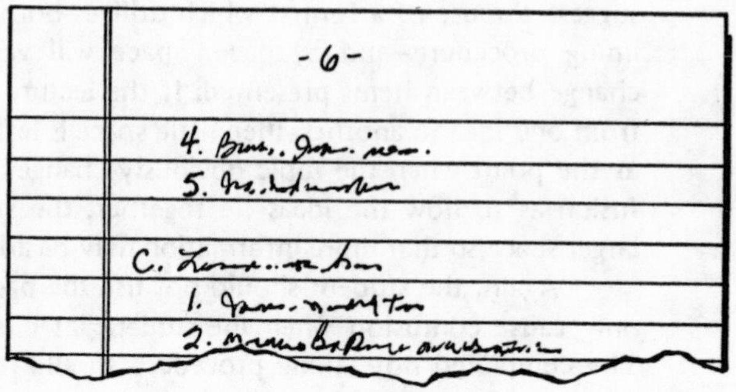

Figure 2-2.

3. Studying

The Notetaking System for Learning not only provides a simple means for recording ideas, but also provides a systematic approach to the study of the notes. Since both lecture and reading notes are recorded within the system, the student will have no need to return to the text material or to shuffle back and forth between two sets of notes.

For study purposes, the notes are removed from the loose-leaf binder and spread out so that only the left hand margin of each page is visible. The labels now become the focal point for the study session.

The type of exam for which the student is studying can dictate the manner in which the notes are approached. For an objective test, it is suggested that the student might approach the labels at random, thus approximating the multiple choice, true-false, and matching questions on this type of exam. For an essay test, the student would approach the study task in a more organized manner, usually starting at the beginning of the notes and moving through them in the order in which they were presented.

As in the question stage of the SQ3R method of study described in this unit, the labels in the left hand margin become the question stems for the purpose of study. A label is transformed into a question, which the student proceeds to answer. Verification is obtained by lifting the next page of notes and reading the information written to the right of the label. This procedure is followed throughout the study period. As the information on a page is learned, it can be returned to the loose-leaf notebook. Study concludes when all of the pages are back in their proper place in the notebook.

Cautions and Comments

Secondary teachers and college professors often complain about the inability of their students to take adequate notes. Yet it is rare indeed to find the word "notetaking" in a secondary text or in a school district's curriculum guide. Very simply, the skill is not taught; rather, it is "assumed" the student will develop it.

Teachers at the secondary level who rely heavily upon the lecture method may want to spend a portion of their instructional time teaching the students how to take notes efficiently. The time investment should pay off in students more completely understanding the subject. Teachers will also be developing an important survival skill that their students will be sure to need in other course work.

In teaching a strategy such as the Notetaking System for Learning, it is important that it be presented early in the school year. To determine if the class as a whole needs such instruction, the teacher might conclude a lecture near the beginning of the first unit by asking the students to turn in their day's notes for the purpose of an informal evaluation. Two questions should be asked as each individual's notes are skimmed: (1) Has this student noted the essential concepts and supporting detail emphasized in the unit? (2) Is the material organized in a way that will lead to successful study of the material for testing purposes?

If the answer to either question is "no" for the majority of the students, then the decision to teach the process must be made. It is also cautioned that knowledge of main ideas and/or outlining may be prerequisite skills to the Notetaking System for Learning. Therefore, effective implementation of NSL may not be accomplished before such abilities are developed. In conclusion, it must be emphasized that better notetaking practices do not necessarily result simply by urging students to do a better job.

REFERENCES

Palmatier, R. A. "Comparison of Four Notetaking Procedures." *Journal of Reading* 14 (1971): 235-240, 258.

Compares four notetaking procedures for relative effectiveness and efficiency.

Palmatier, R. A. "A Notetaking System for Learning." *Journal of Reading* 17 (1973): 36-39.
Presents a detailed explanation for a notetaking procedure that has proved useful to secondary and college students.

HERRINGBONE TECHNIQUE

Purpose

The Herringbone technique is a structured outlining procedure designed to help students organize important information in a text chapter.

Rationale

For many students, the quantity of information contained within a twenty-page content chapter can be overwhelming. By providing structure, a content teacher can assist students in remembering the important information within the chapter. The Herringbone strategy suggests that the important information can be obtained by asking six very basic comprehension questions—Who? What? When? Where? How? and Why? By providing an outline to record this information, the teacher provides the structure for notetaking and for future study of the recorded information.

Intended Audience

The Herringbone technique is intended for use with students in the fourth through twelve grade levels. As with several strategies within this unit, the procedure appears most appropriate for those students whose reading levels are below the difficulty level of the adopted text.

Description of the Procedure

The classroom teacher must first prepare for instruction. The important preparation questions (Herber, 1978) discussed elsewhere in this unit include the following: (1) What are the major concepts that I want my students to understand at the conclusion of this chapter? (2) What are the important vocabulary terms that relate directly to these major concepts? (3) How will my students learn this information? and (4) As I consider the major concepts I have identified (see Question 1), and as I consider the ability and performance level of my class, which of the identified concepts do I expect all of my students to master and which do I expect only my better students to achieve?

Completing this preparation step gives the teacher a perspective as to what information will be important as the students are guided in the use of the Herringbone procedure.

Students may be prepared for the assignment by following the suggestions outlined in the preparation stage of the instructional framework discussed earlier in this unit, or in the readiness stage of the Directed Reading Activity discussed in Unit One. Once this has been accomplished, the students are introduced to the Herringbone form and its use.

Introduction of Form

The Herringbone form, which can be mimeographed in large quantities on standard 8½" X 11" paper, appears in Figure 2-3.

The students are instructed that they will be seeking the answers to these questions and will be recording their answers on the Herringbone form as they read the chapter.

Initially, the classroom teacher could put the Herringbone form on a transparency and display it on a screen for all students to see. As the whole class "walks through" the strategy, the teacher would write in the information on the transparency as the students fill in their forms. With some groups or with whole classes, this "walk-through" procedure may involve only the first couple of chapter subtopics, while with other groups the teacher and students may complete the whole chapter together.

Using the Form

After the students have been sufficiently prepared for learning the information within the chapter and after they understand the structure of the form, they are ready to begin the reading and recording process. The students are advised to read the information seeking answers to the following expanded questions:

1. Who was involved? (Answer should yield the name of one or more persons or groups.)
2. What did this person or group do?
3. When was it done (the event discovered in Question 2)?

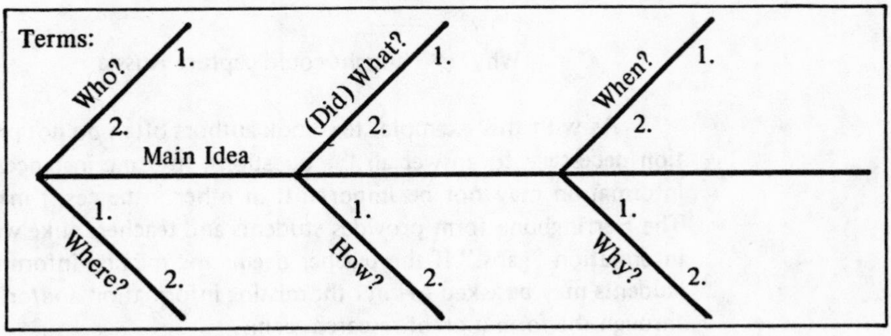

Figure 2-3.

4. Where was it done?
5. How was it accomplished?
6. Why did it happen?

As students work through this procedure and record their answers, they should discover the important relationships within this information.

EXAMPLE

For a chapter on "The War against Germany" in a United States history text, students were advised to read the first main topic and record their answers to the six key questions. Thus, the first main topic, "The United States Enters the War," resulted in the recorded information in Figure 2-4.

Some subtopics will yield more than one important set of facts, as Figure 2-4 illustrates. Others may provide only one important piece of information.

Note also in the above example that two terms which might cause some problems with some students were noted on the left-hand column of the form. By instructing students to record unfamiliar terms, the teacher discovers those terms which, even though they may have been pretaught, are confusing to the students and thus need to be taught, retaught, emphasized, and/or reinforced.

Follow-up

In addition to traditional follow-up activities, the Herringbone strategy appears to present some unique possibilities. In the chapter on "The War against Germany," students recorded the following information on their forms:

Who?	Germany
What?	Invaded U.S.S.R.
When?	June 1941
Where?	Leningrad, Moscow, Stalingrad
How?	——
Why?	Thought could capture Russia

As with this example, textbook authors often do not provide all the information necessary to answer all the questions. In some instances the particular bit of information may not be important; in other instances it may be very significant. The Herringbone form provides students and teachers alike with a visible display of information "gaps." If the teacher deems the missing information important, then students may be asked to infer the missing information and/or to pursue the answers through the formation of research teams.

Other answers provided by the text authors would be pursued in the same way. For example, the text authors' answer to the question, "*Why* did Germany

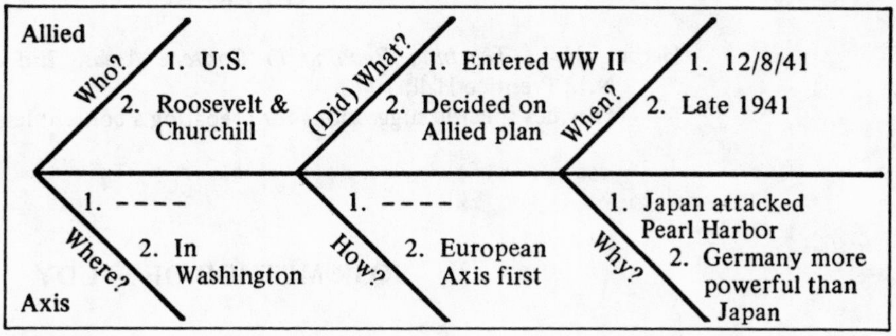

Figure 2-4.

invade the U.S.S.R.?" might be considered rather superficial. The authors simply state that Germany invaded the U.S.S.R. because Germany thought it could capture Russia. The classroom teacher might want to extend the search for understanding by asking, "But why did Germany think it could capture Russia?" Predictions could be made by students, followed by attempts to search out information in other sources.

Finally, the Herringbone form contains the term "Main Idea" on its mid-line (see Figure 2-3). After the students have completed the chapter and their outline, they are asked to make a statement that would represent the main idea of the chapter. This step is similar to the final step in the survey technique described later in this unit. Using the history book example, the teacher might ask, "What one statement can you make that would tell what the authors are saying about the war against Germany?" One student's response: "The war was long and costly in terms of money and lives, but eventually resulted in the defeat of Germany by the Allied Forces."

Cautions and Comments

As described above, the Herringbone technique provides students with a structure for taking notes from a textbook chapter, for observing relationships, and for studying and remembering information. This high amount of structure appears valid only in situations where students might profit from such assistance. In particular it would appear to be most effective when used alternatively with a number of techniques described in this unit and some described in Unit One. Otherwise, where students need to develop their own strategies or where the text material is not "meaty," this technique may be inappropriate.

Again, in the initial stage of teaching this strategy, the teacher may need to "walk through" part or all of a chapter so that the students gain a sense of the type of information they should be seeking. With some groups or with whole classes, this form may become the structure for class learning; that is, it is possible that the teacher will use the "walk-through" approach each time the Herringbone technique is used.

REFERENCES

Herber, H. L. *Teaching Reading in Content Areas,* 2nd ed. Englewood Cliffs, N.J.: Prentice-Hall, 1970.
Provides specific suggestions for preparing a content lesson.

SQ3R METHOD OF STUDY

Purpose

The purpose of the SQ3R method of study as developed by Robinson (1946) is to:

1. Provide students with a systematic approach to study type reading
2. Promote more efficient learning of assigned reading materials

Rationale

High school and college instructors have for years lamented the fact that the majority of their students lack an efficient, systematic method for studying a textbook assignment. It would appear that some general method of study would be better than no method at all. One of the first, and by far the most popular, study methods described in the professional literature was developed by Robinson (1946). The SQ3R method of study is designed to lead students systematically through the study of an assigned text chapter by taking advantage of the format of most textual material and using reading techniques assumed to be efficient and effective for these purposes.

Intended Audience

As a viable study procedure, the SQ3R method of study appears best suited for those students who are studying content chapters in a self-contained classroom or in a departmentalized situation in the upper grades. Although the survey portion of the procedure can be presented in the earlier grades, the total technique appears most suitable for students in grades four and above.

Description of the Procedure

As stated in the Rationale section, the SQ3R method of study was designed to take advantage of the consistent format in most traditional content textbooks. Each chapter generally contains a title, an introduction, a number of headings and subheadings, a concluding or summary statement, and some questions or problems posed by the textbook author(s) at the end of the chapter. This format leads naturally to the five steps which make up the SQ3R procedure:

1. Survey
2. Question
3. Read
4. Recite
5. Review

1 Survey

Perhaps the most important single element in the procedure is the initial survey or preview step. The survey should provide each student with an overview of the chapter content. The survey step should take the students logically through the chapter, seeking to answer these questions: "What is this chapter about?" "What kind of information does the author tell us about this subject?"

The survey step then requires the student to read and think about the chapter title, the introductory paragraph(s), the headings and subheadings, the concluding paragraph, and the end-of-chapter questions. In addition, students are encouraged to survey the pictorial information within the chapter.

At the conclusion of this step, the students should have a general understanding of the chapter content. The amount of time devoted to the survey of a particular chapter will depend upon the length and complexity of the topic and upon the reader's own skill. Something in the range of five to fifteen minutes generally appears appropriate.

2. Question

Students now should be ready for a more detailed study of the chapter. The question step provides a purpose for reading the material in more detail. Very simply, the student selects the first boldface topic in the chapter, reads it, and proceeds to restate it in the form of a question. An example may help to illustrate this procedure. The subtopic "Causes of World War I" would become in question form, "What were the causes of World War I?" The student now is ready to move to the third step.

3. Read

The first of the three "R" steps is to read the material immediately following the first subtopic. The purpose of this reading will be to find the answer to the question posed in step two. With this very specific question in mind, students will tend to move fairly rapidly through the material in pursuit of the answer. Once they have finished reading the material under the first heading, students are ready to move to step four of the procedure.

4. Recite

In steps two and three above, each student formulated a question using the first subtopic in the chapter and then read to find the answer to the question. At this point, students are asked to pause and reflect on the answer. Students are encouraged to answer their question in their own words. This recitation is also the point at which students may record brief notes in their notebook for later review and study. Students then would repeat steps 2-4 as they work through the remainder of the chapter.

5. Review

Immediately upon the completion of steps two, three, and four for the final subtopic of the chapter, the student should spend approximately five minutes reviewing the notes and attempt to recall the main points of the chapter. The student then reads each main heading and tries to remember the supporting or explanatory information. Later reviews will also be helpful aids for long-term remembering.

Cautions and Comments

One of the major difficulties associated with the SQ3R method of study has been the inability of teachers to convince students of the value of such a procedure. Although a number of upper-level teachers have taught the method to their students, the question remains, "how many students regularly use the procedure?"

Indeed, the use of SQ3R must be developed in relevant situations. As the need arises, one approach might be to begin by using the survey technique (discussed in this unit) with the whole class, then add the question and read steps when the students have seen the value of the survey step and are using it on their own.

Finally, it should be mentioned that there are numerous alternatives to the SQ3R method. Some of these may be more appropriate than SQ3R for a particular subject area. Among the alternative study procedures are: (1) OK4R (Pauk, 1974); (2) Panorama (Edwards, 1973); (3) PQRST (Spache and Berg, 1966); and (4) PQ4R (Thomas and Robinson, 1977).

REFERENCES

Edwards, P. "Panorama: A Study Technique." *Journal of Reading* 17 (1973): 132–135.
Source for Panorama (Purpose, Adaptability, Need to Question, Overview, Read, Annotate, Memorize, Assess) study technique.

Pauk, W. *How to Study in College*, 2nd ed. Boston: Houghton Mifflin, 1974.
Source for OK4R (Overview, Key Ideas, Read, Recite, Reflect, Review) study technique.

Robinson, F. P. *Effective Reading.* New York: Harper and Bros., 1962.
Describes a wide range of study skills, including SQ3R, to enhance the reading ability of students in subject matter areas.

Robinson, F. P. *Effective Study.* New York: Harper and Bros., 1946.
Introduces the use of the SQ3R method to aid students in their study.

Robinson, F. P. *Effective Study,* rev. ed. New York: Harper and Bros., 1961.
Revised edition of the previously cited text with examples of diagnostic tests and practice exercises.

Spache, G. D., and Berg, P. C. *The Art of Efficient Reading.* New York: MacMillan, 1966.
Source for PQRST (Preview, Question, Read, Summarize, Text) study techniques.

Thomas, E. L., and Robinson, H. A. *Improving Reading in Every Class,* 2nd ed. Boston: Allyn and Bacon, 1977.
Source for PQ4R (Preview, Question, Read, Reflect, Recite, Review) study technique.

SURVEY TECHNIQUE

Purpose

The survey technique (Aukerman, 1972) is intended to:

1. Provide the students with a systematic approach for previewing a content chapter
2. Provide the classroom teacher with an additional approach to use in preparing students to read the text

Rationale

The acquisition of effective study skills is recognized as one of the major goals of upper-level reading instruction. The survey technique described by Aukerman (1972) provides the content teacher with a systematic means of walking the students through the first step of Robinson's (1961) SQ3R method of study. Specifically, the survey technique is designed to prepare the students for the reading of a text by arranging a whole-class overview of the textual material. By using the technique on numerous occasions throughout the school year, the teacher attempts to lead the student to understand the importance of previewing prior to reading.

Intended Audience

Although probably more useful at the secondary level, the survey technique may also be used at the upper elementary level. It could certainly be useful at this level when the students are scheduled to tackle an especially difficult chapter. As with most highly structured procedures, the technique would appear most valuable for those students who might have difficulty with the text material.

Description of the Procedure

The survey technique serves as a substitute for the readiness stage of the Directed Reading Activity or the preparation stage of the instructional framework. The objective is to prepare the students for the actual reading of the text by arranging a whole-class overview procedure that will result in an understanding of the total chapter content.

As with other instructional strategies discussed in this book, decisions must be made by the teacher as to what particular information to emphasize. By identifying the major understandings the students are to acquire in a given chapter, the content instructor becomes aware of those portions of the chapter to emphasize during the class survey.

Aukerman (1972) outlined a six-step procedure that may be used with any traditionally designed content textbook. The technique follows easily when the text chapter contains the following format: chapter title; introduction; main headings with subtopics; summary; review questions and exercises.

With that format in mind, the teacher may adapt Aukerman's six-step procedure in this way:

1. Analysis of Chapter Title

After reading the title with the students, the instructor might ask questions such as, "What do you think this chapter is going to be about?" "What do you already know about this topic?" "How do you see this chapter relating to the unit we just completed?" Regardless of reading ability, all students can participate in this type of activity.

2. Analysis of Subtitles

The teacher will note each of the subtitles so that each student will understand the overall outline for the chapter topic. This preview may also involve the second step in Robinson's (1961) SQ3R method—the question step. Students could be asked to turn each of the headings into a question. The resulting questions will provide the students with specific purposes for reading the text under each of the headings. For example, the subtitle "Advantages of Cotton Production" would result in the question "What were the advantages of cotton production?"

Questions may be developed by the class as a whole and placed on the chalkboard or on an overhead projector. After using the survey technique on several occasions, the content instructor might request that each student develop his or her own set of questions. Whether as a whole-class or as an individual activity, the development of questions results in a student-produced guide that should be extremely valuable when students are later asked to read and study the chapter in more detail.

3. Analysis of Visuals

Often some of the most important information in a chapter may be found in the visuals of the chapter. Many students ignore these aids, while others may not possess the necessary skills to interpret the pictorial information. This third step in the survey technique gives the content teacher an opportunity to stress the importance of these visual aids and, if necessary, to teach the students how to obtain information from them. The following bar graph example, Figure 2-5, might appear in a seventh grade geography book.

The teacher would ask questions to determine if the students were able to glean information from the bar graph. Two questions might be: "What is the major cotton producing state in the United States?" "What do you suppose the authors of our text meant by the term 'Expressed in 1,000-Bale Units?'" If the students have difficulty with these two questions, the teacher could take a brief period of time to describe the major features of a bar graph and to show students how much information may be obtained from such a simple figure. With the graph shown in the particular example, it would probably be necessary to explain the numerical system so that students would understand that they would need to multiply the number of units depicted on the graph times 1,000 to determine the actual number of bales produced by each state; i.e., in 1974, California actually produced 1,000 X 2,595 = 2,595,000 bales of cotton. Other questions might include

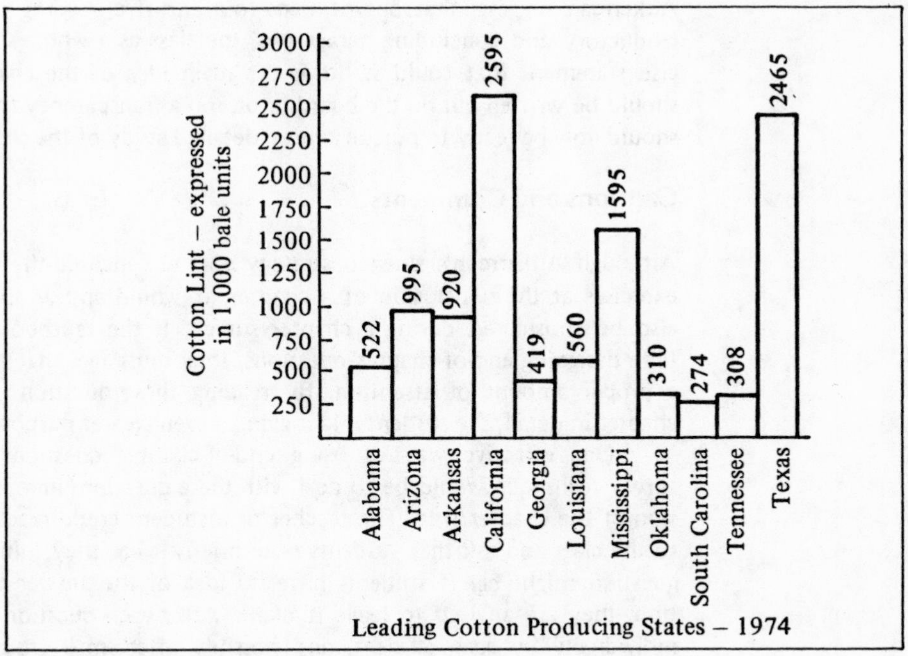

Figure 2-5.

the following: "Where are the majority of the leading cotton producing states located?" "Why do you think Kentucky is not one of the major cotton producing states?"

4. Introductory Paragraph(s)

Many textbook authors use one or more introductory paragraphs to set forth the important ideas within the chapter. Students might be asked to read this information silently. The discussion that follows should concentrate on how the information in the introduction fits with the information discovered in the first three steps of the procedure. A question like the following might be used: "Now that we have read this introductory material, can you see how this information supports some of the things we discovered as we surveyed the chapter?"

5. Concluding Paragraph(s)

Generally, the final paragraphs of a content text chapter provide a summary of the chapter content. By reading the summary before reading the total chapter in detail, students receive additional confirmation of what they discovered in all the previous steps of their survey.

6. Deriving the Main Idea

Aukerman suggests that out of steps four and five, reading and discussing the introductory and concluding paragraphs, the class as a whole should develop a concise statement that could stand as the main idea of the chapter. The statement should be written out on the board or put on a transparency for all to see. Students should now be ready to pursue a more detailed study of the chapter content.

Cautions and Comments

Although Aukerman's six-step strategy does not include the review questions and exercises at the conclusion of a chapter, it would appear that these aids should also be considered during a chapter survey. If the textbook authors have spent time designing end-of-chapter questions, they must feel that these questions merit a proper amount of attention. By reading these questions prior to reading the chapter in detail, the student might gain an even clearer purpose for reading.

One effective way of using end-of-chapter questions within Aukerman's survey technique would be to deal with these questions immediately after a discussion of the chapter title. The teacher or a student could read aloud each question to the class and ask that students note briefly what they think the answer to that question might be. If students have no idea of the answer to a particular question, they are advised to leave it blank. After each question has been considered individually by each student, and possibly after small group discussion, the instructor can deal with the questions in a whole-class discussion. By using the chapter questions in this manner, the teacher is saying to the students, "Let's find out what the author thinks is important in this chapter and let's see how much of this information we already know." Thus, students have an opportunity to review their previous knowledge of the topic before they move to more detailed study of the unit.

Following this procedure, the remaining five steps of the survey technique could be used to gain further information on the topic. After the main idea has been derived, the class could return to the questions at the end of the chapter to discover how many new answers resulted from the survey procedure. It is not unusual for students to answer correctly 20 or 30 percent of the questions during their initial attempt at them and answer another 20 or 30 percent after surveying the chapter.

The procedure, then, becomes an excellent means of introducing students to the initial phases of the SQ3R method of study while demonstrating the value of this technique for studying content material. As instructors observe students using the survey technique more effectively, instructors could gradually withdraw this structure, thus allowing the students to take more responsibility for their own learning.

REFERENCES

Aukerman, R. C. *Reading in the Secondary School Classroom.* New York; McGraw-Hill, 1972, pp. 47–62.
Presents a detailed discussion of how the survey technique might be used by the content teacher.

Robinson, F. P. *Effective Study*, rev. ed. New York: Harper & Row, 1961.
Provides a detailed description of the SQ3R method of study.

3

Strategies and Practices for Teaching Reading as a Language Experience

UNIT OVERVIEW

The Unit and Its Theme

For many years teachers have recognized the worth of the child's own oral language and experiences as basic ingredients in beginning reading instruction. As far back as 1908, Edmund Huey reported the use of a sentence method which drew upon the child's language and experiences to describe pictures. Through the first half of this century, numerous educators cited and recommended an experience-based approach to teaching reading (e.g., Storm and Smith, 1930; Gans, 1941; Lamoreaux and Lee, 1943). In recent years, interest in using the language and experience of children has continued to grow. Researchers and educators have searched for the one best method for teaching reading and turned their attention to language acquisition and the psycholinguistic nature of the reading process. In the middle of the 1960s, the approach became widely recognized and identified by its now familiar label, "the language experience approach."

The rationale of this approach is based upon the notion that children are born with a prowess for language acquisition and that this prowess can and should be applied to the acquisition of reading abilities. To this end, proponents of the language experience approach advocate taking advantage of the experiences children bring to reading. By conveying these experiences through language, children can move from oral to written expression. From this foundation children can develop the ability and interest to read widely, deeply, and fluently.

The Strategies

The present unit describes three strategies for teaching reading as a language experience. These strategies represent several of the major variations of this approach.

Allen's Language Experiences in Communication

The Language Experiences in Communication represent an attempt by Roach Van Allen to develop a comprehensive language-based approach to reading. Most people credit Allen with nurturing the evolution of the language experience approach. Allen's intent has been to develop an approach which provides the language competencies essential to promote reading. In comparison with others, this approach provides the most comprehensive and detailed suggestions for teaching reading as a language experience.

Ashton-Warner's Organic Reading

Organic Reading is an experience-centered approach to reading instruction based upon Sylvia Ashton-Warner's teaching experiences with Maori children in New Zealand. It is designed to bridge the gap between the language world of the child and the language world of books through the use of each child's key vocabulary.

Stauffer's Language-Experience Approach

The Language-Experience Approach represents Russell Stauffer's conceptualization of the language experience approach for teaching beginning reading. His approach focuses on the use of individual- and group-dictated stories, the use of word banks and the use of creative writing activities. As a beginning reading approach, it can serve either to supplement or to substitute for traditional basal reading programs.

Utilization

The implementation of the language experience approach requires teacher understanding of students' experiences and language abilities. The language experience approach involves facilitating, rather than teaching, children "how to learn to read" or "how to read." In other words, to teach reading as a language experience requires that the teacher respond to students as they teach themselves about reading. Teacher-directed activities should neither hinder learning nor distort appropriate reading behavior. With these ideas in mind, teachers might review the suggestions of Allen, Ashton-Warner, and Stauffer, and possibly generate their own strategies.

REFERENCES

Gans, R. *Guiding Children's Reading through Experiences.* New York: Teachers College, 1941.

Huey, E. G. *The Psychology and Pedagogy of Reading.* New York: Macmillan, 1908.

Lamoreaux, L., and Lee, D. M. *Learning to Read through Experiences.* New York: Appleton-Century-Crofts, 1943.

Storm, G. E., and Smith, N. B. *Reading Activities in Primary Grades.* Boston: Ginn, 1930.

ALLEN'S LANGUAGE EXPERIENCE APPROACH IN COMMUNICATION

Purpose

The Language Experience in Communication represents the language experience approach as advocated by Roach Van Allen (1976). It is designed to develop the language competencies essential for the promotion of reading. To this end, it provides each child with opportunities to:

1. Experience communication in various situations
2. Study aspects of communication
3. Relate the ideas of others to self

Rationale

Historically, the writings and material of Roach Van Allen have been largely responsible for this approach's recognition and evolution. Allen's rationale for the language experience approach stems largely from a project sponsored by the Department of Education, San Diego County, California, where researchers pursued the question, "Of all the language experiences available for study in the elementary school years, which ones have the greatest contribution to make to reading?" This work served to identify twenty essential language experiences and give the approach its now familiar label, "language experience."

With the approach's evolution, these twenty experiences have been organized into a design for a total language arts/communication curriculum. Figure 3-1 shows its design (Allen, 1976, p. 13). Within the design, the twenty language experiences fall within a framework of three strands and occur through the development of four types of activities. The three strands are: experiencing communication, studying communication, and relating communication of others to self. The four types of activities integral to the development of these experiences are: language acquisition, language prediction, language recognition, and language production.[1]

1. Language acquisition is directed toward increasing students' inventory of words, knowledge of ways to express themselves, and ability to explain the unfamiliar. Language prediction entails developing students' abilities to anticipate aspects of language and language patterns in their reading ang listening. Language recognition is directed toward having students see the relationship between their language and the printed language of others. It includes developing their awarenesses of the characteristics of print and certain word identification skills. Language

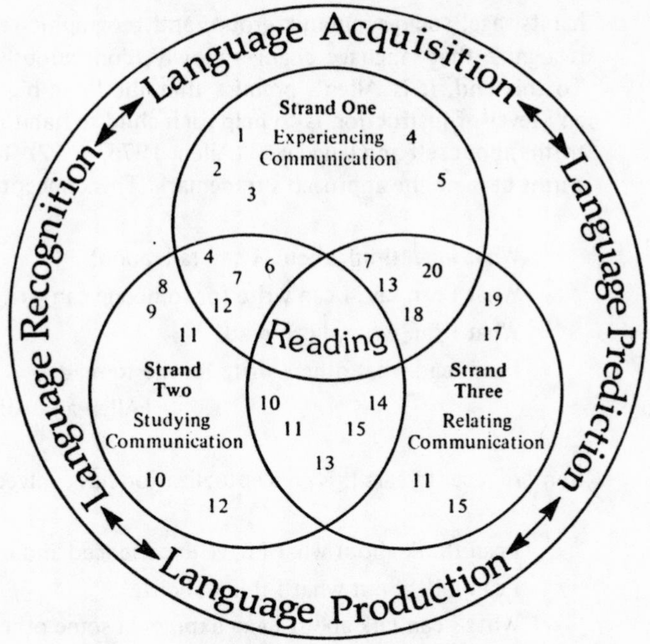

Reading in a Language Experience Approach

I. Experiencing Communication	II. Studying Communication
1. Oral sharing of ideas	8. Recognizing high-frequency words
2. Visual portrayal of experiences	9. Exploring spelling
3. Dramatization of experiences	10. Studying style and words
4. Responding rhythmically	11. Studying language structure
5. Discussing and conversing	12. Extending vocabularies
6. Exploring writing	13. Reading non-alphabetic symbols
7. Authoring individual books	

III. Relating Communication of Others to Self

14. Listening to and reading language of others
15. Comprehending what is heard and read
16. Organizing ideas
17. Assimilating and integrating ideas
18. Searching out and researching multiple sources
19. Evaluating communication of others
20. Responding in personal ways

Figure 3-1.

From: Roach Van Allen, *Language Experiences in Communication.* Copyright ©1976 by Houghton Mifflin Company. Reprinted by permission.

The implementation of Allen's curriculum design is guided by certain principles and assumptions about language and the learner, and the interactive nature of the two. The assumption is that students acquire reading and writing skills in the same way they acquire oral language skills. It is suggested that teachers recognize that students vary in language and language acquisition in accordance with their

production involves having the student communicate through a variety of different media, associating most communications with speaking and writing, and realizing that ideas can be expressed, written, and read.

habits, age, socio-economic group, and geographic region; teachers should further recognize that language changes slowly, continuously, creatively, and personally. To this end, it is Allen's premise that the "one big responsibility of a teacher at any level of instruction is to help each child to habituate, and to internalize certain truths about self and language" (Allen, 1976, p. 52). The conceptualization of these truths became the approach's trademark. This conceptualization was:

What I can think about, I can talk about.
What I can say, I can write (or someone can write about).
What I can write, I can read.
I can read what others write for me to read.

(Allen and Allen, 1966, Level 1, p. 6)

In more recent years this conceptualization has evolved into the following:

I can think about what I have experienced and imagined.

I can talk about what I think about.

What I can talk about I can express in some other form.

Anything I can record I can tell through speaking or reading.

I can read what I can write by myself and what other people write for me to read.

As I talk and write, I use some words over and over and some not so often.

As I talk and write, I use some words and clusters of words to express my meanings.

As I write to represent the sounds I make through speech, I use the same symbols over and over.

Each letter of the alphabet stands for one or more sounds that I make when I talk.

As I read, I must add to what an author has written if I am to get full meaning and inherent pleasure from print.*

*From: Roach Van Allen, *Language Experiences in Communication.* Copyright ©1976 by Houghton Mifflin Company. Reprinted by permission.

Intended Audience

Allen's language experience approach can be used with students of all ages and abilities. It provides for a total language arts curriculum which can be implemented within a single group, a whole classroom, or across a whole school. The approach works with whole-class, group, or individual instruction.

Description of the Procedure

According to Allen, it is not his intention to suggest exactly how to develop a language experience approach, but to suggest ways it might be implemented. In so doing, he assumes that teachers understand the philosophy of this approach, its curriculum rationale, learning center organization, and the use of multiple materials.

The language classroom proposed by Allen can be characterized by direct and indirect teaching activities within the framework of an instructional schedule. The direct and indirect teaching procedures entail the use of:

1. Patterns of teacher-pupil interaction
2. Learning centers
3. Planned programming

These provide the skeleton or organizational framework upon which the instructional schedule clings. For purposes of discussion, the organizational framework will be presented, and a presentation of specific teaching suggestions will follow.

Organizational Framework

1. *Patterns of Teacher-Pupil Interactions.*

Depending upon the nature of the activity, Allen suggests whole-class, group, or individual organizational patterns. Whole-class activities are suggested for the following:

a. Reading aloud to or by children
b. Oral discussion of topics of interest
c. Oral composition of stories
d. Films, filmstrips, and other audiovisual presentations
e. Introduction and demonstrations of games or learning centers
f. Seminars on various skills
g. Singing, rhymes, choral reading, or unison reading.

Group activities are suggested for the following:

a. Teacher taking dictation for one child
b. Children working, reading, or playing games with each other
c. Teacher reading with individuals or groups
d. Meeting a group's skill needs
e. Completing work initiated with class
f. Editing manuscripts for publication
g. Planning and rehearsing dramatizations

Individual activities are suggested for the following:

a. Conferring with students about writing individual books
b. Conferring with students concerning their progress

c. Helping with spelling or word recognition
d. Taking dictation from individuals for whom sharing would be inappropriate

2. Learning Centers.

To meet the specific needs of the approach, Allen suggests and describes a variety of permanent and temporary learning centers for the language classroom. Several of his suggestions are described below.

a. *Strand learning centers.* Once children have internalized the curriculum rationale, large centers made up of subcenters are suggested for each strand. For example, within a larger center for self expression (Strand One), there might be various subcenters for directing art expression, creative writing, and creative dramatics. Within a center for language study (Strand Two), there might be subcenters for editing manuscripts, review of language skills, and dictation experiences. Within a third, larger center for reflection (Strand Three), there might be subcenters for leisure reading, puppets, listening, and reading instruction.
b. *The discussion center.* Allen sees the discussion center as the hub of the language classroom. It is where the teacher would introduce activities, stimulate interest, share stories, establish classroom procedures, and evaluate the program. It is where the students would share and present ideas to other classmates.
c. *The arts and crafts center.* An arts and crafts center is suggested to provide the students a "treasure house" of creative materials and to serve as a "launching pad" for expression. This center is where children would express themselves through various media within a recreational setting. Allen sees this expression as furnishing the raw materials essential for speaking, listening, reading, and writing.
d. *The discovery center.* A discovery center serves to highlight the language of science and encourages children to discover new things or look at familiar things with new perspectives. Toward these ends, it would be equipped with microscopes, magnifying glasses, and collections of plants, insects, and minerals.
e. *The dramatization center.* A dramatization center serves to encourage children to discover themselves and relate to others through dramatization. The center would be equipped with masks, puppets, and clothing.
f. *The language study center.* A language study center provides students a variety of different activities by which to acquire aspects of language, such as word study, language anticipation, grammar, and sight words.
g. *Reading research center.* A reading research center provides the students a place to browse, research, and read a variety of material. Intended for relaxation reading and research, it would contain reference material, recreational reading materials, books written by the children, and magazines.
h. *Writing/publishing center.* A writing/publishing center is a place where children find both resources and motivation. Here children

would be stimulated to write, edit, review, and publish manuscripts. Here, newspapers, magazines, and previously published books of other children might be located.

Allen provides a number of other suggestions for learning centers which might be activated with program planning. Among his major suggestions are a music center, a cooking center, a viewing/listening center and, for relaxation and contemplation, a quiet place. Unit Eight includes a discussion of the use of learning centers and gives examples.

3. *Program Planning.*

Program planning is another essential aspect of Allen's organizational framework for teaching reading as a language experience. Program planning serves to structure learning experiences; for this purpose, Allen provides guidelines for recording, charting, and implementing the language experience program. His specific guidelines include the following suggestions.

a. Major language goals should be selected and implemented regularly and systematically. For example, language goals should be selected from each of the three strands and emphasized for no less than one week. Over a month or six weeks, each of the twenty language experience substrands should be emphasized by the teacher.
b. To serve the language concepts being emphasized, the teacher should develop learning centers to meet the students' needs and adjust the class grouping plans to afford maximum benefits.
c. Teacher-pupil interactions should be suited to the activities and needs of the students.
d. Evaluation procedures should be selected that can assess the program in terms of its objectives.

The chart in Figure 3-2 is suggested by Allen to guide program planning (Allen, 1976, p. 88).

Specific Teaching Suggestions

In addition to the organizational framework, Allen makes several specific teaching suggestions for establishing certain learning experiences. In an effort to provide a representative and detailed examination of some essential aspects of Allen's approach, his suggestions for dictated stories are presented.

Suggestions for dictated stories. Dictated stories are an integral part of Allen's language experience approach. They afford students the opportunity to learn about language through experiencing, studying, and reflecting upon oral communications

Name__________________ Class______________ Dates__________ to__________

Theme or language emphasis:____

Activities from the Three Strands	Classroom Organization*			Learning Centers Activated† (with materials and equipment needed)	Evaluation‡			
	TC	SG	I		In	CR	St	PC
Experiencing communication								
Studying communication								
Relating communication of others to self								
Other activities								

*TC – total class
SG – small group
I – individuals

†Learning centers available: Discussion, Arts and Crafts, Cooking, Dramatization, Game, Reading/Research, Viewing/Listening, Writing/Publishing, A Quiet Place

‡In – informal inventory
CR – criterion reference
St – standardized test
PC – personal conference

Figure 3-2.

From: Roach Van Allen, *Language Experiences in Communication.*

Allen breaks his suggestions for dictated stories into thirteen basic steps. They are:

- *Step One.* Visit with the student for the purpose of discussing a topic of interest. Have students tell the names for things and describe their color, size, shape, function, parts, feelings, taste, smell, quantity, and related actions or events.
- *Step Two.* Decide whether the goal is for the student to provide description, or to tell a story of some kind. If telling a story is the goal, have the student tell the whole story; then decide whether to write all of the student's ideas or some of them. Allen points out that often the goals for the dictation can be served by writing only one or two of the student's ideas. As the stories or labels are writ-

ten, the teacher and student should talk about the letters, their names, their formation, the sounds they represent, and their structure. As Allen (1973) suggests:

> Talk about alphabet symbols you are using to represent the sounds the child made. (Let other children listen.) Let it be known that the letters have names, that some words begin with capital letters, that the same letters are used over and over as the first letters of words, that the same words appear over and over, that some ending sounds appear over and over, and they may tell us "how many" or "when". (p. 1)

- *Step Three.* After writing the story or the student's ideas, read the text back to the student and ask if the text is what the students said. The student might be asked to read along or to read some words or sentences alone.
- *Step Four.* Display the students' ideas or stories in the room and invite the students either to tell about their ideas or stories or to read them to the group. Some sentences might be read in unison to show the proper phrasing during reading. Have students compare their stories for word study. For example, students might study two or three characteristics of words, such as words that are the same, words that rhyme, words that begin or end the same, words with similar meanings, and words that are names. Allen suggests that teachers and students might identify these characteristics by underlining with different colored pens.
- *Step Five.* Students might be invited either to read words, phrases or sentences, or to read along in unison. Allen points out that involvement is more important at this point than correctness or the identification of poor readers.
- *Step Six.* The teacher or students might identify words that appear five or more times in students' stories and place them on a chart entitled "Words We All Use." Allen suggests this chart can be used as an aid for developing a reading vocabulary, as a source for word games, as a resource for the correct spelling of words, and as a way to determine if the student is ready for book reading. In terms of the latter purpose, Allen suggests a student is ready for book reading only when the vocabulary on this chart matches the vocabulary of books.
- *Step Seven.* The students' dictated stories are copied onto ditto masters, duplicated, bound, and distributed to each student. Eight or ten stories are suggested for each book.
- *Step Eight.* When students become interested in writing, Allen suggests they trace their recorded story.
- *Step Nine.* After tracing, students might be encouraged to copy stories on spaces left between each line.
- *Step Ten.* The students move from copying below each line to copying on a separate sheet of paper.
- *Step Eleven.* The students write their own stories on the chalkboard.

- *Step Twelve.* A group or the whole class listens to the stories and makes suggestions for editing. The edited story is written on a story strip and displayed.
- *Step Thirteen.* Students involve themselves in writing and refining their own stories at the Writing Center. The Writing Center can include for those students who cannot write, independent tracing, copying, and other activities.

Cautions and Comments

Allen (1976) suggests that there are certain features about the language experience approach to teaching communication that distinguish it from traditional approaches to reading and from other aspects of language experience approaches. These include:

1. Students' oral language grows and is used to develop language acquisition, production, recognition, and prediction abilities.
2. Vocabulary control occurs naturally rather than artificially through the students' natural use and acquisition of the vocabulary they use.
3. Students' vocabulary acquisition is accelerated through developing an understanding of words and language, rather than through drills.
4. Individualization, grouping, and teaching patterns vary with students' individual and group needs and not solely with their abilities.
5. In comparison with other language experience approaches, the language experience approach to teaching communication affords a comprehensive curriculum design for creating learning environments and for screening activities.
6. Word identification skills are taught directly and in relationship with writing and spelling.
7. Students initially read familiar rather than unfamiliar story material. This provides them with a basis and the confidence for reading other material.
8. Students read initially within the context of their own linguistic environment, rather than within a language environment that is unfamiliar to them.
9. Students learn about language through expression and through exposure to the various language media. These experiences afford them an understanding of language patterns and the writing system.
10. Students gain exposure to a wide variety of reading material including newspapers, magazines, recreational reading material, reference material, and stories written by their peers.
11. The use of a variety of multi-media materials stimulates the students' interests and expression.

12. Students are afforded opportunities to become fully involved in personalized learning experiences. Their ideas are valued and used as the basis for these experiences.
13. Students internalize a pattern of thinking about reading. This pattern suggests that ideas can be spoken, written, or read.
14. Students learn to read as a result of their increased sensitivity to their environment, their language, and their discovery of how reading meets their personal needs.

The approach does distinguish itself from other traditional approaches to teaching reading and from other language experience approaches. It does, as Allen suggests, provide teachers a wealth of suggestions for implementing a comprehensive language-arts-based approach to teaching reading. But there are certain of these suggestions that might be questioned. For example, Allen states that reading, writing, speaking, and listening are closely interrelated. However, he assumes that in practice these activities can be taught concurrently and interchangeably. During the dictation of a story, the teacher would refer students to a study of how letters are formed and how they sound. As Smith (1973) suggests, reading, writing, speaking, and listening should not be taught concurrently when the interchange detracts from meaningful and purposeful communication. The emphasis upon the mechanics of writing would tend to do just that.

Other exampies of questionable practices include Allen's suggestions for direct rather than indirect word identification skills instruction, his emphasis upon words and the acquisition of a sight vocabulary, and his suggested use of choral and unison reading. Again, advocates of a psycholinguistic notion of reading (Smith, 1973) would claim this approach over-emphasizes the machanics of word-perfect reading.

Research evidence to support Allen's approach is rather limited, and that which is available tends to be negative (Kendrick and Bennett, 1966). In defense of Allen, the research that has been implemented has seemed rather insensitive to the subtleties of the goals he outlined. Measurement procedures and analysis techniques have seemed inadequate to truly evaluate the effectiveness of this approach.

Allen did not invent the language experience approach, but he should be given a great deal of credit for its emergence, popularity, and evolution. His language experience approach to teaching communication represents his most recent efforts and his response to demands for a more comprehensive and structured language experience approach. The enigma of the approach may be that while it is not sufficiently prescriptive for some teachers, it may be too prescriptive for others.

Check appendix for the following:
Suggestions for book making
Suggestions for stimulating creative writing

REFERENCES

Allen, R. V. "How a Language Experience Program Works." In E. C. Vilscek, (ed.), *A Decade of Innovations: Approaches to Beginning Reading.* Newark: International Reading Association, 1968.
Provides a brief overview of the approach's rationale and guiding principles.

Allen, R. V. *Language Experiences in Communication.* Boston: Houghton Mifflin, 1976.
Provides a detailed discussion of the approach's rationale and methods of implementation.

Allen, R. V. "Suggestions for Taking Dictation." Unpublished paper, University of Arizona, 1973.
Describes his suggestions for taking students' dictation.

Allen, R. V., and Allen, C. *Language Experience Activities.* Boston: Houghton Mifflin, 1976.
Contains more than 250 activities for use with the approach and in learning centers.

Allen, R. V., and Allen, C. *Language Experiences in Early Childhood.* Chicago: Encyclopedia Brittanica, 1969.
Provides extensive resource material, including suggestions for lessons, teaching methods, materials and activities for use in first grade or early childhood programs.

Allen, R. V., and Allen, C. *Language Experiences in Reading, Levels I, II, and III.* Chicago: Encyclopedia Brittanica, 1966-1968.
Provides extensive resource material, including suggestions for lessons, teaching methods, materials and activities, for use with elementary school students.

Aukerman, R. C. *Approaches to Beginning Reading.* New York: John Wiley and Sons, 1971, pp. 302-311.
Provides a detailed discussion of the approach's development, rationale, methods, and materials.

Hoover, I. W. "Historical and Theoretical Development of a Language Experience Approach to Teaching Reading in Selected Teacher Education Institutions." Ed.D. thesis, College of Education, University of Arizona, Tucson, 1971.
Presents a survey of the language experience approach's historical development and its introduction in teacher education institutions.

Kendrick, W. M., and Bennett, C. L. "A Comparative Study of Two First-Grade Language Arts Programs." *Reading Research Quarterly* 2 (1966): 83-118.
Reports a research study comparing the language experience approach with a traditional basal method.

Lee, D. M., and Allen, R. V. *Learning to Read Through Experience.* New York: Appleton-Century-Crofts, 1963.
Presents a 146-page overview of the language experience approach.

Smith, F. "Twelve Easy Ways to Make Reading Difficult." In F. Smith, ed., *Psycholinguistics and Reading.* New York: Holt, Rinehart and Winston, 1973, pp. 183-196.
Discusses the problems associated with selected instructional principles and practices.

ASHTON-WARNER'S ORGANIC READING

Purpose

Organic reading (Ashton-Warner, 1958) is an experience-centered approach to reading instruction based upon Sylvia Ashton-Warner's twenty-four years of teaching experiences with New Zealand Maori children. It is designed to provide a bridge from the known to the unknown, a bridge that can help students move from their own experiences to sharing the written experiences of others.

Rationale

In her various books, *Spinster* (1958), *Teacher* (1963), and *Spearpoint* (1972), Ashton-Warner presents the rationale and details of her procedure. She states that organic reading is derived from the notion that learning experiences should begin with the "intrinsic" rather than with the "extrinsic;" she suggests that students should relate to their own innermost thoughts before relating to the thoughts of others. Her goal as a teacher is to "release the native imagery and use it for working material" (Ashton-Warner, 1972, p. 17).

Along this line of reasoning, the student's initial exposure to reading should afford an organic, instinctive reaction to reading. As Ashton-Warner suggests:

> First words must mean something to a child. First words must have intense meaning for a child. They must be a part of his being.
>
> How much hangs on the love of reading, the instinctive inclination to hold a book! Instinctive. That's what it must be. The reaching out for a book needs to become an organic action, which can happen at this yet formative age. Pleasant words won't do. Respectable words won't do. They must be words organically tied up, organically born from the dynamic life itself. They must be words that are already part of the child's being. (Ashton-Warner, 1963, p. 30)

Ashton-Warner claims that the longer the student's reading is organic, the stronger it will become. She suggests that teachers should reach into the minds of students to touch this key vocabulary; when a number of words are acquired, students should be given opportunities to write and read stories based upon this vocabulary. Ashton-Warner suggests that in so doing the foundation to a lifetime of reading can be laid.

Intended Audience

Organic reading is suited for use on either an individual, a group, or a classroom basis with any student. It was proposed as a beginning reading method with children from divergent cultures, specifically New Zealand Maori children, but it has also been used in the United States.

Description of the Procedure

Sylvia Ashton-Warner describes the organic reading approach as integral to the total curriculum. Organic reading would be one aspect of the organic teaching program. During a school day, students would be scheduled to do "organic work" and "standard work." Both these aspects of the school program would involve what Ashton-Warner refers to as "input" and "output" periods. As suggested by Ashton-Warner, the typical school day would entail the following activities (1963, p. 101):

TYPICAL DAY'S ACTIVITIES

Morning
- Organic Work
  - Output period (approximately 1 hour 45 minutes)
    - conversation, art activities, craft activities, singing, creative dance, key vocabulary, organic vocabulary, etc.
  - Input period (approximately 1 hour)
    - key vocabulary (for little ones), organic vocabulary, organic discussion, stories, pictures, etc.

Afternoon
- Standard work
  - Output period (approximately 1 hour)
    - nature study and numbers
  - Input period (approximately 50 minutes)
    - standard vocabulary, standard reading, Maori book vocabulary and reading, supplementary reading, stories, songs, poems, letters (for little ones)

Organic reading involves four movements or periods in the student's development. The first movement begins with the students generating words they wish to learn. The latter movements involve the students in writing and reading stories.

First Movement

The first movement entails, as Ashton-Warner puts it, reaching into the child's "inner mind" to discover the child's key vocabulary. Ashton-Warner suggests that each student has a key vocabulary, which, if it is to be reached, requires a great deal of teacher sensitivity and patience. It is probed during the morning output period when the teacher holds personal conferences with each student. The teacher elicits these key words from the student and writes each on a twelve-by-five-inch card as it is spoken. The student then takes the work, traces it, studies it, and, when ready to move on to other activities, places it in the teacher's word box.

Later that same morning, each student is given further experiences with these same words. Namely a check is made to see if the words are remembered. An opportunity is given for the student to use them in organic writing and spelling activities. In the latter activities, the student will:

a. Write either a sentence or a story using the key vocabulary words
b. Be presented with the words for either naming or spelling

The chalkboard rather than paper is used extensively for these activities.

Several other techniques are used to learn and check each student's key vocabulary. At the beginning of each school day, students receive their cards mixed together and emptied on the classroom floor. When the students enter, they have to scramble to find their own word cards. Ashton-Warner suggests that the recalled cards represent the student's "living" key vocabulary. Following this line of reasoning, words that are not recalled are removed and destroyed. To facilitate further learning, each student then sits with a partner, and they hear and help each other say their words.

According to Ashton-Warner, each student's key vocabulary reflects the student's inner self. The words in this key vocabulary center upon the student's primitive instincts. Specifically, they reflect ideas related to fear and sex. Among the fear words often suggested were *ghost*, *frightened*, *cry*, and *wild*. Among the sex words often suggested were *kiss*, *love*, *dance*, and *together*.

Second Movement

As the students' vocabulary develops, they progress through the other movements. By the time the second movement has been reached, the student has acquired a sizeable key vocabulary and has begun suggesting words from "outside" rather than "inside," such as *happy days* and *snowy mountains*. In this movement, the use of two words replaces the use of single words; longer, yellow cards replace the white word cards. The student again traces the words written on the card, puts them in a story, and, during the morning input period, writes them on the chalkboard and spells them. Early every morning, the students will once again arrive to find their new cards piled on the floor and will begin a search for them. During this movement, the students begin to read either homemade or teacher-made books which use key vocabulary words. These are the students' stories, made from their own words by their teacher or their parents. The students read these books to themselves and each other.

Third and Fourth Movements

As the students continue to progress, they move through Ashton-Warner's third and fourth movements. During these movements, the student progresses from writing his or her own small stories with teacher assistance to writing small stories without teacher assistance to writing rather sophisticated stories.

During these movements the student's vocabulary is ever changing; Ashton-Warner suggests words appear and disappear with their changing appeal. Whenever the student adds a new word, the teacher writes it in the back of the student's own story book. These back pages assume the role of a personal dictionary for the student.

During these movements, time is also alloted to vocabulary building, reading, sharing, and discussing stories. During vocabulary periods, students write their words on the chalkboard and spell them aloud. During organic reading and sharing, students not only read and master their own stories, but also share them with others. Following organic reading and sharing, the students discuss each other's stories, then proceed to use the Maori readers. These readers contain stories collected from the work of previous children. They are intended as an introduction to reading published books.

During the afternoon input and output periods, the students are presented with standard school experiences in accordance with their level of development. These experiences purport to introduce the students to the culture at large. Experiences would include nature study, numbers, standard vocabulary, standard reading, listening experiences, songs, and poems. For students at the key vocabulary level, they would also include letter writing activities.

Cautions and Comments

There have been a number of evaluations of Ashton-Warner's ideas (Packer, 1970; and Duquette, 1972). These evaluations have yielded mixed results in terms of the carry-over of the approach to published reading programs, but they do support Ashton-Warner's claim that her approach affords a more enjoyable and meaningful approach to developing beginning readers' attitudes and abilities. As she suggests in her own evaluation of the use of the approach with American children (*Spearpoint,* 1973), organic reading may have differential success in accordance with the general attitude and desire of children for learning.

Teachers should recognize that the approach necessitates a great deal of daily preparation. Teachers would have to be aware of and record each student's developmental level and scheduled activities, and, in particular, to teach the student's key vocabulary. Teachers would need to be able to provide the mechanisms for generating stories based upon the students' vocabularies and for having students write their own stories.

Finally, it should be noted that certain aspects of Ashton-Warner's approach lack adequate development. For example, while her suggestions for using and generating key vocabulary seem reasonable, some of her proposed methods are ill-defined and poorly reasoned. In places her approach lacks sufficient definition to be understood or implemented, and some of her suggestions lack a base either in theory or in research, e.g., her procedures for spelling and writing words.

Check appendix for the following:
- Suggestions for word box use
- Suggestions for book making
- Suggestions for stimulating creative writing

REFERENCES

Ashton-Warner, S. *Spearpoint.* New York: Alfred A. Knopf, 1972.
Describes Ashton-Warner's experiences with her method while teaching in Colorado.

Ashton-Warner, S. *Spinster.* New York: Simon and Schuster, 1958.
Describes aspects of her life as a teacher of New Zealand Maori children and refers to her organic teaching methods.

Ashton-Warner, S. *Teacher.* New York: Simon and Schuster, 1963.
Provides a detailed description of her organic teaching methods, their rationale and their use with New Zealand children.

Aukerman, R. C. *Approaches to Beginning Reading.* New York: John Wiley and Sons, 1971, pp. 320–324.
Provides a summary description and discussion of the organic teaching methods.

Duquette, R. J. "Research Summary of Barnette-Duquette Study." *Childhood Education* 48 (1972): 438–440.
Presents a summary of a research study in which Ashton-Warner's key vocabulary concept was used with students of varying reading ability in different United States cities.

Packer, A. B. "Ashton-Warner's Key Vocabulary for the Disadvantaged." *Reading Teacher* 23 (1970): 559–564
Presents the findings of a United States study in which words in students' key vocabulary were compared with basal word lists.

Veatch, J. *Reading in the Elementary School,* 2nd ed. New York: John Wiley and Sons, 1978, pp. 343–357.
Discusses key words and its relation to beginning reading.

Veatch, J., Sawicki, F., Elliot, G., Barnette, E., and Blakey, J. *Key Words to Reading: The Language Experience Approach Begins,* 2nd ed. Columbus: Charles E. Merrill, 1979.
Provides a description of how key vocabulary can be integrated into an individualized reading program.

Wasserman, S. "Aspen Mornings with Sylvia Ashton-Warner." *Childhood Education* 48 (1972): 348–353.
Describes a teacher's exposure to organic teaching through a workshop run by Ashton-Warner.

STAUFFER'S LANGUAGE-EXPERIENCE APPROACH

Purpose

The purpose of the Language-Experience Approach advocated by Russell Stauffer (1970) is to take advantage of the linguistic, intellectual, social, and cultural wealth a student brings to school so that the transfer from oral language to written language can be made.

Rationale

In the preface to his book, *The Language-Experience Approach to the Teaching of Reading* (1970), Stauffer makes the following statement:

> The best label that can be applied to the Language-Experience Approach is "The Eclectic Approach to Reading Instruction." It embraces the best practices regardless of their sources and does so in a functional communication-oriented way.

He suggests that essential to the Language-Experience Approach are the relationships which exist among language, thought, and experience, and among the communicative skills of reading, writing, speaking, and listening. More specifically, he suggests:

1. Reading, writing, speaking, and listening occur within the context of purposeful communication
2. The interests, curiosities, creativity, culture, capacity, percepts, and concepts of each individual are used
3. The use of word recognition and word identification is developed in a meaningful context ensuring the use of meaning clues
4. Reading skills which are taught are assimilated and used

5. Individual interests and understandings are extended and refined
6. An appreciation of the value and uses of reading is afforded

To these ends, the Language-Experience Approach is a total language arts approach which relies heavily upon dictated stories, word banks, and creative writing.

Intended Audience

The Language-Experience Approach is designed for use as a beginning reading approach with students of various ages and abilities. It is appropriate for use either on a one-to-one, a group, or a whole-class basis.

Description of Procedure

The following description of Stauffer's Language-Experience Approach is not intended to be exhaustive, but instead to represent its major characteristics. The interested reader is directed to Stauffer's book, *The Language-Experience Approach to the Teaching of Reading* (1970), for further details. Those aspects we will discuss include:

1. Dictated experience stories
2. Word Banks
3. Creative writing

1. Dictated Experience Stories

Dictated experience stories are the core of Stauffer's Language-Experience Approach. They provide students with the opportunity to learn to read much as they learn to talk. They also provide a means of getting started with reading and for developing, refining, and extending reading skills.

As a way of getting started, Stauffer suggests the use of whole-class dictated stories. During the first few weeks, the whole-class dictated stories provide the students an opportunity to become familiar with the procedure and to get acquainted with each other linguistically, culturally, and socially. Once familiar with the procedure, the students engage in group-dictated stories and, ideally, individual-dictated stories.

Across whole-class-, group-, and individual-dictated experience stories, the procedures used by the teacher are quite similar. For this reason, they will be discussed together.

a. *Generating the dictated experience story.* To generate the dictated experience story requires that the teacher locate a stimulus with which the student can associate and through which, Stauffer suggests, students can "examine more carefully the world about them, to see new horizons, to view the past and the future, and to act upon it intellectually" (Stauffer, 1970, p. 55). The stimulus might be an event, an idea, or a concrete object. It might involve something the students can see, touch, or feel, and, with the help of teacher questioning, discuss.

When the teacher feels the students are able and willing to generate some dictation, the stimulus is put aside and the students gather around a chart set up for dictation. For class-dictated stories, a lined chart approximately two feet by three feet is suggested; for group-dictated stories a chart approximately twelve inches by fifteen inches. For individual-dictated stories, letter-sized paper is suggested.

The teacher now asks the students to tell about the stimulus; as the students offer ideas, these are recorded by the teacher. In a whole-class or a group situation, only selected students would be given an opportunity to dictate sentences. Once the several sentences are recorded, the teacher might terminate the generation activity and reread the sentences to check if the recorded ideas are stated appropriately.

b. *Reading the story and follow-up activities.* Once the students' dictated story is completed, it is read. First the teacher reads the story; then the teacher and students read the story in unison. As the story is read and read again, the teacher points to each word. The teacher may then direct the students to draw a picture depicting their story, to identify known words in the story, or to begin other activities.

On the second day, the students are again referred to their dictated experience story. If the story is a class effort, the class is first divided into groups, with at least one child who contributes to the story in each group. Typically, the activities of the second day are sequenced in this way:

1. Each student follows along, either individually or in groups, as the teacher reads their individual, group or class stories.
2. As the teacher points to each word, the story is read by the teacher and student in unison.
3. The whole story or portions of the story are read by selected individuals or by the author of the story.
4. The students match, name, or locate selected words.
5. The students locate and underline words they know or the whole group knows.
6. To check on known words, the teacher has the student(s) reread the dictated story orally. If the student fails to recognize a word previously underlined, the underlining is crossed, e.g., donkey. This marking indicates "donkey" is no longer a known word.

On the third day, students in the class are given the opportunity to do more intense study of their stories. When stories were dictated with the whole class, the teacher reproduces the story and distributes it to each student. Individually, students read over the story and underline known words. Stories are then placed in class and personal folders. The students whose stories are generated individually or in a group are given an opportunity to reread their stories and check (after a reasonable "forgetting period") whether they still remember their words from the previous day. For the purpose of providing a schedule for group dictation, Stauffer (1970) suggests the following activities across a week:

GROUP DICTATING SCHEDULE

	Group I (least mature)	Group II	Group III	Group IV (most mature)
Monday	dictating	other activities	other activities	dictating
Tuesday	re-reading and word study	dictating	dictating	re-reading and word study
Wednesday	re-reading and word study	re-reading and word study	re-reading and word study	other activities
Thursday	dictating	re-reading and word study	other activities	dictating
Friday	re-reading and word study	dictating	dictating	re-reading and word study

2. Word Banks

As Stauffer describes the word-bank file, it is "a personalized record of words a pupil has learned to read or recognize at sight" (Stauffer, 1970, p. 74). The file of words emanates from the dictated stories generated by the student. It includes only words that the student has identified as being known across successive days. These are words that have been underlined at least twice. As a check on the students' recognition of these words, the teacher has them identify their words. For this purpose, a small window card is suggested. (See diagram) The window frame is placed over each underlined word in random order. The random ordering of presentation prevents the student's use of context.

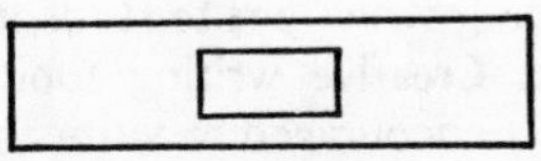

Window Card

Henry

Henry is my very best friend.
He is an ant that I keep in an
ant house beside my bed. He has
six legs and is brown and red.

The students' known words form the deposits and reserves of their individual word banks. Each known word is written or typed on a card (approximately 3/8 by 1 1/2 inches) and filed. As the word bank expands beyond thirty cards, an alphabetic filing system is introduced. Thus, each student gains a personalized file of known words, which acts both as a resource and as a dictionary. To use the word bank cards as a resource, Stauffer suggests a variety of activities: composing stories, word attack activities, discrimination activities, categorization activities, and finding other occurrences of the words in print.

3. Creative Writing

Another facet of Stauffer's Language-Experience Approach grows out of the students' word banks—creative writing. Stauffer defines creative writing as "a composition that reflects a child's own choice of words, ideas, order, spelling, and punctuation" (Stauffer, 1970, p. 78).

The students' first encounter with writing is expected to occur with the writing of names and recognition of words. But creative word usage begins with the construction of sentences from words in the word banks. Using their word cards, students' first creative writing experiences occur when they lay out simple sentences and stories with their cards. When a word not in their word bank is required, they begin to learn to write and spell, using their new word recognition skills.

To begin creative writing experiences, Stauffer suggests the use of twelve- by eighteen-inch paper. To provide a space for illustration, he suggests leaving the top half unlined. To guide lettering and to afford ample spacing between lines, he suggests ruling five lines with 3/4-inch spacing, and lines 3/8-inch wide between each two of these lines across the bottom of the page.

As described by Stauffer (1970, pp. 82–83), the following guidelines may help the teacher in developing creative writing abilities from these beginnings:

a. Students should want to write rather than be coerced into writing
b. Instructions to students should be simple and direct
c. Creative writing topics may be suggested, but students should be encouraged to write about anything they wish
d. Students should be encouraged to write legibly and spell accurately, but not at the expense of interferring with the flow of their ideas
e. Students' ideas should be encouraged to flow freely through teacher assistance and questioning when needed
f. Students' writing should be evaluated in terms of quality of expression and not purely by "adult standards"

Cautions and Comments

Stauffer's language-experience approach provides the teacher with a comprehensive, well-articulated, and experience-based language arts program for initial reading.

The approach seems suitable for use with students of varying ages and capabilities. It provides for a variety of language-experience activities in all four facets of the language arts. It may be used either to eventually supplement or to substitute for a total reading program. Stauffer's approach affords incidental instruction for the development, extension, and refinement of word identification skills, spelling skills, writing skills, concept development skills, and general comprehension.

As evidence of the approach's use and value, Stauffer provides a wealth of actual examples taken from teachers in different settings and also cites theory and research. Several related research studies are abstracted in the appendices to his book (Stauffer, 1970).

However, the approach does seem to have at least one major shortcoming. Namely, it appears that the approach places an undue emphasis upon the recognition of isolated words. This emphasis occurs in the pointing to words during reading, in the identification and mastery of single words, and in the word banks composed of single, known words. Students with whom the approach is used are in danger of becoming non-fluent readers and word callers, if they give each word the power these activities suggest. If reading for meaning is our goal, the approach should place less emphasis upon word-perfect reading and the acquisition of single known words and give more emphasis to reading with understanding.

Check appendix for the following:
Suggestions for word box use
Suggestions for book making
Suggestions for stimulating creative writing

REFERENCES

Stauffer, R. G. *Directing Reading Maturity as a Cognitive Process.* New York: Harper & Row, 1969, pp. 186–238.
Presents a detailed discussion of aspects of Stauffer's language-experience approach.

Stauffer, R. G. "The Language-Experience Approach." In J. Kerfoot, ed., *First Grade Reading Programs.* Newark: International Reading Association, 1965.
Provides additional information concerning Stauffer's language-experience approach.

Stauffer, R. G. *The Language-Experience Approach to the Teaching of Reading.* New York: Harper & Row, 1970.
Presents a detailed account, with examples, of the rationale and procedures of this approach.

Stauffer, R. G., and Hammond, W. D. "The Effectiveness of Language Arts and Basic Reader Approaches to First Grade Reading Instruction—Extended into Second Grade." *Reading Teacher* 20 (1967): 740–746.
Presents research findings in which Stauffer's approach is compared favorably with basic reading program instruction.

Stauffer, R. G., and Hammond, W. D. "The Effectiveness of Language Arts and Basic Reader Approaches to First Grade Reading Instruction—Extended into Third Grade." *Reading Research Quarterly* 4 (1969): 468–499.
Presents an extension of previous research findings concerning the Stauffer approach.

4

Recreational Reading Strategy

UNIT OVERVIEW

The Unit and Its Theme

Each of the previous units contains descriptions of numerous strategies designed either to teach students how to read or how to read better. This strategy unit provides a description of just one strategy, but perhaps it is more important than any other single strategy in this text.

One of the major goals of education should be the development of life-time readers—individuals who not only can read, but who do read. Children and adults discover the joy of reading not by being told that reading is exciting and stimulating, but by being given the opportunity to read materials of their own choosing in a quiet, nonpressured environment.

The Strategy—Uninterrupted Sustained Silent Reading

The Uninterrupted Sustained Silent Reading period could be one of the major components of a successful reading program. Very simply, time is set aside during the school day to provide students with an opportunity to read. Students, as well as their teacher, read materials of their own choosing in a quiet, relaxed atmosphere.

Utilization

Specific information related to the implementation of Uninterrupted Sustained Silent Reading may be found in the section entitled "Description of the Procedure." The strategy is generally successful when the classroom teacher recognizes the true value of the technique and prepares the students properly for the reading period.

UNINTERRUPTED SUSTAINED SILENT READING

Purpose

Generally recognized objectives of Uninterrupted Sustained Silent Reading (USSR) are:

1. To provide students with a quiet time to practice their silent reading
2. To provide students with models of good silent reading behavior
3. To increase students' abilities to sustain silent reading for longer periods of time.

Rationale

Much time is spent teaching students *how* to read; however, it is here argued that few classroom teachers provide students either a model for reading, or the opportunity to read materials for pleasure. USSR is intended to provide students the opportunity to practice the art of reading—an opportunity to become actively involved in the reading act with materials of their own choosing. Just as playing golf and seeing others play golf gives a neophyte golfer the opportunity to learn to play, USSR is intended to provide the reader with the opportunity to become a better reader by reading and seeing others read. McCracken and McCracken (1978) suggest USSR provides students with the following messages:

> "Reading books is important.
> Reading is something anyone can do.
> Reading is communicating with an author.
> Children are capable of sustained thoughts.
> Books are meant to be read in large sections.
> The teacher believes that the pupils are comprehending (because he or she doesn't bother to check).
>
> The teacher trusts the children to decide when something is well written, when something important has been read (because the teacher expects pupils to share after USSR)". (p. 408)

Intended Audience

Uninterrupted Sustained Silent Reading is appropriate for kindergarten students through those at senior high school level. College and adult reading programs also could profit from the use of the technique. The technique may be used by an elementary teacher with a self-contained classroom, by a content teacher in a departmentalized program, or by a total school staff during a predetermined period of the school day (Ganz and Theofield, 1974; Petre, 1971).

Description of the Procedure

It would appear that USSR contains three vital elements:

1. Preparation
2. The Reading Period
3. Follow-up

1. *Preparation*

Perhaps the key to the success of a USSR program is this vital first step. Students should understand what they are going to be doing during the activity, why it is important, and how it will be carried out.

The idea of USSR should be discussed with students several days in advance of the first reading session. The emphasis at this stage should be on the fact that the students will be allowed to select whatever reading material they desire to read during this period. Although students should be encouraged to bring their favorite reading material to class for USSR sessions, several students obviously will forget on occasion; therefore, the teacher should collect a variety of reading materials that will remain in the classroom and can be used during USSR sessions. The collection should be changed occasionally to provide a variety of offerings.

Teachers also should be sure to inform their administrator(s) and colleagues of what they are doing and should inform them not to interrupt unless an emergency arises.

It is essential that all students in the class understand the rules of USSR. Presentation of the rules a day or two before the start of USSR will allow students and teachers to discuss why these particular regulations are necessary. It is suggested that the rules be reviewed just prior to the first USSR session. The three cardinal rules of USSR follow:

a. Everybody reads. Both students and teacher will read something of their own choosing. Completing homework assignments, grading papers, and similar activities are discouraged. The reading should be for the pleasure of the reader.
b. There are to be no interruptions during USSR. The word "uninterrupted" is an essential part of the technique. Interruptions result in loss of comprehension and loss of interest by many students; therefore, questions and comments should be held until the silent reading period has concluded.
c. No one will be asked to report what they have read. It is essential that students feel that this is a period of free reading with the emphasis on reading for enjoyment.

2. *The Reading Period*

The USSR period begins as soon as the students have been given a sufficient amount of time to select their reading materials and the teacher has reviewed the rules briefly. Following the first session, it may be only necessary occasionally to remind the students of the rules.

a. *Setting the time.* The time length of the very first USSR session should be such that the majority of the students within the class can easily sustain their silent reading. For the lower grades, this may mean something in the neighborhood of three to five minutes; for upper elementary grades, five to ten minutes; and for secondary classrooms, ten to fifteen minutes. It is probably better initially to underestimate students' ability to sustain silent reading, since one of the goals of USSR is to increase gradually the time devoted to the activity. Depending upon the ability and interest level of the students, reasonable goals might be fifteen to twenty minutes for primary level classrooms; twenty to thirty minutes for the middle grades; and thirty minutes for high school classes. These times should be considered as only guidelines.
b. *Timing USSR.* Most teachers have found that a kitchen timer or an alarm clock works best as the timing device for USSR sessions. The timer should be set for the agreed-upon time and then placed in such a position that students are unable to see the face of the device. This procedure solves the problem of the "clock watchers" within a classroom. For this same reason, a large classroom clock should not be used as the timing device. Another advantage of the alarm clock or kitchen timer is that it provides a definite end to the USSR session. The sound of an alarm clock leaves no doubt that the reading period has come to an end, and that it is time to move on to other activities.
c. *The role of the teacher.* During the USSR period, the teacher is doing exactly what all the students in the class are doing–reading for pleasure. The teacher has the very important role of showing good, sustained silent reading behavior. For some students within the classroom, this may be the first opportunity to observe an adult who is reading for pure enjoyment.

   It is important to keep this one activity in mind. There are a number of things that a teacher should *not* do during USSR. The class instructor should not correct papers, plan lessons, take attendance, or perform similar school-related activities. By doing this type of activity, teachers are, in effect, saying to students, "Reading is an important activity for you, but not for me." Likewise, the teacher should not move around the classroom to seek out those students who are not reading or those students who are potential trouble makers. Besides not serving as an adequate model, a teacher in the monitoring role becomes a potential "interrupter" of the reading process.

d. *Interruptions during USSR.* It is not unusual for interruptions to occur occasionally, especially in the initial phase of using the procedure in the classroom. Interruptions that cause the classroom teacher and a large number of students to look up from their reading should generally result in an end to the reading period for that day. However, persons guilty of interrupting should not be reprimanded; rather, the classroom teacher may simply say, "I'm sorry, but that concludes our USSR session for today. Please put your reading material away and we will proceed with our next lesson." The instructor should be prepared to move quickly to the next scheduled activity without providing the individual who interrupted with the attention that the student might be seeking. The activity immediately following the USSR also should not appear to be arranged as a means of punishment; i.e., tests and other equally unpopular activities are best scheduled at other times.

After the habit of silent reading has been firmly established, minor and unintentional interruptions may be handled smoothly without resulting in an end to the reading session. In these situations, the teacher might respond in this manner: "I hope that the interruption did not cause you to completely lose your train of thought. Do you think you can return to your reading without any problems?" If most students respond affirmatively, then the teacher provides a model by returning immediately to reading. Very minor disturbances that cause the instructor and only one or two students to look up from their reading should be ignored. After quickly evaluating the situation, the teacher should return immediately to the reading. This action has the effect of saying, "No problem. Let's continue our reading."

e. *Concluding the reading period.* USSR ends with the sound of the timer. The instructor should be prepared to move to the next scheduled activity. Occasionally, teachers may provide students a few additional minutes of reading time. This "buffer" period allows students an opportunity to read until a more appropriate stopping point is reached.

3. *Follow-up*

McCracken (1971) suggests that after the first week of USSR, the teacher may begin to think of ways to encourage sharing what has been read during the silent reading sessions. The teacher can set an example by making a brief comment about interesting ideas the students have read, by keeping a log of the books and the number of pages read, and by similar actions that show a sincere interest in the reading act. These sharing activities can result in greater student interest in reading.

It must be emphasized that such sharing activities should not begin until after the USSR activity has been firmly established. If the teacher begins to prompt students to share too early in the beginning sessions, USSR might deteriorate into something other than reading for enjoyment.

Cautions and Comments

To reiterate, the key to success of USSR is the role of the teacher. The teacher, by the very act of reading, is communicating the *value* of reading to the students. Conversely, any lack of interest or enthusiasm by the teacher can result in a similar reaction by the students.

In the beginning stages of implementation of this activity, it is probably best to proceed slowly and to take small steps. USSR should be undertaken at the classroom level before any consideration is given to a school-wide program. Even though there have been some successful school-wide USSR programs, there are also reservations regarding programs that insist that everyone read at the same time of day and for the same amount of time. Certainly, differences in the amount of time allocated for the lower primary grades versus time allocated for the upper intermediate grades are one consideration.

Finally, though USSR is a simple technique and can easily be implemented in the classrooms at any level, it is very difficult to evaluate. Certainly, increasing the length of time the students are able to sustain their silent reading is one way to evaluate the success of the activity. Perhaps the only other means to evaluate the success of USSR sessions is how receptive the students become to the follow-up periods initiated by the teacher. Though this is a very subjective means of evaluation, a willingness of students to share what they have been reading during USSR is one indication of its value.

REFERENCES

Evans, H. M., and Towner, J. C. "Sustained Silent Reading: Does It Increase Skills?" *The Reading Teacher* 29 (1975): 155–156.
Describes a study comparing the use of USSR with the use of basal supplements.

Gambrell, L. B. "Getting Started with Sustained Silent Reading and Keeping It Going." *Reading Teacher,* 32, no. 3 (1978): 328-331.
Discusses preparation for and management of the USSR.

Ganz, P., and Theofield, M. B. "Suggestions for Starting USSR." *Journal of Reading* 17 (1974): 614–616.
Provides recommendations for initiating a USSR program on a school-wide basis.

Hunt, L. C. "Six Steps to the Individualized Reading Program (IRP)." *Elementary English* 48, no. 1 (1971): 27–32.
Describes the intent and procedures for implementing USSR.

McCracken, R. A., "Initiating Sustained Silent Reading." *Journal of Reading* 14 (1971): 521–524; 582–583.
Recommends six rules teachers must follow to implement USSR successfully.

McCracken, R. A., and McCracken, M. J. "Modeling Is the Key to Sustained Silent Reading." *Reading Teacher* 31, no. 4 (1978): 406–408.
Describes how and what a teacher does during and after silent reading; also defines what students do.

McCracken, R. A., and McCracken, M. J. *Reading Is Only the Tiger's Tail.* San Rafael, Calif.: Leswing Press, 1972.
Provides recommendations for initiating a USSR program.

Petre, R. M. "Reading Breaks Make It in Maryland." *Journal of Reading* 15 (1971): 191–194.
Describes a sustained reading program used throughout the state of Maryland and the benefits resulting from it.

5

Oral Reading Strategies and Practices

UNIT OVERVIEW

The Unit and Its Theme

Current practices seem to indicate that much instructional time in our elementary classrooms is devoted to oral reading. Although there is value in oral reading for beginning reading instruction, there is some question as to the effectiveness of the way the activity may be conducted in the classroom.

The most frequent oral reading activity is that of "round-robin" or "circle" reading. In this activity, each student in turn reads a small portion aloud to his or her reading group or to the class as a whole, while the other students follow along silently. This practice is used primarily in conjunction with the basal reading program.

The issue at hand is whether oral reading activities conducted in this manner are justifiable. Spache and Spache (1977) have noted that "round-robin" reading is merely a word-calling practice, not a meaning-oriented activity as it should be. Additionally, Harris (1970) has emphasized that this method has only limited utility as a rapid, but inefficient, method of evaluation.

Oral reading is a communication skill. It is a way of delivering information or providing entertainment to listeners. If used in this way, oral reading would seem best done for a specific purpose, and a student's performance would seem best evaluated in terms of its communicative value.

The Strategies

The four strategies discussed in this unit are designed to aid the teacher in planning oral reading activities that have specific purposes. Three of the strategies are mainly developmental in nature and focus on the communicative aspects of oral reading. The other strategy tends to be used with students who may be having difficulty in reading. As a preview of this unit, a brief summary of the strategies follows.

Choral Reading

Choral reading is a strategy designed to give students practice in reading with the proper expression. Useful as a whole-class reading activity, choral reading provides students with active involvement in print and puts prime emphasis on interpreting meaning.

Radio Reading

Providing practice for students in both reading and listening, radio reading focuses instruction on the ultimate goal of oral reading—communicating a message. It is useful throughout the grades wherever oral reading is one of the teaching methods, particularly as a substitute for "round-robin" reading.

Paired Reading

Paired reading accomplishes a dual purpose: it provides practice for students in reading for meaning, and it aids the teacher in grouping for instruction. Along with peer tutoring, paired reading is suited for use with students in the elementary grades.

Echo Reading

Echo reading is designed to foster the acquisition of vocabulary and oral fluency. It is most effective in a one-to-one instructional situation and primarily with students in the elementary grades.

Utilization

Since oral reading pervades reading instruction in the elementary grades, it is imperative that teachers understand that its effectiveness as an instructional tool is limited if emphasis is placed on word-perfect reading. The success or failure of oral reading instruction is dependent upon an examination of its actual purpose and an understanding of its intent—a tool to communicate a message. In such a context, word-perfect oral reading may detract from effective communication.

REFERENCES

Harris, A. J. *How to Increase Reading Ability*, 6th ed. New York: David McKay, 1975.
Spache, G. D., and Spache, E. B. *Reading in the Elementary School*, 4th ed. Boston: Allyn and Bacon, 1977.

CHORAL READING

Purpose

The purpose of choral reading is to:

1. Provide practice for students in reading with the expression necessary to add to meaning
2. Develop self-assurance by giving every student a chance to function as part of a group
3. Aid students in developing an appreciation for oral expression

Rationale

Artificial barriers are sometimes created by students and between students when oral reading occurs. For example, poorer readers may not like to read orally, and the shy student who rarely volunteers in any class activity will often be hesitant about oral reading. On the other hand, the overly-confident student, if given the opportunity, might dominate an oral reading exercise.

Choral reading provides the teacher with a socialization tool. Poor readers as well as shy ones can use the whole-group format to avoid humiliating corrections while they gain confidence in themselves. The obstrusive student may be tempered through the same whole-group format, which discourages that student from showing off.

Additionally, choral reading can develop students' interest in the creative forms of language such as poetry, where previously students might have had negative feelings toward poetry.

Finally, choral reading provides students with the opportunity to become actively involved with print, placing the prime emphasis on interpreting and expressing meaning. Many times, words and not meaning are emphasized in reading activities. Choral reading develops students' abilities to read for meaning—the eventual goal of the act of reading.

Intended Audience

Choral reading is suitable for any school population. Grade level and achievement level are inconsequential, because of the group approach of this strategy. Class size also matters little, as the teacher can divide any large group into smaller, more manageable, choral groups.

Description of the Procedure

As a substitute for oral reading as commonly practiced, choral reading presents the teacher with a unique instructional activity that can unite all readers, regardless of ability, in a common reading experience. At the same time, this strategy can provide students with entertainment, group involvement, and practice in reading with self-expression.

In order that choral reading be carried out effectively, the teacher must be prepared to deal with the following components of this strategy:

1. Developing Rhythmic Sensitivity
2. Casting

1. Developing Rhythmic Sensitivity.

Before choral reading can be accomplished successfully, the students should be guided by the teacher through progressive steps to develop their sensitivity for rhythm. The teacher should not make any assumptions concerning students' ability in choral reading. By guiding them through the activity first, the teacher is assured that students have the framework to establish eventual independence in that activity.

The concept of modeling is very appropriate with this activity. One way to impress young children is for the teacher to be an example. By showing students that poetry and other creative forms are enjoyable, by sharing these things with the class, and by demonstrating the desired self-expression, the teacher should find students experience little difficulty in beginning choral reading.

A variety of selections should be used for choral reading, to aid students in acquiring a sensitivity for rhythm, mood, and voice modulation. The teacher should demonstrate proper phrasing, tempo, and enunciation with the selections for choral reading, and, through discussion, emphasize the importance of proper expression in conveying a poem's mood and meaning.

Choral reading might begin with short selections, preferably memorized. Eventually, longer selections, possibly with the rhythm marked, may be introduced.

To provide additional reinforcement for students, a tape recorder may be used for evaluative purposes. Students may also participate as critical listeners by separating themselves from the choral groups and providing feedback. After a few successful experiences, students may begin, and be encouraged, to suggest other ways selections might be interpreted and read. Sound effects and pantomiming may also be used.

Finally, when selecting material for choral reading, care should be taken to ensure selections have an easily understandable theme and a distinct rhythm.

2. Casting

Casting is a term used in choral reading to refer to the way a selection is divided into parts and assigned to members of the class for reading (Dallmann, 1976). Once the rhythm and tempo of a particular selection are understood, the teacher and students should choose from the following methods of organization for choral reading:

a. Refrain
b. Dialogue
c. Line-a-child or line-a-choir
d. Cumulative
e. Unison

a. *Refrain.* With certain poems that have a chorus, either the teacher or a designated group can recite the narrative, with the rest of the class responding in the chorus. The refrain provides a good beginning for choral reading.

b. *Dialogue.* Poems with considerable dialogue (often a question-and-answer format) readily lend themselves to a two-part casting. Alternate responses can be made between boys and girls or between high and low voices.

c. *Line-a-child or line-a-choir.* This arrangement engages three or more individuals or choirs in rhythmic response. Some lines also may be spoken in unison by all participants. This type of choral reading has variety and provides a challenge for students to respond in the exact tempo.

d. *Cumulative.* In this form of choral reading, the intent is to create a crescendo effect. Unlike the line-a-choir method, the introduction of a new group to the presentation is permanent, not temporary. This is a more difficult form of choral reading because voice quality, rather than volume, is necessary to attain a significant climax.

e. *Unison.* This is the most difficult type of choral reading, even though it has the simplest structure. An entire group or class reads every line together. The potential for problems in blending and timing is very great in unison reading. Monotonous reading often results if the children are inexperienced and insufficient direction has been given by the teacher. This method is best suited for intermediate level students.

The following verse from a poem provides an example of how one type of casting may be used in a choral reading exercise.

The Triantiwontigongolope[1]

1st child	There's a very funny insect that you do not often spy,
2nd child	And it isn't quite a spider, and it isn't quite a fly;
1st child	It is something like a beetle, and a little like a bee,
2nd child	But nothing like a woolly grub that climbs upon a tree.
1st child	Its name is quite a hard one, but you'll learn it soon, I hope.
1st child	So, try:
Chorus	Tri—
All	Tri—anti—wonti—
Children	Triantiwontigongolope

The refrain in this selection can be used with one group of students reciting the narrative while the other recites the chorus. Individual lines or stanzas of the poem may also be assigned to groups of students and the line-a-choir, cumulative, or unison casting may be implemented, depending on the sophistication of the students.

Cautions and Comments

Choral reading provides students with a unique and valuable language experience, since it integrates reading with two other linguistic skills: listening and speaking. Additionally, choral reading builds positive attitudes toward participation in groups and develops students' imaginative abilities.

However, choral reading can contribute little to the reading and language development of students if it is not used properly. Smith (1972) stated that a common practice with choral reading has been for the teacher to select a passage for choral reading, teach it to students who either read it well or memorize it, assign parts of it to groups, and then "drill" the students until the passage sounds good according to the teacher's conception of "good" choral reading.

This practice negates the instructional objectives of: (a) making the selection meaningful to the students, (b) developing creativity, and (c) developing self-expression. Strict, tense drill directed by the teacher does not set the proper learning conditions, but active involvement on the part of the students does.

Another area of concern in choral reading is maintaining the students' focus on the meaning being conveyed. Students have a tendency to focus attention on their delivery of the selection and sometimes lapse into overdramatics. It must be emphasized that it is the choral reading that is on display, and not the students themselves.

A further meaning-related concern in choral reading is that all students should have a similar understanding of the selection. This is essential

1. "The Triantiwontigongolope" from *A Book for Kids* by C. J. Dennis is reprinted by permission of Angus & Robertson Publishers.

in order to convey effectively, as a group, a depth of feeling and sensitivity to words.

A last area of concern is voice quality. Each word must be enunciated at the same time by the whole group—a difficult task to accomplish for some students. Finally, students must also learn that it is not necessary to read loudly when expressing themselves; rather, they should read with warm but firm voices; the choral reading itself will take care of the volume.

REFERENCES

Allen, R. V. *Language Experiences in Communication.* Boston: Houghton Mifflin, 1976, pp. 150–154.
Discusses the value of choral reading in the language arts program.

Dallmann, M. *Teaching the Language Arts in the Elementary School.* Dubuque, Iowa: Wm. C. Brown, 1976, pp. 310–314.
Lists the instructional values of choral reading and supplies guidelines for its implementation.

Donoghue, M. R. *The Child and the English Language Arts.* Dubuque, Iowa: Wm. C. Brown, 1975, pp. 125–133.
Provides examples for using choral reading in the language arts program.

Petty, W. T., Petty, D. C., and Becking, M. F. *Experiences in Language: Tools and Techniques for Language Arts Methods.* Boston: Allyn and Bacon, 1976, pp. 119–123.
Explores the use of choral reading as an enjoyable way to interpret literature.

Smith, J. A. *Adventures in Communication: Language Arts Methods.* Boston: Allyn and Bacon, 1972, pp. 183–193.
Offers suggestions for creative and effective choral reading activities.

Spache, G. D., and Spache, E. B. *Reading in the Elementary School.* Boston: Allyn and Bacon, 1977, pp. 244–254.
Examines the use of oral reading in the primary program and cites claims for and against its use.

RADIO READING

Purpose

The purpose of radio reading (Greene, 1979) is to provide practice for students in:

1. Accurately communicating a message through oral reading
2. Comprehending at the listening level
3. Summarizing and restating an orally read message

Rationale

Radio reading provides the teacher with a viable alternative to the common practice of "round-robin" reading. Too often, oral reading situations deteriorate into word-attack sessions. Unlike "round-robin" reading, radio reading does not allow for prompting or correcting. Rather, it focuses instruction on the ultimate goal of oral reading—to comprehend and communicate a message.

Radio learning derives its name from the analogy between a radio announcer talking to a listening audience and the oral reading situation. The reader functions as the radio announcer with a script, and the listeners serve as the audience listening to a radio program. It is the purpose of the reader to communicate accurately a message in oral reading. The listeners respond by discussing and restating the message and evaluating whether the passage was clearly rendered.

Intended Audience

Radio reading is appropriate throughout the grades, whenever oral reading is used in instruction. It is particularly suitable in the elementary grades as a substitute for "round-robin" reading; however, it is also useful in the content areas, especially where interpretive reading is done. Radio learning may be used in either a one-to-one or a group setting.

Description of the Procedure

Radio reading creates a "safe," nonthreatening atmosphere for the reader, in which comprehension, not word-perfect reading, is the primary instructional goal. In order to implement a radio reading lesson properly, Searfoss (1975) recommended that four steps be followed:

1. Getting Started
2. Communicating the Message
3. Checking for Understanding
4. Clarifying an Unclear Message

1. Getting Started

In this step of the lesson, the teacher sets the tone for the proper atmosphere by explaining the procedure to the students. The simple ground rules of radio reading are these: the reader reads and the listener(s) listen(s).

The teacher leads the activity by explaining the remaining three steps of the strategy to the students. Emphasis is placed on the responsibility of the reader to communicate a message to the listeners, just as a radio announcer communicates to his audience. Since the audience (listeners) will not have a copy of the material, the teacher instructs them to attend closely to the oral reading.

It is also the job of the teacher to select materials for radio reading which are appropriate in difficulty and length. The materials should be challenging, though not frustrating, and should be narrative or expository in nature. For example, short stories or selections from basal-type readers would be appropriate. The material should be of reasonable length so as not to overwhelm the listener. As a guideline, Searfoss (1975) recommended that each reader should orally read only a paragraph or two in the lower grades, progressing up to as much as a page in the intermediate grades.

2. Communicating the Message

Since the job of the reader is to convey a clear message, the reader is permitted to change words, insert new words, or omit words where warranted. The role of the reader in this activity is similar to that of the fluent, silent reader; both are attending to meaning rather than to individual words. The reader is responsible, however, for deciding when he or she needs help with an unknown word. Greene (1979) stated that when giving directions for radio reading, the teacher should say, "If you come to a word you need and you cannot figure it out, put your finger beside it and ask, 'What is that word?' "

Again, since radio reading is comprehension-oriented, and further delay on a word would increase the probability of short-term memory interference, the teacher or other listeners should refrain from prompting or beginning a word-attack lesson. The reader should be given the word immediately so he or she can continue, with as little interruption as possible, to process meaning.

3. Checking for Understanding

The listening audience has control over the student's oral reading and, if necessary, over rereading. If an accurate message has been communicated by the reader, the check for understanding will be brief. The discussion of what was heard, whether teacher-led or student-initiated, will move quickly. After a quick summary has been volunteered, other listeners can confirm the message. Allowances are made for inferences and rewording, as long as accuracy is maintained.

Thus, the reader earns the right to continue reading by communicating a clear message. In a group situation, the role of the radio reader may rotate to give every reader an opportunity to read; the same procedure is followed.

4. Clarifying an Unclear Message

If the listeners give conflicting information or are able to detect errors during the discussion, the reader has not communicated a clear message. It is the radio reader's responsibility to clear up the confusion by returning to the story and rereading the portions of concern.

It is still the reader's job to achieve clarity in the passage. The listener may decide that the reader needs assistance to achieve that goal. However, as before, prompting must be avoided to maintain the necessary atmosphere for radio reading.

Cautions and Comments

Since radio reading differs greatly from current oral reading practices, the teacher should be certain the four steps outlined are followed. Two areas of caution warrant discussion to enable the teacher to maintain the proper instructional climate for radio reading.

One area of caution concerns the students' response to the procedural steps of radio reading. Ideally, the students will quickly understand the rules and follow them. Radio reading will then be performed smoothly, i.e., the students will read as well as they can, requesting help when necessary. In reality, students may manifest other types of responses to this instructional format, causing possible difficulties for the teacher in its implementation.

One possible difficulty is for the reader to request help at an inappropriate time. Such an occasion arises when it is apparent that the reader already knows the word or has adequate word-attack skills to decode the word. The only recourse the listener has in this situation is to tell the reader the requested word.

It is most likely correct to assume that the reader is testing the rules concerning the reader's and the listener's responsibilities for unknown words, rather than simply displaying deficiencies in reading. Thus, not responding to a request for help, or prompting the reader, violates the contract between the reader and the listener and makes the rules of radio reading worthless. If the reader requests help, it must be immediately supplied.

An additional response that a student may manifest is not to request help when he or she does need it. The reader then will be redirected to render a clear message after the oral reading. On the other hand, failure to respond at all presents the listener with an entirely different situation. In either an individual or a group situation, the appropriate response for the listener, after waiting a reasonable length of time, is simply to say, "What's the rule?"

In an individual situation, it may be necessary for the listener to restate the rule concerning unknown words. If a response is still not elicited, then radio reading should be ended for the day. A clarification of the procedural steps is then in order. In a group setting, a no-response situation is much easier to deal with. Anytime the radio announcer (reader) ceases to broadcast, the listeners will tune to a new "station," i.e., the first reader's right to continue reading ceases, and a new radio reader takes over.

A second caution concerning the instructional climate for radio reading is the tendency of teachers to prompt, to correct, or to initiate a word-attack lesson when a reader encounters difficulty or requests help. Such tactics are inappropriate with this strategy. It disrupts the process of reading and converts the activity into a word-attack lesson.

If the reader makes an error and the teacher corrects it, the responsibility for "correctness" shifts to the teacher and deprives the reader of the responsibility for meaningful reading. Prompting also removes from the reader the responsibility for relaying the message.

There is clearly no place for prompting or for correcting in radio reading. If an error is made in an oral rendering, the burden of dealing with it rests with the listener, who must be skillful enough to pick it out and remember it until the passage has been read. It is the reader's responsibility alone to render a clear, comprehensible message from the assigned passage.

REFERENCES

Greene, F. P. "Radio Reading." In C. Pennock, ed., *Reading Comprehension at Four Linguistic Levels.* Newark, Del.: International Reading Association, 1979, pp. 104–107.
Discusses the concept of radio reading and describes the procedure.

Searfoss, L. W. "Radio Reading." *The Reading Teacher* 29 (1975): 295–296.
Outlines four basic steps in implementing radio reading.

PAIRED READING

Purpose

The purpose of paired reading (Greene, 1970) is to:

1. Give students practice in meaningful oral reading
2. Aid teachers in individualizing instruction
3. Create a non-threatening instructional atmosphere conducive to learning.

Rationale

Paired reading is intended to provide an opportunity to increase the amount of oral reading activity in a group situation, within the structure provided by the teacher. Based upon ideas used in peer tutoring, paired reading involves the pairing of two children of differing reading fluency. Its purpose in the context of oral reading is to entertain and teach. Paired reading uses students as peer-models for other students of lesser reading competence, within a relaxed, non-threatening atmosphere.

Intended Audience

Paired reading activities would be appropriate as a grouping aid in most reading situations throughout the elementary grades. This strategy also lends itself well to situations where peer, rather than teacher, instruction would enhance the confidence of the reader.

Description of the Procedure

Paired reading is a method of instruction in oral reading that allows the teacher to use an educational tool of great potential—the student. This strategy eliminates the pressure on the teacher to "produce," by substituting a peer of sufficient reading competence that he or she is able to provide guidance when necessary.

This technique requires that the teacher pair two students of different reading competence in an oral reading situation. The students may be of the same chronological age, or the more competent reader may be slightly older. A pairing which involves a more competent younger student and a less competent older one is not advised. Each student in the pair reads from materials suited to his or her own reading ability.

To provide for maximum effectiveness, the two students sit side by side, so that one can follow while the other reads. When the less competent one reads, it is suggested that the more competent student refrain from any premature prompting. If the less competent student does encounter a word that proves difficult to decode, this student should ask the more competent reader to pronounce the word.

Another difficulty that may arise when the less competent student is reading, is the failure to communicate a message accurately. Through a combination of self-monitoring and retelling, the paired readers can focus on comprehending and communicating the message. Both readers should be taught to ask themselves continually as they read, "Does that make sense?" Additionally, at the finish of the oral reading, the reader is asked to retell what has just been read. Retelling is an appropriate means to monitor comprehension; it lacks the pressure and anxiety usually associated with answering questions at the end of a passage.

At a point halfway through this activity, the more competent student begins to read. Suggested times for changing readers are ten to fifteen minutes in the primary grades and twenty to thirty minutes in the intermediate grades.

While the more fluent one is reading, the role of the less competent student becomes that of a listener following along in the text. That student is thus continually exposed to new vocabulary, seeing and hearing the new word and, perhaps, assimilating it into his or her sight word vocabulary. The more fluent reader acts as a model of meaningful oral reading for the other student, using the proper rhythm and phrasing.

Cautions and Comments

If implemented properly, paired reading will be a worthwhile activity for both readers in the pair and a boon for the teacher, since the method provides for more responsive instruction in oral reading. Perhaps the key to its successful implementation is careful pairing of the students and preparation of the more competent reader.

The psychological and emotional benefits of paired reading are clear. The more competent reader gains prestige from becoming a "teacher;" this student's self-esteem is boosted. The less fluent reader profits from the relaxed atmosphere of the situation and gains more confidence in reading through working with a more knowledgeable reader.

Almost every student can contribute something to a tutoring situation; however, the teacher must be careful to select students who will be compatible in a paired situation. In addition to knowing the reading capabilities of the students, the teacher also has information available concerning their behavioral and emotional make-up. Using this information, the teacher can match the needs of the less competent reader to the cognitive and affective strengths of the more fluent reader.

Regardless of native strengths and abilities, the more competent reader needs guidelines from the teacher to enable this student to work effectively in a paired reading situation. The student needs to know the overall goals and purpose of paired reading, as well as his or her role in the strategy. In particular, the more fluent reader needs to be aware that prompting and correcting the less competent reader are not appropriate in paired reading. Emphasis should also be placed on the more fluent reader's role as a model. The teacher will have to monitor each pair occasionally to insure that proper working relationships are being established and maintained.

Finally, teachers are cautioned that having a reader follow visually as well as aurally may present a situation where a conflict arises between the rate information is received visually and is received aurally. This conflict may cause unnecessary difficulties, especially for the nonfluent reader.

REFERENCES

Boraks, N., and Allen, A. R. "A Program to Enhance Peer Tutoring." *The Reading Teacher* 30 (1977): 479–484.
Describes a training program for peer tutoring with emphasis on effective teaching interaction and positive interpersonal relations.

Ehly, S., and Larsen, S. C. "Peer Tutoring in the Regular Classroom." *Academic Therapy* 11 (1975–76): 205–208.
Provides a rationale and guidelines for implementing a general peer tutoring program.

Ehly, S. W., and Larsen, S. C. "Peer Tutoring to Individualize Instruction." *Elementary School Journal* 76 (1976): 475–480.
Offers a variety of suggestions for designing a tutoring program as an aid in individualizing instruction.

Greene, F. P. "Paired Reading." Unpublished paper, Syracuse University, 1970.
Discusses the rationale and implementation of paired reading.

ECHO READING

Purpose

The purpose of echo reading is to increase the reading fluency of students who have had difficulty in reading.

Rationale

Echo reading was originally conceived by Heckelman (1969) and is also known as the "neurological impress method," or the "impress method." Heckelman hypothesized that current reading methods allow a student to commit many mistakes, which become very deeply imprinted and are not easily corrected. Because of the time and difficulty involved in correcting these mistakes students do not make any progress in reading.

Heckelman believed that implementing a new learning procedure could suppress the older methods of learning and thus enable children to read. As a result of this thinking, the impress, or echo, method was used. Its intent was to expose readers only to accurate, fluid reading patterns. After a certain length of time for instruction, the correct reading patterns would become deeply "impressed" and would replace previously learned patterns.

Intended Audience

Echo reading has been used almost exclusively with readers who have had difficulty progressing in reading. The procedure should be employed in a one-to-one instructional situation.

Description of the Procedure

The echo method is a technique which involves the student's visual, aural, oral, and tactile abilities in the process of learning to read. It is recommended that the procedure be used for fifteen minutes a day in consecutive daily sessions. After a total instructional time of seven to twelve hours, there is often a significant rise in achievement by the reader.

At the start of echo reading, the reading material used should be at a level slightly lower than what the reader is able to handle adequately. By using material on which the reader has already experienced success, the teacher increases the probability that the echo method will get off to a successful beginning. Material to be used with the procedure should be varied to maintain the student's interest. Newspapers, magazines, and other types of fiction and nonfiction books might be used.

Before echo reading starts, some preliminary instructions are given to the student. The student is told to disregard accompanying pictures in the story. The teacher also indicates to the student not to be concerned with reading at all; rather, the student is asked to do as well as possible in terms of just saying the words. The student is told only to slide his or her eyes smoothly across the line of print without stopping or going back. At no time does the teacher attempt to correct any mistakes the student may make.

As echo reading begins, the reader is seated slightly in front of the teacher with both participants jointly holding the reading material. Both read in unison; the voice of the teacher is directed into the reader's ear at this close range. In beginning sessions, the teacher is supposed to read slightly louder and faster than the student. This aspect allows the reader to make maximum use of the aural and visual senses involved in this strategy.

As the student begins to master the material and gains confidence in saying the words, the teacher may choose to read with a softer voice or even lag slightly behind the student. If the student should falter, the teacher should resort to immediate reinforcement by increasing loudness and speed.

In the beginning sessions, the goal is to establish a fluent reading pattern. Therefore, it is often necessary for the teacher and student to repeat sentences and paragraphs several times until that goal is reached. Once this is accomplished, the teacher and student may move on to more difficult materials. Usually no more than two or three minutes of repetitive reading is required before a fluent reading pattern is established. It is recommended that the teacher regularly reinforce any success the student meets.

To accompany their voices, the teacher's finger simultaneously moves along the line of print. The finger is placed directly under the word as it is spoken, in a smooth, continual fashion. It is emphasized that the flow of the teacher's finger must coincide with the speed and flow of the oral reading.

Once accustomed to the echo method, the student can begin to take over this function from the teacher. At first, the teacher may need to help the student by guiding the student's finger until a smooth, continuous movement is established.

The coordination of the movement of the finger with the flow of the oral rendition is essential. It is argued that if the teacher's finger is not placed under the word as it is spoken, the aural and oral sensory modes will not be operating in conjunction with the visual and tactile modes (Heckelman, 1969).

The major concern of the echo method is the style, not the accuracy, of the oral rendition. At no time during the reading is the student questioned on the material, either for word recognition or comprehension. However, if the student volunteers any information, the teacher permits it.

If success with the method has not been achieved by the fourth hour of its use, the procedure should be terminated. A changeover to another method is then suggested.

Cautions and Comments

Particularly in the beginning stages of echo reading, a student may experience some difficulty, due to the novelty of the situation, or to the conflict that can arise between aural and visual input. A teacher might counter student complaints of not being able to keep up by urging the student to disregard mistakes and to continue reading. Slowing down slightly to a more comfortable speed or rereading some initial lines may eliminate student discomfort with the technique. However, forcing students to process visual and auditory information concurrently may require them to change their natural processing procedures for these types of input. This change may cause undue difficulty and warrant termination of this time-consuming procedure.

Echo reading seems to place an undue emphasis upon the psychomotor skills involved in reading, rather than upon the reading-thinking processes which direct those skills. If reading-thinking processes direct the use of aural and visual skills, then, logically, reading improvement should begin with these reading-thinking processes. In other words, the emphasis given psychomotor skills within echo reading seems misplaced and in danger of detracting from meaningful reading experiences by which the student might acquire visual and aural skills both naturally and incidentally.

REFERENCES

Heckelman, R. G. "A Neurological-Impress Method of Remedial-Reading Instruction." *Academic Therapy* 4 (1969): 277–282.
Introduces and describes the concept of the impress method.

Hollingsworth, P. M. "An Experiment with the Impress Method of Teaching Reading." *The Reading Teacher* 24 (1970): 112–114; 187.
Reports the results of a study designed to overcome some limiting factors of the impress method.

Hollingsworth, P. M. "An Experimental Approach to the Impress Method of Teaching Reading." *The Reading Teacher* 31, no. 6 (1978): 624–626.
Describes results from the use of the impress method.

Langford, K. "An Examination of Impress Techniques in Remedial Reading." *Academic Therapy* 9 (1974): 309–319.
Reviews the literature concerning the impress method and offers a theoretical explanation of the approach.

Trela, T. M. *Fourteen Remedial Reading Methods.* Belmont, Calif.: Lear/Siegler Feron, 1967, pp. 6–8.
Reviews the procedures and rationale of the impress method.

6

Strategies for Improving Word Identification

UNIT OVERVIEW

The Unit and Its Theme

No aspect of reading instruction has been the subject of more debate than that dealing with word identification instruction. These debates suggest that instruction in word identification, particularly in phonics, is the single most important ingredient in the entire reading program. Such arguments seem to disregard the notion that word identification includes skills other than phonic skills. These arguments ignore the notion that word identification and phonics are only a means to an end: reading for understanding. The issue addressed in this unit is not whether to teach, but how to teach, word identification skills. This unit addresses the problem of preparing readers to deal with unknown words they encounter as they read.

The unit presents the theoretical bases and procedures for some of the alternative ways to teach word identifcation. In so doing, it provides a backdrop for examining alternatives.

The Strategies

Four strategies designed to improve the reader's word identifcation skills are presented in this unit. The strategies represent both traditional and contemporary suggestions for developing word identification abilities. A brief summary of the strategies will provide a preview of the unit.

Analytic Method

The analytic method is among the most widely used of the traditional methods for teaching phonics. This method is designed to have readers use known words to discover strategies for decoding unknown words.

Synthetic Word Families

The synthetic word families approach is another widely used traditional method for developing phonic and word identification abilities. It is designed to serve three purposes: to help readers learn the sounds represented by letters and some methods of blending these sounds into words; to increase the student's sight vocabulary through the use of consonant substitution; and to aid students in word identification skills through the use of blending and minimally contrasting word elements.

Syllabaries

The syllabaries strategy has evolved in recent years. This approach is designed to improve word identification skills through the use of the syllable as the unit of pronunciation.

Goodman's Reading Strategy Lessons

Reading strategy lessons represent an attempt to translate the theories of Kenneth Goodman (1967, 1975) into practice. Advocates of Goodman's psycholinguistic perspective on reading have designed these lessons to help readers focus on and strengthen their use of the syntactic or grammatic, the semantic or meaning, and the graphophonic or sound-symbol cueing systems involved in reading.

Utilization

Each of the strategies discussed represents different theoretical viewpoints on the teaching of reading. To ensure adequate implementation, teachers should study each strategy carefully, especially its intent and rationale. In so doing, each strategy should be considered in terms of its efficacy in actual reading situations. Specifically, the strategies should be judged in terms of how well they prepare the child to read material with understanding.

ANALYTIC METHOD

Purpose

The analytic method of phonics instruction is designed to provide students with strategies for decoding unfamiliar words; in this method, students are encouraged to employ their knowledge of the phonic elements within familiar words.

Rationale

The analytic method of phonics instruction is based on the premise that words can be analyzed into their common phonic elements. The student is introduced to a number of "common" words, from which an analysis of component parts can follow. That is, when the student has a bank of words with the same phonic features, phonics instruction begins. For example, students might be asked to "discover" this generalization: common sound of the letter *b* as in *bat, ball*, and *boy*.

In essence, this method places stress on meaning and on the importance of building a bank of known words as the basis for acquiring certain phonic understandings. Letter sounds are never learned in isolation, thus avoiding the distorted notion that isolated letters have sounds. Phonic elements are learned through discovery, rather than through rote memorization.

Intended Audience

The analytic method of phonics instruction is suggested for use with beginning readers, where the emphasis is placed on learning sound/symbol relationships. The method may be used in conjunction with existing classroom materials or as a substitute for them, either in a group or in an individual situation.

Description of the Procedure

The discussion of the actual teaching of an analytic phonics lesson will focus on the following steps, as recommended by Karlin (1975):

1. Auditory and Visual Discrimination
2. Auditory Discrimination
3. Word Blending
4. Contextual Application

1. Auditory and Visual Discrimination

Hearing and seeing the likenesses and differences in sound and letters are essential parts of phonics instruction. It is from this base that an analytic phonics lesson begins. If a teacher were to present a phonics lesson concerning the single consonant *d*, the first thing to do would be to put a sentence on the board, underlining the word containing the target element in this way:

The *dog* bit the boy.

Rather than call attention to the sentence at this time, the teacher writes other words on the board that have the same phonic element. The words should all be known words. Children are asked to look at the words and read them. It is suggested that the students, *rather than the teacher*, pronounce the words. Since language differences may exist between the teacher and the children, the sounds produced by the teacher may differ from those produced by the children; some confusion may arise.

Words that might be listed could include:

Dick
dot
dig
duck

Emphasis is placed upon the beginning sound as each is pronounced, but the phonic element is never separated from the word. Through questioning and discussion, the teacher would elicit the following from the students:

a. The words all start alike
b. The words all sound alike in the beginning

2. Auditory Discrimination

Now that students have seen and heard that the words start alike, the next step is to reinforce further the targeted phonic element through the student's listening vocabulary. A new group of words is read by one of the students, rather than by the teacher, again to avoid possible language confusion caused by differences in sound production between the teacher and the students. The students are now asked to decide whether or not these words begin like the group of words on the board. The new words are not written on the board. Words that might be used here could include:

dock	bank	deep
went	dark	rich

Finally, students are asked to generate words that begin the same way as the targeted phonic element:

dumb	do	Doug	dear

3. Word Blending

If students are successful with the first two steps of the teaching procedure, they will be ready to learn to generalize from known words how the targeted phonic element sounds in new words. A sight word is written on the board, and below this word, another one with the targeted element:

mad
dad

Students are asked to focus on the similarities and differences between the word that they know and the new word with the phonic element which they are learning. They should observe that:

a. The words end alike.
b. They sound alike at the end.
c. They differ in the beginning.

Once students have observed the above, the teacher draws their attention to the fact that the new word starts like the group of words on the board.

Students are now asked to interchange the beginning consonant elements; thus, the *m* is replaced with a *d*. Students must remember how words with *d* sound in order to pronounce the new word, *dad*. This process is continued with a few more pairs of words, to insure that students can use their newly learned phonic element. Other pairs that might be used are:

bay	rip	fairy
day	dip	dairy

4. Contextual Application

The last step in this teaching strategy requires that students apply their new learning in an actual reading situation, where phonic learning is more natural than in isolation. Students are now asked to read their newly acquired words in short sentences:

My dad is at work.
What day is today?
Dip your brush in the paint.
Milk comes from a dairy.

After reading these sentences successfully, the students are asked to go back to the original sentence which started the lesson and read it:

The *dog* bit the boy.

Students may respond to the original sentence in different ways. Some may rhyme "log" with "dog," substituting the initial consonant; others may have mastered the sound of *d* and use it in conjunction with context clues to decode *dog*. The important thing to remember is that nowhere in the lesson was the *d* separated from real words, thus avoiding any distortion that may result when the students sound letters in isolation.

Cautions and Comments

Substantial claims have been made by proponents of both synthetic and analytic phonics approaches as to which is the better method. Certainly, the more holistic approach taken by analytic phonics seems to be the more appropriate learning strategy. However, at this time there is no well-founded longitudinal research that would enable us to choose between the two approaches.

Two comments are in order concerning the use of either analytic or synthetic phonics. First, some professionals argue that the exclusive use of one approach over the other limits students' chances to master phonic principles. Moving back and forth between the two approaches may be a productive procedure if it enhances the students' abilities to deal with the abstract principles of phonics. It also may prove to be nonproductive, causing confusion rather than developing understanding.

Secondly, no matter which approach is chosen, it must be remembered that the ultimate test of a student's ability to use phonics is whether or not the student is able to read successfully for meaning and to apply such skills in contextual situations. Regardless of the method used, it is possible that a student would acquire adequate phonic skills and still remain a poor reader. With respect to either the analytic or the synthetic phonic method, it would seem imperative that students' newly acquired phonic understandings be applied to actual reading situations.

For an extended discussion of this strategy, the reader is directed to the Cautions and Comments section under Synthetic Word Families.

REFERENCES

Durkin, D. *Teaching Them to Read,* 2nd ed. Boston: Allyn and Bacon, 1974, pp. 251–321.
Describes both the content of and the various teaching procedures used in phonics.

Durkin, D., *Phonics, Linguistics, and Reading.* New York: Teachers College, 1972.
Provides a complete description of the content of phonics.

Johnson, D. D., and Pearson, P. D. *Teaching Reading Vocabulary.* New York: Holt, Rinehart and Winston, 1978.
Examines word identification in both the analytic and the synthetic approaches.

Karlin, R. *Teaching Elementary Reading: Principles and Strategies,* 2nd ed. New York: Harcourt Brace Jovanovich, 1975, pp. 179–193.
Compares the analytic and the synthetic phonic approaches and provides sample lessons.

Mazurkiewicz, A. T. *Teaching about Phonics.* New York: St. Martins, 1976.
Provides a thorough description of teaching phonics.

Miller, W. H. *The First R: Elementary Reading Today,* 2nd ed. New York: Holt, Rinehart and Winston, 1977, pp. 97–117.
Examines phonic analysis in depth and explores advantages and disadvantages of both the analytic and the synthetic approaches.

SYNTHETIC WORD FAMILIES

Purpose

The purpose of synthetic word families is to:

1. Increase vocabulary through the use of consonant substitution
2. Aid students in word identification skills by employing the strategy of blending better sounds with contrasting word elements

Rationale

Word families are word elements that contain both vowel and consonant elements, to which can be synthetically blended an initial consonant element. For instance, the word family-*at* can be blended or "slid" with the sounds of *b,c,f,* and *h* to form *bat, cat, fat,* and *hat* (Guszak, 1978). Word families have also been variously referred to as phonograms, graphemic bases, and spelling patterns; they form the basis for reading systems claiming a linguistic approach.

The use of word families is based upon the principle that English is an alphabetic writing system employing a methodical code which is easily broken. This code consists of many contrasting patterns (word families), which the student can take advantage of when learning to read. Therefore, reading instruction centered around the patterns of language and the contrasting elements that may be generated from those patterns might be highly conducive to success in identifying unknown words and in learning to read. Less importance is placed on learning words in context, since instruction with synthetic word families begins with parts and proceeds to form wholes.

When using word families in conjunction with consonant substitution, the instructor can capitalize on the principle of minimal contrast and the student's knowledge of letter sounds. After a model word (a known word) has been explored for its elements, the word family (vowel and consonant elements) can be used to generate new words through consonant substitution. Learning is accomplished by building upon what is already known, varying that known element only minimally. Thus, the identification of new words is centered around maximum similarity and minimum difference—the maximum similarity being the word family, and the minimum difference being the synthetically blended consonant.

Intended Audience

The use of synthetic word families is commonly associated with beginning reading instruction in the primary grades. Although there is a variety of instructional materials that use the concept of synthetic word families and are intended as total reading programs, word families may be used in group or in individual situations as a substitute or as a supplement for other materials designed to teach word identification skills.

Description of the Procedure

Some background information is in order before dealing with the teaching procedure. The following would be representative of the use of synthetic word families in books known as linguistic readers:

Nat is a cat.
Is Nat fat?
Nat is fat.
Nat is a fat cat.[1]

The above is a prime example of the use of initial consonant substitution and minimal contrasts within the word family-*at*.

Aukerman (1971) has described the variety of ways word families are used in linguistic readers. Synthetic word families are built upon a base sound which may be a sound in any position—beginning, medial, or ending. For instance, using the short vowel sound of *a* (aah) with both initial and final consonant substitution, a number of combinations may be generated:

fa (fat)	pa (pal)	na (nab)
da (dad)	sa (sad)	va(van)
ma (mad)	ba (bat)	la (lap)
	of	
at	ax (axe)	ap (apt)
am	ad (add)	ak (ack)
an (ant)	ag	as

1. C. C. Fries, A. C. Fries, R. Wilson, and M. K. Randolph. *Merrill Linguistic Readers: First Reader.* (Columbus, Ohio: Charles E. Merrill, 1965) p. 4.

Nonsense combinations are encouraged in linguistic material, since they may be parts of meaningful words that the student may meet later.

A second method would be to use a medial position word family, such as *an*, and build words or nonwords that are larger in length:

ban	bans	band
bant	banx	banp
bang	banz	bank

Using different initial consonant sounds, numerous other combinations may be built, both with and without meaning.

Word pairs may also be used as follows:

lamp	belt	tilt	band
ramp	felt	pilt	cand

On the other hand, if more regularity is desired, an identical base with the five short vowel sounds could be used, to which initial consonant sounds might be added:

b-all	g-all	p-all
c-all	h-all	s-all
f-all	m-all	t-all

or

b-ell	j-ell	p-ell
d-ell	m-ell	s-ell
f-ell	n-ell	t-ell

Used in the previously mentioned ways, the synthetic word family concept can produce innumerable word combinations.

To present a more manageable application of synthetic word families, and to show how they may be fit into a teaching procedure to augment other types of instruction in word identification, we will focus our discussion of synthetic word families on these:

1. Prior Concepts
2. Teacher Guidance
3. Student Independence

1. Prior Concepts

There are certain prior concepts or learnings that students may need to have before the teacher can initiate a synthetic word families approach. These include: (1) a small bank of known words; (2) rhyming words; and (3) consonant sounds.

A first pedagogical principle is that learning proceeds from the known to the unknown. In accordance with this principle, the synthetic word families approach begins with a small bank of known words to serve as a referent from which to generate new words. It is recommended that whole words, rather than elements of words, be used to initiate this procedure. For example, *b-ell* might be easier to learn than *-ell*.

Students must be sensitive to rhyme. They must be able to recognize that those words which look alike at their end (possess the same word family) probably rhyme in most cases. Additionally, students must know which parts of rhyming words sound alike, and which parts do not. To this end, students should be given auditory discrimination activities to ensure that they can differentiate between the rhyming and non-rhyming words.

Finally, knowledge of individual consonant sounds is necessary, so that students may effectively synthesize these sounds with word families. Needless to say, it will be difficult to rhyme words without a knowledge of consonant sounds.

2. Teacher Guidance

Again, as with most teaching procedures, it must not be assumed that even if students have mastered all necessary prerequisites, they will be thus able to use word families effectively to improve word identification abilities. The teacher must guide the students toward independence.

Initially, teachers should select a model word which is part of the student's known vocabulary. New words generated by using (1) the same word family as the model word; and (2) differing beginning consonant sounds, may be placed next to the model. An example might be:

dog
bog
fog
hog
log

Through observation and teacher encouragement, students will see that the new words look like the model except for the initial consonant. Students who have mastered consonant sounds will be able to read the minimally contrasting words. By doing this, students will recognize that all words sound alike. The teacher may point out that detecting word family elements can aid in pronouncing unfamiliar words.

Exercises as described above should be continued by using other words the students know as a basis and blending known consonant sounds to them. Gradually, the teacher should allow the students to generate new words. Later on, the use of digraphs and blends as possible initial substitutes should be explored and demonstrated.

By going through these exercises diligently, the teacher can be confident that the students are able to use the concept of synthetic word families in substitution exercises. However, there may not be any transfer to "real" reading and to student independence from these exercises alone.

3. Student Independence

Exercises like these do not necessarily insure that students will be able to match mentally the word families they know with the unfamiliar words they encounter in reading. To help students gain independence in using word families, Cunningham, Arthur, and Cunningham (1977) have recommended a teaching procedure to aid students in mentally processing word matches to identify unfamiliar words in their reading.

The first step in this strategy is to create five cards with known words for each student. For instance, the five word cards may be: *tell, can, dog, it,* and *bump.* The teacher writes a word on the board, such as *bell*, and students are expected to find a match among their cards. This is followed by the teacher, or more preferably, by a student volunteer, demonstrating how the words look alike (word family), how they differ (initial consonant), and pronouncing both words. Searching through their small bank of word cards to secure a match will aid students in eventually gaining the facility to match words on their own when reading print. Word cards are continually added, and this procedure is continued, until students have mastered fifteen word cards as well as possible matches.

The second step of this strategy is for students to match a word printed on the board without the aid of the word cards. This is the point where students start to use their total mental processes to provide a match. All fifteen words are used in this step.

The third step involves the extension of the fifteen words to include all the words the students know. A new model word is given, and students are asked to figure out the unknown word by attempting to match it with a known word in their heads. In this way, they gain further independence in using synthetic word families to decode unknown words.

The fourth and final step is for students to apply this concept to their reading. When a student encounters difficult words, the teacher should encourage the student to think of a word family which ends like the unknown word, to aid in identifying it. It is here that students face the true test of using synthetic word families, i. e., word families to aid in decoding unknown words.

Some further specific examples of strategies which support the use of synthetic methods of word identification are described in Unit Seven, which deals with multisensory strategies for teaching reading.

Cautions and Comments

When using synthetic word families as an aid to improving word recognition, teachers need to be aware of some possible problems. To reiterate, using word families in isolation without helping students use them in actual reading situations may be valueless. Students need to be shown the relevance of word families to the thought-getting aspect of reading. Indeed, the use of word families may deteriorate into a "game of word-calling" if students are merely asked to play with words, no matter how exciting this activity may become.

Some problems may arise in generating new words using word families. Nonsense words, though advocated by linguistic approaches to reading, should be avoided. By definition, these words are meaningless, despite the linguistic consistency they provide. For this reason, they may or may not be an aid to reading with understanding. The second area of concern is that of irregular words. For instance, does *bow* rhyme with *cow* or *row*? Furthermore, consonant sounds may become distorted when sounded separately, as with the sound of *b-buh*. Should *bat* be pronounced as *bah-at*?

An alternate use of synthetic word families has been developed by LaPray (1972) for use with poor readers. Those students who have mastered little else in reading except their name are asked to list spontaneously their names and other words which they may know. Utilizing the few words generated, new words can be built from their known parts. For example, if a student lists only *Bill*, *dog*, and *mom*, new words may be built and learned, first by sound and then by context, by putting them into a short phrase or sentence.

Finally, to leave the reader "some food for thought," Kenneth Goodman's (1976) comments on the efficacy of phonic instruction are worthy to note.

> You have to put skills in the context of meaning. That's where they have the most value. That's where they maintain their proper proportion. And there they won't lead to the development of problems which eventually interfere with learning to read. In fact, children learn best this way because skills taught in context don't result in incorrect generalizations which then have to be overcome.
>
> Take the common emphasis on phonic skills. When you isolate a letter or a sound, you make it more abstract, and you also change its relative value. If I give kids the sentence, "The girl is in the garden," I can talk about the initial letter of girl and the sound that it relates to. But if I give the lesson backwards, if I start with the sound of g, then I'm saying that each letter has a value—a meaning. That's not true. The value is dependent on the sequence that it's in. And the importance of noticing and using a particular graphic cue is exaggerated because in context it works together with everything else.
>
> *Reading: A Conversation with Kenneth Goodman.*
> Glenview, Ill.: Scott, Foresman and Company, 1976,
> p. 7.

REFERENCES

Aukerman, R. C. *Approaches To Beginning Reading.* New York: John Wiley and Sons, 1971, pp. 9-88.
Discusses the use of synthetic word families as one basic approach to phonics instruction. Also describes, in detail, linguistically-oriented materials used in beginning reading instruction.

Cunningham, P. M., Arthur, S. V., and Cunningham, J. W. *Classroom Reading Instruction K-5: Alternative Approaches.* Lexington, Mass.: D. C. Heath and Company, 1977, pp. 74-77.
Advocates the use of consonant substitution with word families to build sight word vocabulary.

Guszak, F. J. *Diagnostic Reading Instruction in the Elementary School.* New York: Harper & Row, 1978.
Suggests using synthetic word families as an adjacent program for some students in word identification.

LaPray, M. *Teaching Children to Become Independent Readers.* New York: Center for Applied Research in Education, 1972.
Advocates the use of synthetic word families as a means to establish success-oriented instruction with students experiencing reading difficulties.

Miller, W. H. *The First R: Elementary Reading Today*, 2nd ed. New York: Holt, Rinehart and Winston, 1977, pp. 119-132.
Delineates numerous advantages and limitations of the various linguistic reading approaches.

Spache, G. D., and Spache, E. B. *Reading in the Elementary School*, 4th ed. Boston: Allyn and Bacon, 1977, pp. 102-120.
Describes the linguistic approach to the teaching of reading, including the concept of synthetic word families.

SYLLABARIES

Purpose

The purpose of syllabaries is to:

1. Teach word identification skills through the use of the syllable as the unit of instruction
2. Use a comparison-contrast strategy to decode words by preceding from known word parts to unknown word parts

Rationale

The syllabary method of improving word recognition skills is based upon the use of the syllable as the unit of pronunciation. It is an alternative to traditional phonics which is based upon the use of phoneme/grapheme correspondence.

Phonemes, the basic sounds of language, become distorted when pronounced in isolation, i.e., the sound of the letter *b* pronounced in isolation is *buh*. Some students seem to have difficulty learning to pronounce these units and even more trouble blending them together, i.e., *buh-ah-tuh = bat.* Though the use of phonics to decode unknown words presents difficulty to some, most students do have the facility to segment words into syllables (Gibson and Levin, 1975).

The syllabary, seemingly a more natural unit of pronunciation for some students, may provide a sound means to overcome those phonological problems by beginning with those units (syllables) which are more easily recognized and pronounced in isolation (Gleitman and Rozin, 1973). To illustrate this point with the word *paper*, note the difference in ease of pronounciation between *puh-aper* (only first letter sound in isolation) versus *pa-per* (two syllables in isolation). This premise and the use of a comparison-contrast strategy to decode unknown words form the basis of the syllabary, which was developed as a means to teach word recognition skills.

There are some differences among the teaching strategies advocated by the various materials for teaching beginning readers decoding skills; however, it can be inferred that: (1) certain rules must be applied by readers to identify unfamiliar words; and (2) they must be applied in some certain order. To identify an unknown word, readers are taught to apply an ordered set of syllabication rules and then to apply phonic rules with each of the individual syllables.

Cunningham provides this example with the word *recertify* to illustrate the word identification processes a reader might typically use:

1. Reader decides on the number of syllables by counting the vowels (remembering that the *y* at the end of a word is a vowel): four vowels = four syllables.
2. Reader divides the word into syllables by applying the following ordered rules:

   a. Divide between a root word and a prefix: *re certify*.
   b. Divide between two intervocalic consonants (except consonant, of course): *re cer tify.*
   c. Divide before a single intervocalic consonant: *re cer ti fy*.

3. Reader applies rules to the letters in each syllable.

   a. *re*: ends in a vowel–long *e* sound; think long *e* sound–blend with *r*–pronounce *rē*.
   b. *cer*: *c* before *e*, *i*, or *y* usually has the *s* sound; *e* is controlled by *r*. Blend *c* with *er*–pronounce *ser*.
   c. ti: just like first syllable, if it ends in a vowel; try the long sound–pronounce *tī*.
   d. *fy*: when it is a vowel rather than a consonant, *y* can be pronounced as in *cry* or as in *daddy*. Try *fī*.

4. Reader blends all four syllables together: *re ser ti fi.* Reader does not recognize word as one he or she has heard before or knows a meaning for, so reader tries different sound correspondences.
5. Reader tries a different sound for the syllables. Perhaps it is a *y* as in *Daddy: rē ser tī fē.* Still not a word reader knows; perhaps this is a word the reader has never heard of before?
6. Finally, reader remembers about unaccented syllables and tries a schwa in different places until he happens upon the correct pronunciation: *rē ser t'fī.* "Oh, like what happens if you forget to renew your license and have to be recertified to get another license."
7. Reader continues reading. (Cunningham, 1975–1976, pp. 129–130. Reprinted with permission of the International Reading Association.)

Though it may seem difficult, if not impossible, for this process to take place in a reader's mind as he or she attempts to identify an unknown word, this is the current mode of word identification processes which is advocated and taught to elementary school students.

To provide an alternative to the theory that students apply an ordered set of rules in word identification, Cunningham (1975–76) proposes a synthesized theory of mediated word identification, based upon these premises:

1. Words and word parts are stored in the human memory
2. Word identification does not involve the application of teacher-taught rules; rather, it involves a search through this memory-store, comparing the unknown with the known
3. Unfamiliar words not recognized on sight are segmented into units
4. These units are compared/contrasted with known words, with word parts, or with fragments, for identifcation
5. Recombining the units results in a word for which the reader knows a meaning or a sound referent
6. Readers form their own rules (they are not taught rules) for decoding unfamiliar words by comparing/contrasting the unknown with the known

Applying the synthesized theory of word identification to previous example with *recertify*, it can be assumed that the reader has numerous words and word parts in his memory-store and has also developed the ability to compare the unknown to the known. Segmenting an unfamiliar word occurs not by successively applying adult-taught syllabication rules, but by recognizing known parts in the unknown whole.

The reader can identify the unfamiliar whole *recertify* through a variety of comparisons such as:

1. If *certify* is in the reader's-memory store, along with either the word part *re* or other words beginning with *re* (*reexamine; relay*), the resulting combination of the two parts is tested against words for which the reader has sound and/or meaning referents.

2. If *certify* is not in the reader's store, it might be segmented into more manageable units. For instance, the reader might have *identify* or *sanctify* segmented *tify*. The reader could identify *re* as described. *Cer* might be secured from parts of *certainly* or *ceramics*. Again, the reader would combine parts for comparison against the reader's sound and/or meaning referents.
3. If a wrong match is chosen from the reader's word-store (*recreation* instead of *relay*, or *ceremony* instead of *certainly*), the reader will be unable to identify it as there will be no sound or meaning referent. The reader will reenter his or her memory store for a more appropriate match.

Intended Audience

Gleitman and Rozin (1973) suggested three possible ways to incorporate the use of the syllabary in reading instruction in the elementary grades. First, it may be used as an introductory system to make phonics utility more accessible to students. Secondly, the syllabary may be used as a substitute for teaching many phonics principles, thus minimizing the quantity of instruction in that area. Finally, Gleitman and Rozin recommend that the syllabary could be used as a remedial approach to word recognition in cases where students cannot master phonics principles. It is the latter use that Cunningham (1975–76) demonstrated successfully in a study investigating the use of the syllable as a means to improve word recognition skills. Therefore, the syllabary seems most appropriate for augmenting other forms of word recognition instruction for beginning readers or for readers experiencing difficulty with sound/symbol relationships.

Description of the Procedure

To employ the syllabary strategy to improve readers' word identification skills, the teacher would follow these steps:

1. Teacher-Dominated Training
2. Student-Oriented Practice
3. Meaningful Reading

1. Teacher-Dominated Training

The teacher must not assume that students will readily grasp the thrust of the syllabary. Teachers should start with familiar one-syllable words before moving on to less familiar polysyllabic words. Beginning the training with familiar monosyllabic words insures students will be able to call upon their own word-store.

The teacher might begin with words like *pen, sill, for,* and *wind* to illustrate how words like *penny, pencil, silly, before, windy, window,* and *windowsill* may be identified. In this way, words or word parts that are known become established in the word-store, enabling the students to use these known words in comparing unknown polysyllabic words. For example, knowledge of the words *wind* and *silly* will enable a student to make the appropriate comparisons to identify the word *windowsill.* Teacher questioning should accompany this step of acquainting students with the use of the syllabary to insure the match between syllables and the known word parts. Gleitman and Rozin (1973) have recommended the use of pictures as an aid to identifying unknown words by their syllabic parts. Some examples are shown.

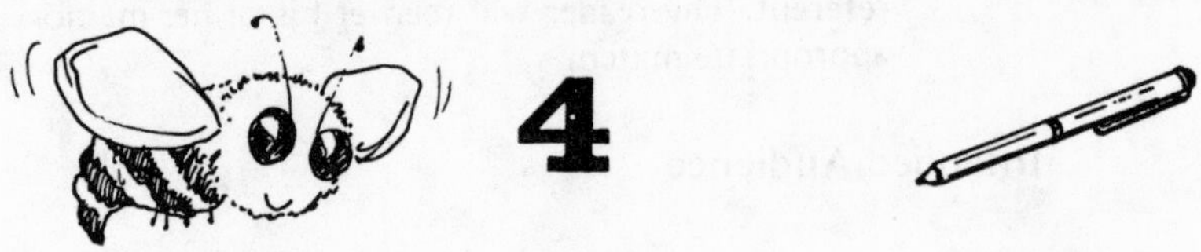

be fore penn y

2. Student-Oriented Practice

At this point in the strategy, the students are ready to begin more independent work with the concept of the syllabary. Polysyllabic words are introduced for students to decode using the comparison/contrast strategy. Work may be done individually, but is probably best accomplished in pairs or in small groups, until students have a firm grasp of the concept. An illustration of this type of practice follows.

Words like *sleepless, blanket,* and *pillow* might be introduced. The teacher is cautioned that it may be necessary to guide the students through a few practice words before they can work independently. For instance, using the syllabary to decode *sleepless,* the teacher can show children *less,* which might be a word in their memory-store or a word part, as in *unless.*

Again, the teacher is illustrating how to compare unknown words to known words or word parts in the students word-stores. As students gain skill and confidence in using the comparison/contrast strategy, more complex words may be introduced. It is suggested that as students are exposed to new words, these words be written on word cards for review and reinforcement. The comparisons students have made from their word-stores may be written on the back of the card and may be referred to by the student if any difficulty arises during the review. Review with flash cards may be accomplished by pairing the students.

3. Meaningful Reading

It is to be remembered that the implementation and usage of the syllabary has occurred only when unknown words were seen in isolation. The ultimate test of any form of word identification occurs when the student becomes able to decode unknown words from a meaningful context. Hence, the follow-up step in the use of the syllabary is to develop students' ability to deal with unknown words in story reading.

It is recommended that a short story consisting of a few paragraphs be constucted, using many of the words students have studied in isolation. Variations of those words or similar words should also be incorporated. For example, the polysyllabic words used in Section 2, Student-Oriented Practice, should be used, but the teacher should attempt to use the variations (*sleeping; pill*) as well. In this way, the teacher can be assured that the comparison/contrast word identification strategy is being successfully implemented and has been transferred to "real" reading. An illustration of a short story using these words is included.

Nim looked very sleepy.
He threw his pillow on the floor.
He removed his blanket.
He had not gotten to sleep.
It had been a sleepless night.

Cautions and Comments

There are apparent merits to a word identification strategy employing the syllabary; however, there are also a number of cautions that teachers should be aware of. First, although the syllable may be more easily pronounced in isolation than a phoneme, there are thousands of separate syllables in the English language. The task of dealing with each of these units might be overwhelming. For this reason, it should be used in conjunction with sound/symbol relationships.

Second, dialect differences in readers make for differences in syllable pronounciations. What may seem to be an obvious comparison with an individual's word-store may be obvious only to the teacher who also has a particular dialectical pattern. The students may not necessarily be contemplating the "obvious" comparison, because of differences in their speech.

Third, the syllable is very much influenced by the stress it receives, i.e., the sound shifts with the stress (Goodman, 1973). For example, *site* becomes *situate* by adding more meaning units to the original word. This could very easily produce confusion for the young reader.

Finally, it is cautioned that nonsense words be avoided in teaching the syllabary. Cunningham (1975–76) found no differences between a group trained to use the syllabary concept and a control group, when both groups attempted to decode unknown words. This result probably occurred because students did not have a sound or a meaning referent to use when comparing their attempts to decode nonsense words.

REFERENCES

Cunningham, P. M. "Investigating a Synthesized Theory of Mediated Word Identification." *Reading Research Quarterly* 11 (1975–76): 127–143.

Reports the results of an experiment designed to improve the word identification abilities of second graders using a syllabary approach. Subjects pronounced significantly more one- and two-syllable words correctly than did control subjects, thus supporting the use of the syllabary.

Gibson, E. J., and Levin, H. *The Psychology of Reading.* Cambridge, Mass.: MIT Press, 1975.
Describes the use of the syllabic method as a means to learn to read in various languages.

Gleitman, L., and Rozin, P. "Teaching Reading by Use of a Syllabary." *Reading Research Quarterly* 8 (1973): 447–483.
Reports the successful use of the syllabary with pictures as an introductory method to teach reading to both inner-city and suburban children.

Goodman, K. S. "The 13th Easy Way to Make Learning to Read Difficult." *Reading Research Quarterly* 8 (1973): 484–493.
Challenges the use of the syllabary as a means of teaching word identification skills.

Rozin, P., and Gleitman, L.R. "The Structure and Acquisition of Reading II: The Reading Process and the Acquisition of the Alphabetic Principle." In A. Reber and O. Scarborough, eds., *Toward a Psychology of Reading.* Hillsdale, N.J.: Lawrence Erlbaum Assoc., 1977, pp. 55–142.
Describes research, theory, and practice built around the syllabary approach.

GOODMAN'S READING STRATEGY LESSONS

Purpose

The purpose of the reading strategy lessons (Goodman and Burke, 1972) is to increase students' awareness of the language and thought clues available during reading. The lessons are intended to:

1. Help readers focus on aspects of written language not being processed effectively
2. Support and strengthen readers' use of clues already being used

Rationale

Reading strategy lessons are based upon Kenneth Goodman's (1967; 1975) notions of reading that suggest there are certain universal reading processes. These processes are applied by all readers with varying levels of proficiency across different reading material. Toward the end of acquiring meaning, these processes include:

1. The reader selecting the appropriate and necessary language cues to make predictions

2. The reader verifying these predictions
3. The reader reprocessing language cues if predictions prove untenable

A diagram developed by Y. Goodman and Burke (1974) depicts these notions.

Proficient Silent Reading Model*

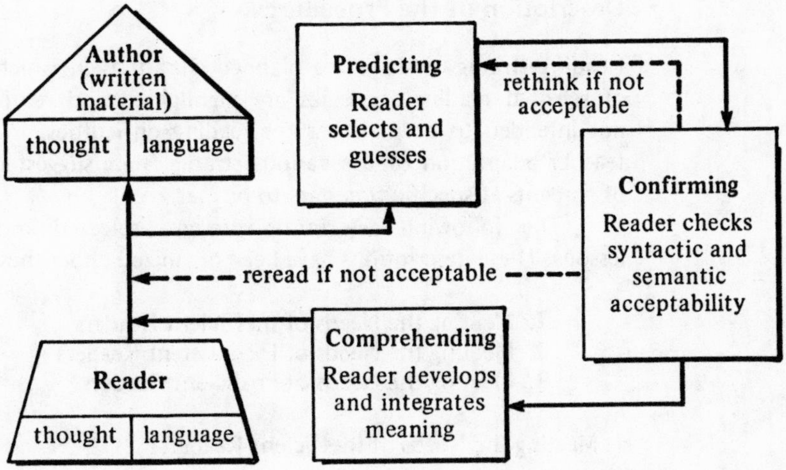

The general goal of the reading strategy lessons is to involve students in a meaningful reading situation which does not distract them from reading with understanding. To this end, some general guidelines are suggested:

1. The language of the material used should be similar to the language of the reader and of worthy literary quality
2. The language of the material should not be ambiguous.
3. The language of the material should use redundant information naturally.
4. The content of the material used should be both interesting and significant to readers.
5. Lessons should afford students the opportunity to apply learnings from strategy lessons to actual reading situations
6. Lessons should be related to students' ongoing learning experiences
7. Lessons should be initiated when students' needs arise and terminate with students' boredom, disinterest, or accomplishment.

*The reader selects the appropriate language cues in order to *predict* as best he can, based upon his knowledge of language and his background experience. He *confirms* his predictions by testing these hypotheses or predictions. He does this by checking the syntactic and semantic acceptability of what he thinks he is reading against his knowledge of language and the world. Finally, he *comprehends* those items he believes to be significant. He integrates this new meaning or knowledge into established meaning system. He then interacts with the print again. The process is continuous, and as we read, we constantly add, alter, or reorganize the meanings. (Y. M. Goodman, Burke, and Sherman, 1974, p. 18. Used by permission of the author.)

Intended Audience

It is suggested that almost all readers can benefit from reading strategy lessons. The lessons may expand proficient readers' actual reading experiences and help them to build confidence. They can improve and support the strategies used by readers who exhibit evidence of effective, but inconsistent, use of strategies, *or* for whom the development of effective strategies has been disrupted.

Description of the Procedures

Reading strategy lessons are planned situations in which the use and availability of selected reading strategies are highlighted and reinforced. The situations are not intended to be panaceas for reading difficulties. Instead, teacher insight and teacher adaptation of the various strategies are suggested as essential if the needs of students at specific times are to be met.

The following description presents selected and representative strategy lessons. These descriptions have been organized under these headings:

1. Meeting the Needs of Inefficient Readers
2. Meeting the Needs of Inconsistent Readers
3. Meeting the Needs of Proficient Readers

1. Meeting the Needs of Inefficient Readers

Y. Goodman (1975) describes inefficient readers this way:

> They use effective reading strategies occasionally in short phrases or sections of written material, but in most reading situations, these readers tend to omit words they think they do not know; they do not predict acceptable grammatical or semantic structures as they read; they read word for word using sounding out techniques without concern for meaning. They do everything they were taught to do in an isolated and unrelated fashion. They look for little words in big words and find fat/her an acceptable solution for father. They separate words between two middle consonants and often read lit/tul for little and prit/tee for pretty. When they do make occasional effective use of reading strategies, they lack confidence in deciding which strategy is most effective. They regress and correct in situations when it is inefficient to do so. For example, if such a reader reads can't for cannot because of the use of an appropriate predicting strategy, this is corrected when the reader picks up additional graphic cues. Such readers often think that graphic input is the most significant aspect of reading. Reading is not to discover something new or for enjoyment, it is to satisfy another person.*

*From: Yetta M. Goodman, "Reading Strategy Lessons: Expanding Reading Effectiveness." In W. Page (Ed.), *Help for the Reading Teacher: New Directions in Research.* NCTE and ERIC, p. 39. *

According to Goodman (1975), inefficient readers need first to realize that they are effective language users and that these abilities can help in reading. To this end, strategy lessons by which students become aware of the utility of their language cueing systems are suggested. For example, cloze procedures similar to the following are suggested to enable students to become more aware of their use of grammatical and meaning cues:

> "Stop!" said John. "Stop! Stop!" He could see that the little red ________ was heading straight for the bridge that had been washed away in the last storm. The driver of the ________ must have heard John. He hit the brakes and the ________ stopped. Its motor stopped and the driver jumped out.

To deal with some of the specific inefficiences of readers, other strategies are suggested.

a. For readers whose omissions or substitutions result in meaning loss, teachers are urged to encourage them to make meaningful substitutions for omissions. Students might produce words that have some related meaning or words with a close meaning. This might be done incidentally, by encouraging the reader to ask, "What word could go in this spot?" "Why do you think so?" The teacher might take a more systematic approach too, using exercises like these:

1. Present the students a passage with systematic deletions of words or phrases and encourage readers to use the context to suggest alternative possibilities.

   They ________ around the pool.
   ________ enjoyed swimming.

   The children ran for the bus. They had slept late. Just as they arrived at the bus stop ________.

2. Present the students with a passage containing nonsense words for significant verbs or nouns and have students replace these with real words.

   The buemt hopped through the grass and disappeared into its burrow. The buemt had a little tail of white fur and long ears. The buemt loved to nibble on leaves.

3. Present the students either a passage containing intentional significant miscues, or have the students prepare a passage containing certain intentional miscues. The readers task would be to locate these miscues.

b. For the readers who have developed habitual associations between words or phrases that have close graphic or phonic similarities, such as *for-from, saw-was, though-thought,* lessons using carefully controlled linguistic material are suggested. For example, the students might be asked to read or write stories which use or elicit one of the confused words or use both words nonambiguously.

The following is an example of a suggested method for dealing with students' confusions between *was* and *saw*. First, present the student with sentences containing one of the habitually associated words. For example, "It was father." In this setting, it is not likely that students will produce "It saw father." When the students show evidence of being able to handle one of the habitually associated words, introduce the students to material in which both words are used nonambiguously.

2. Meeting the Needs of the Inconsistent Reader

Y. Goodman (1975) describes inconsistent readers in the following statement:

> These readers use effective reading strategies when the material is highly interesting to them or when it is easy because it has a low concept load. However, when these readers find themselves reading material which is complex, they use less efficient reading strategies. They stop searching for meaning and end up sounding out or word calling. When asked how they handle any particular reading problem, such readers often say they sound words out; they may be unaware that they use context to read or they may believe the teacher disapproves of it. Strategy lessons help these readers become aware of the various effective reading strategies they already use when reading easy material, permitting them to transfer effective reading strategies to more difficult reading materials.
> From: Yetta M. Goodman, "Reading Strategy Lessons: Expanding Reading Effectiveness." In W. Page (Ed.), *Help for the Reading Teacher: New Directions in Research.* NCTE and ERIC, p. 138. Copyright © 1975 by the National Council of Teachers of English. Reprinted with permission.

As described by Goodman and Burke in the manual *Reading Miscue Inventory* (1972), inconsistent readers include the reader who makes some effective use of reading strategies and the reader who makes moderately effective use of reading strategies. In natural reading situations, it is suggested that these readers be encouraged to make judgments while reading. They should be encouraged to ask self-monitoring questions, such as, "Does what I am reading make sense?" "If it doesn't, what should I do about it?" If the material is not making sense, it is suggested that the readers be encouraged either to continue to see if the selection will begin to make sense, or to judge whether to move to an alternative selection.

Strategy lessons for these readers are designed to develop their awareness of the transfer value of effective reading strategies from easy to difficult material. For example, in the context of easy material, readers might become aware of the strategies used to deal with unfamiliar words and to differentiate the significance of words.

Here is an example of a strategy lesson serving these purposes. It is taken from Goodman's article, "Reading Strategy Lessons: Expanding Reading Effectiveness" (1975). This story uses a concept or word which is probably not well known.

> The boy was looking for Petoskies. He was walking slowly to make sure he wouldn't miss them. He usually found a number of them each time

> he went looking for them. They were not easy to find because they were the same color as the sand. He enjoyed looking for Petoskies on the beach. He was helping his mother, too, since she used them in her work. She was an artist and made jewelry with them. Petoskies are usually bluish gray in their natural state with the fossils in them somewhat darker. When Petoskies are polished, the gray color becomes lighter and the fossils take on a brown character. Petoskies are found only on the shores of the Great Lakes.

To aid students gain meaning for the unknown word, the teacher would:

> Put this story on an overhead projector and use it with a small group of readers. Tell them not to worry about pronouncing every word as they read. Cover the entire story and move the cover down, exposing one more sentence with each move. As each sentence is exposed, ask the children to tell what the word (point to Petoskies) means. After each sentence, ask the children to revise their guesses about the word. Do not pronounce the word for the children, nor should you ask them to pronounce it. If any reader does say the word, the pronunciation should be accepted without comment. Only after the story is completely exposed and the meaning of Petoskies fully discussed should you ask for variations in pronunciation and finally tell the group how you think it may be pronounced. This is an interesting lesson because many teachers may not pronounce Petoskies the same way the people who polish and sell these stones do.
>
> From: Yetta M. Goodman, "Reading Strategy Lessons: Expanding Reading Effectiveness." In W. Page (Ed.), *Help for the Reading Teacher: New Directions in Research.* NCTE and ERIC, p. 138. Copyright © 1975 by the National Council of Teachers of English. Reprinted with permission.

Other strategy lessons for these readers might be to have students judge the significance or insignificance of words, phrases, or sentences contained in a selection. For example, students might be asked to read a selection and either delete or underline redundant words.

3. Meeting the Needs of Proficient Readers

Proficient readers are considered to be using reading strategies effectively. Therefore, reading strategy lessons afford these readers an opportunity to develop confidence in the use of these strategies. Specifically, strategy lessons might broaden and deepen their reading experiences. To deepen the readers' experiences, they might be encouraged to anticipate plot, theme, and events, to perceive subtleties and inferential meaning, to realize the influence of background and experience upon interpretation, and to appreciate that other readers have different interpretations about the same reading experience. To broaden their reading experiences, such students might be given the opportunity to read a variety of different types of reading materials in varying literary styles. Obviously, attention should be centered upon improving their reading-to-learn abilities.

Cautions and Comments

Reading strategy lessons represent an attempt to extend K. Goodman's notions of the reading process to classroom practices. According to this view, learning to read "ought not to be very much more difficult than the process by which one learns the oral mode of language. That is, provided that the same principles of relevance, meaningfulness, and motivation for communication which characterized the learning of oral language have been adhered to" (Cambourne, 1976-1977, p. 610). The ramification of this notion for instruction, specifically phonic instruction, lies in the following assumptions: decoding to speech or sound is not a necessary step between grapheme and reading for meaning; a hierarchy of subskills is not a necessary aspect of learning reading; maximizing the internalized knowledge of a reader should be encouraged; beginning readers use the same process as fluent readers and should learn to read as naturally; and phonics analysis is neither useful nor necessary.

In terms of the latter assumption, Goodman has been critical of both the emphasis upon phonics and the methodologies proposed. He has claimed that phonic approaches to reading are preoccupied with the erroneous notion that reading requires precise letter identification. That is, he disagrees with the notion that reading involves exact, detailed, sequential perception and identification of letters, words, and spelling patterns. His main argument is that we do not and cannot read letter by letter. A good reader is so efficient in sampling and predicting that he uses the least available information necessary. A less proficient reader needs the confidence to engage in sampling and predicting; encouraging less proficient readers to use too many cues, to be cautious, may detract from the readers' addressing meaning.

Along this line of reasoning, the strategy lessons are not intended to be exhaustive, but to illustrate to teachers ways they might develop their own strategies, based upon a reasonable understanding of the reader and the strategy lessons' rationale. In this regard, the suggestions are sufficiently explicit for appropriate instructional adaptations at most levels. They do need further amplification, though, especially to meet the needs of primary-level and advanced high-school students. Finally, those teachers needing more background before they construct their own strategy lesson with Goodman's ideas are directed to the reference section that follows.

Unfortunately, further details of Goodman's reading strategy lessons were being developed at the time of completion of this unit. Therefore, the present description of Goodman's reading strategies may already be dated. The interested reader should refer to Y. Goodman and C. Burke, *Reading Strategies: Focus on Comprehension*, Holt, Rinehart and Winston, (in press) for further information.

REFERENCES

Allen, P. D., & Watson, D. J., eds. *Findings of Research in Miscue Analysis: Classroom Implications.* National Council for Teachers of English and Educational Resources Information Center, 1976.

Includes a collection of articles addressing an extended discussion of the research base of Goodman's ideas and its relevance to instruction.

Cambourne, B. "Getting to Goodman: An Analysis of the Goodman Model of Reading with Some Suggestions for Evaluation." *Reading Research Quarterly* 12 (1976–1977): 605–636.

Describes the major features of Goodman's model, its implications and how it might be reevaluated.

Goodman, K. S. "A Linguistic Study of Cues and Miscues in Reading." *Elementary English* 42 (1965): 639–643.

Presents aspects of Goodman's research and the bases for reading strategy lessons.

Goodman, K. S. "Reading: A Psycholinguistic Guessing Game." *Journal of the Reading Specialist* 6 (1967): 126–135.

Presents Goodman's original definition of reading and describes its ramifications.

Goodman, K. S. "The Reading Process." In S. S. Smiley and J. C. Towner, eds., *Language and Reading.* Bellingham: Western Washington State College,1975.

Presents an updated model of Goodman's reading process which revises and expands upon the earlier model.

Goodman, K. S., and Burke, C. L. "When a Child Reads: A Psycholinguistic Analysis." *Elementary English* 47 (1970): 121–129.

Describes the reading process using data collected on students' miscues during reading.

Goodman, Y. M. "Reading Strategy Lessons: Expanding Reading Effectiveness." In W. Page, ed., *Help for the Reading Teacher: New Directions in Research.* National Council of Teachers of English and Educational Resources Information Center, 1975, pp. 34–41.

Presents the rationale for and several examples of reading strategy lessons.

Goodman, Y. M., and Burke, C. L. *Reading Miscue Inventory.* New York: Macmillan, 1972.

A manual with suggestions for using strategy lessons, based upon students' identified needs.

Goodman, Y. M., Burke, C. L., and Sherman, B. W. *Strategies in Reading.* New York: Macmillan, 1974.

A handbook of reading strategies which provides the theory and practice of strategy lessons.

Smith, F., ed. *Psycholinguistics and Reading.* New York: Holt, Rinehart & Winston, 1973.

Presents a series of articles addressing the relevance of psycholinguistics to reading.

7

Multisensory Strategies for Teaching Reading

UNIT OVERVIEW

The Unit and Its Theme

Starting from the premise that stimulation of several channels of sensory input reinforces learning, a number of specific variations of multisensory techniques have developed over the years. Indeed, multisensory strategies for teaching reading date back to ancient Greek and Roman education, where methods of tracing were used and recommended by notables such as Plato. In these various strategies, visual, auditory, kinesthetic, and tactile modalities are stimulated; therefore, they are often referred to as VAKT methods. Although the acceptability of using these processes without any emphasis upon comprehension may be questioned, the VAKT approaches described herein have had some reported success. While techniques suggested in the VAKT strategies could be incorporated into a classroom reading curriculum, they are designed and suggested for use when there are students with severe reading disabilities. Most of these approaches include techniques to improve spelling and writing skills, as well as reading skills. In the present unit, however, only the reading aspects of some of the more noted multisensory strategies will be presented.

The Strategies

In this unit, six representative techniques have been labeled multisensory strategies and selected for inclusion. Three of the six techniques described here involve what might be considered traditional VAKT strategies. The remaining strategies place a heavy emphasis upon phonics instruction in association with traditional VAKT learning techniques.

Fernald Technique

With respect to multisensory approaches, the Fernald technique has been perhaps the most widely used VAKT approach. It represents a comprehensive approach to developing reading abilities from low to normal ability.

Cooper Method

The Cooper method represents one of several modifications of the Fernald technique, which purports to give students a foothold in reading. This method proposes a variation upon Fernald's tracing technique which proposes tracing in sand and the use of a controlled vocabulary as the initial source for learning words.

Modality Blocking Procedure

The modality blocking procedure was developed by Harriet and Harold Blau; it is based upon the Fernald technique and represents an attempt to avoid over-stimulation of modalities. The technique systematically blocks the visual modality so that over-stimulation of the various modalities will not happen concurrently. This procedure is purported to be successful with "disabled" readers of all ages.

Gillingham-Stillman Method

The Gillingham-Stillman method represents one of several multisensory approaches which emphasizes students' auditory channels in learning to read. Based upon the theories of Samuel Orton, the Gillingham-Stillman procedure provides an alphabetic method by which words are built through associations involving students' visual, auditory, and kinesthetic processes. It purports to provide teachers of "disabled" readers a systematic approach to teach reading in a progression from letters to words, from words to sentences, and from sentences to stories.

Hegge-Kirk-Kirk Method

The Hegge-Kirk-Kirk method represents another multisensory approach which emphasizes learning to read through auditory channels in association with visual and kinesthetic stimulation. As with the Gillingham-Stillman method, it purports to provide teachers of "disabled" readers with systematic drills to teach reading through sound blending, word families, and, eventually, sentence and story reading.

Monroe Methods

The Monroe methods represent still another multisensory approach in which sound blending is merged with kinesthetic responses to ensure learning. For teachers of "disabled" readers, it purports to provide various methods of approach for the difficulties these readers incur in beginning reading.

Utilization

The reader should be cautioned to examine carefully both the theoretical bases and the intent of a multisensory strategy prior to implementation. The effectiveness of a procedure should not be judged in terms of the efficiency with which it programs or sequences experiences. Instead, the effectiveness of an approach should be judged from whether it meets the needs of students who will be expected to read for meaning.

FERNALD TECHNIQUE

Purpose

The Fernald technique (Fernald, 1943) has two basic purposes:

1. To teach the student to write and read words correctly
2. To extend the student's reading to various materials other than personal compositions

Rationale

Fernald claims that many cases of reading disability, both "partial" and "extreme," are due to teachers' failure to use methods which allow students to learn in the manner most appropriate to their individual abilities. Fernald claims the use of limited methods blocks the learning process. As an alternative, Fernald's own procedure, which incorporates a multisensory strategy, purportedly caters to the varied needs of individuals.

Intended Audience

The Fernald technique is intended for use with cases of "extreme" and "partial reading disability." "Extreme disability" refers to the totally disabled student with zero reading ability. "Partial disability" refers to the student with some reading skills, who is unable to acquire adequate reading skills within the instructional framework of the class. It is intended that the teacher use the procedure on a one-to-one basis with each student; however, the technique can be adapted for use with groups.

Description of the Procedure

Fernald divides her technique into four stages in accord with varying levels of individual reading ability and development. In the first stage, the student traces the word with a finger, saying each part of the word aloud as it is traced, until it can be written without looking at the copy. By the final stage, the student is eager to read. The student can begin to generalize about words and to identify new ones.

Stage One

The first stage is highly structured and for this reason will be described in some detail. In this stage, the student selects any word or words that he or she wants to learn, regardless of length. Each word is written with crayon on a strip of paper in large, chalkboard size cursive writing, or manuscript print. The student then traces the word with finger contact, pronouncing each part of the word as it is traced. This tracing procedure is repeated as many times as necessary until the student can write the word on a separate piece of paper without looking at the copy. As new words are learned in this manner, they are placed in an alphabetized word file by the student.

After several words are taught in this way, the student begins to realize that he or she can read and write words. At this time, "story writing" activities are introduced. Subsequent learning of words occurs whenever the student cannot write a word for the story. Sometimes the student may have to learn every word by this tracing technique before the story can be written. After the words are learned and the story is written, the story is typed by the teacher within twenty-four hours. The story is then read by the student, who proceeds to file the words under the proper letter in the word file.

The following points are stressed by Fernald for using this initial stage.

1. As a result of the findings from learning-rate experiments, unknown words should always be traced with the finger in contact with the paper
2. In order to avoid breaking the word into meaningless units, the student should write the word from memory rather than from copy
3. Similarly, if any error or interruption occurs during the student's writing of the word, the word should be rewritten entirely
4. To ensure the student understands the meaning of the word, words should always be used in context

A FERNALD DIALOGUE FOR STAGE ONE

The following dialogue between a student and teacher is presented to illustrate the use of the first stage of the Fernald technique with a "totally disabled" reader.

TEACHER: Good morning, my name is Mr. Stewart and I'm your teacher. Please sit here at my side.

STUDENT: Oh, all right.

TEACHER: I have a new way of learning to read which I'd like you to try. Many bright people have had the same difficulty you have had in learning to read and have learned easily by this new method. Now, give me any word that you want to learn to read.

STUDENT: Dinosaur.

TEACHER: Dinosaur?

STUDENT: Dinosaur.

TEACHER: Now, watch what I do and listen to what I say. Are you ready?

STUDENT: Yeah.

[The teacher should use a crayon and a piece of paper which is approximately four inches by twelve inches.

1. The teacher says the word before writing it.
2. As the word is written, each syllable is said.
3. If the word is written in cursive style (as the word is said again), the *t*'s are crossed and the *i*'s are dotted, etc.
4. As the word is said again, each syllable is underlined.
5. The word is said again.]

TEACHER: Now again, watch what I do and listen to what I say. Are you ready?

STUDENT: Yeah.

TEACHER: [The teacher follows exactly the steps as above, only the teacher uses a finger instead of a crayon.] I want you to do exactly as I did until you think you can write the word without looking at it. Now watch again what I do and listen to what I say. Ready? [Teacher repeats tracing procedure.]

STUDENT: Let me try.

TEACHER: Do what I did and say what I said until you can write the word without looking at it.

STUDENT: [The student traces the word following the procedure demonstrated.]

TEACHER: [Teacher checks student's tracing technique. Whenever the student hesitates or makes an error, the teacher stops the student and, if necessary, demonstrates the technique again. The number of times the student traces the word is recorded.]

STUDENT (After several tracings): I think I know the word now.

TEACHER: [Teacher removes copy of word and places a blank sheet of paper and a crayon in front of the student.] Write the word on this piece of paper using the same procedure. [If the student makes a mistake, the student is stopped immediately. Do not erase the word. Instead, fold or turn paper over and allow the student to try again.]

STUDENT: [Student writes the word using the same procedure followed when tracing the word.] Finished.

TEACHER: Are you correct?

STUDENT: I sure am.

TEACHER: Check and see if you are correct.

STUDENT: [Student turns over the copy and compares attempt.]

TEACHER: Were you correct?

STUDENT: Yeah.

TEACHER: Do you think you can write it correctly twice? Try writing the word again. [The teacher turns copies of the word down and gives student another blank sheet of paper.]

[Student proceeds to write the word correctly a second time.]

TEACHER: Check to see if you are correct again.

[Student checks word.]

TEACHER: Congratulations! That's great! Now place the word in your word file under the proper letter.

[Student proceeds to place word under the letter *d* in the word file.]

TEACHER: Now tell me another word you wish to learn.

Two, three, or maybe four words might be learned using this same procedure during a single session over each of the first few days. As soon as the student realizes that words can be learned by this procedure, "story writing" is started. Words are learned as they are needed for the story the student is writing.

Stage Two

The length of the tracing period (stage one) will vary from student to student and is phased out when the student is able to learn without it. This becomes evident when there is a decrease in the number of tracings required to learn a word, and when some words are learned with single or no tracings. At the point when the need for any tracing disappears, the student is ready to embark upon stage two. On the average, the tracing period lasts about two months, with a range from one to eight months.

During stage two, the student learns words simply by looking at the word while saying it over and over. As with stage one, words to be learned are derived from unknown words in stories the student has written. These words are presented to the student in print or in cursive form for study. The word is learned by saying the word several times, over and over again, until it can be written from memory.

Stage Three

Stage three is basically the same as stage two, except that the student has now reached the stage where learning occurs merely by looking at a word and saying it.

The student is permitted to read anything and as much as he or she desires. Whenever an unknown word is met, the student is told the word. At this stage, the student learns directly from the printed page. It has become unnecessary to write or print each new word on a card. The student looks at the word in print, pronounces it a number of times, and then is able to write it from memory. As with the previous stage, after reading new words are reviewed, filed, and, at a later stage, reviewed again.

Stage Four

In stage four, the student is able to recognize new words from their resemblance to words or parts of words already learned. As with stage three, the student is expected to read a variety of materials. However, unlike stage three, the student is able to work out many words. For example, such words might be learned from the context, or from generalizations about words or word parts. The student is told only those words for which it is not possible to determine the meaning. For purposes of retention, such words are usually written down by the student.

Fernald emphasizes the need for student involvement in the content of what is being read. For this reason, she suggests that the student be encouraged to survey a paragraph to clear up the meaning of unknown words prior to reading. She argues that this will prevent distraction and enable the student to concentrate on the content of the reading material. Toward the goal of reading for meaning, she discourages the sounding-out of words during reading, either by the teacher or by a student, and suggests that any word that the student does not know be provided.

Cautions and Comments

Empirical evidence of the success of the Fernald technique comes from various studies. Kress and Johnson (1970), Berres and Eyer (1970), Enstrom (1970), and Coterell (1972) have all reported positive results with this approach. Fernald herself provides a great deal of documented support for the strategy's success in *Remedial Techniques in Basic School Subjects* (1943).

While there seems to be a consensus that the Fernald technique yields positive results and has several desirable features, there also seems to be agreement that it suffers from some major drawbacks.

On the positive side, the desirable features of the Fernald method include:

1. It appears to provide a fairly well balanced program for guiding the development of word perception skills. It reinforces the acquisition of word form cues, and the ability to use context.
2. Methods seem consistent with aims and take into account variations in the child's rate of learning and specific needs and interests.
3. Motivation and reading of interesting materials are emphasized.

On the negative side, objections to the use of the technique include:

1. The procedure tends to be very time consuming and demanding of the teacher's time, especially in the early stages. Often more expedient methods for teaching "disabled" readers could be developed.
2. Reading books is deemed important, but delayed.
3. Syllabic division within words may distort the pronunciation of certain words, e.g. fat/her.
4. Readers may develop who are too busy sounding out words to either concentrate on meaning or understand the purposes of reading. In this respect, it can be argued that Fernald suggests the need, but not the methods by which students will read for meaning.

REFERENCES

Berres, F., and Eyer, J. T. "John." In A. J. Harris, ed., *Casebook on Reading Disability*. New York: David McKay, 1970, pp. 25–47.
Describes a case history example of the use of the procedure.

Bond, G. L., and Tinker, M. A. *Reading Difficulties: Their Diagnosis and Correction*, 3rd ed. Englewood Cliffs, N.J.: Prentice-Hall, 1973, pp. 498–501.
Presents a brief discussion of the procedure and its uses.

Chall, J. *Learning to Read: The Great Debate*. New York: McGraw-Hill, 1967, pp. 170–172.
Presents a brief discussion of aspects of Fernald's work with disabled readers.

Coterell, G. "A Case of Severe Learning Disability." *Remedial Education* 7 (1972): 5–9.
Describes an example of the procedure's successful use.

Enstrom, E. A. "A Key to Learning." *Academic Therapy* 5 (1970): 295–297.
Describes a successful example using the procedure.

Fernald, G. *Remedial Techniques in Basic School Subjects*. New York: McGraw-Hill, 1943.
Presents a detailed description of the procedure and results of its use.

Gearhart, B. R. *Learning Disabilities: Educational Strategies*. St. Louis: C. V. Mosby, 1973, pp. 76–90.
Presents a detailed discussion of the procedure and provides examples of its use through case histories.

Harris, A. J., and Sipay, E. R. *How to Increase Reading Ability*, 6th ed. New York: David McKay, 1975, pp. 393–396.
Presents a brief discussion of the procedure and its use with students experiencing reading difficulty.

Kaluger, G., and Kolson, C. J. *Reading and Learning Disabilities*. Columbus, Ohio: Charles E. Merrill, 1969, pp. 263–267.
Presents a theoretical discussion of the procedure and its use.

Kress, R. A., and Johnson, M. S. "Martin." In A. J. Harris, ed., *Casebook On Reading Disability.* New York: David McKay, 1970, pp. 1-24.
Describes an example of the use of the procedure through a case history.

Meyer, C. A. "Reviewing the Literature on Fernald's Technique of Remedial Reading." *The Reading Teacher* 31, no. 6 (1978): 614-619.
Reviews studies examining the effectiveness of Fernald's technique.

COOPER METHOD

Purpose

Using a modification of the Fernald technique, the Cooper method (1947) is a multisensory approach for beginning reading instruction with "disabled" readers.

Rationale

Cooper's method is in accord with Fernald's claim for VAKT procedures in the view that many cases of reading disability can be overcome by the use of methods which allow students to learn in the manner most appropriate to their individual abilities. But, as an alternative to the Fernald technique, Cooper proposes a different method of tracing and the use of a controlled vocabulary. With respect to the latter, words the student wishes to learn are selected by the student from a controlled vocabulary list.

Intended Audience

The Cooper method is intended for use with students with reading problems. As with the Fernald technique, it is intended for use on a one-to-one basis, but can be adapted for use with groups.

Description of the Procedure

The Cooper method, like the Fernald technique, involves extensive stimulation of the student's visual, auditory, kinesthetic, and tactile modalities. Unlike the Fernald technique, it consists of having the student select words from a controlled vocabulary list, derived from preprimers, and tracing words in a shallow sand tray. The Cooper method consists of the following steps:

1. Teacher prepares a shallow tray of sand or salt which corresponds in size to a shoebox lid. The bottom of the box or tray may be painted to make the tracings stand out
2. The student is positioned in front of the sand tray at a desk
3. The student is presented with a list of words from which to select

4. With the student watching, the teacher prints the selected word on a small card and pronounces it
5. As the word is pronounced, the student examines the card
6. Using the index and second fingers, the student writes the word in the sand, with teacher guidance of the hand if necessary
7. The student compares the word written in the sand with the word written on the card
8. The sand is shaken to erase the word and the word is written again in the sand
9. If an error occurs, the process is repeated from Step 6 until the word can be reproduced without the copy
10. The student uses the word in a sentence, either orally or in writing

When the student has acquired the vocabulary of three preprimers, book reading is introduced.

Cautions and Comments

Cooper's method differs from the Fernald technique in two major respects: the use of sand and controlled vocabulary. The use of a sand or salt tray for writing words appears to be more efficient, economical, and perhaps more motivating. The benefits of using a controlled vocabulary, however, have yet to be substantiated. Spache and Spache (1977) offer a discussion of the efficacy of controlled vocabulary, and the interested reader might refer to the disadvantages they cite.

As with all of the multisensory approaches described in Unit Seven, the Cooper method proposes procedures for teaching a student to read that appear to contradict what is known about how and why a student reads. In particular, purposeful reading seems delayed until the student has acquired certain word identification skills, which may actually detract from reading for meaning. For a further discussion of these points, the reader should refer to the other Cautions and Comments sections in Unit Seven.

REFERENCES

Cooper, J. L. "A Procedure for Teaching Non-Readers." *Education* 67 (1947): 494–499.
Presents a detailed discussion of his technique and its origin.

Kaluger, G., and Kolson, C. J. *Reading and Learning Disabilities.* Columbus, Ohio: Charles E. Merrill, 1969, pp. 266–267.
Discusses the Cooper method and makes suggestions for its use.

Spache, G. D., and Spache, E. B. *Reading in the Elementary School.* Boston: Allyn and Bacon, 1977, pp. 44–45.
Discusses the problems arising from vocabulary controls.

MODALITY BLOCKING PROCEDURE

Purpose

The purpose of the modality blocking procedure (Blau and Blau, 1968), is to teach "the severely handicapped reader" to read by avoiding interference caused by the visual modality during word identification.

Rationale

Basic to the modality blocking procedure is the theory that, in some cases, learning to read may be blocked by the visual modality. It is argued that, in contrast to reading, students learn to speak because there is no interference from the visual modality. Furthermore, it is argued that whenever two or more types of information, such as visual and auditory, are delivered to the brain simultaneously a breakdown in processing may occur. For these reasons, Blau and Blau (1968) suggest that the visual input must be cut off rather than reinforced, as it tends to be in other multisensory approaches.

Intended Audience

The modality blocking technique is intended for use on an individual basis with students who have difficulty reading. In general, it is suggested for use with either readers who have minimal reading ability or with more advanced readers who are having word identification difficulties. The technique must be administered on a one-to-one basis, but a trained aide can implement it also.

Description of the Procedure

The modality blocking approach represents a modification of the Fernald technique. It entails a nonvisual AKT method for developing word identification. The following steps are involved in the approach:

1. A word is selected from either the student's spelling list, compositions, dictated stories, reading stories, or textbook, or in accordance with structured phonic material. As Blau and Blau suggest, students often learn to spell words several years above their reading level, so there should be few restrictions on their source for words.
2. The student is placed in front of a chalkboard, a flannel graph board, or a magnetic board. The procedure and its purpose are explained to the student.
3. The student is blindfolded, or eyes are closed.
4. The teacher or the aide traces the word to be learned on the student's back. As it is traced, the teacher or the aide spells the word aloud, letter by letter. This continues until the student can identify the letters and spell the word.

5. Usually, if overloading of the sensory modes does not result, or the student masters the procedure with ease, three-dimensional plastic or wooden letters are placed in front of the blindfolded student. As the teacher traces the spoken letters on the student's back, the student traces the three-dimensional letters.
6. The three-dimensional letters are scrambled, and the student, still blindfolded, arranges the letters in proper sequence.
7. The blindfold is removed, and the student sees the word.
8. The student writes the word on paper or at the board, and then on a file card for future review.

Blau and Blau indicate that once a word has been mastered using this technique, it is readily recognized visually. Also, they claim that as a result of the procedure, learning appears to mature and, subsequently, word recognition, spelling, and comprehension appear to improve at a faster rate than might be expected.

Cautions and Comments

Blau and Blau (1968) reported success with students of varying ages using their modality blocking procedure or nonvisual AKT. Without questioning the legitimacy of these claims, both the rationale for this approach and its overall effectiveness need further substantiation.

The strategy is directed toward the improvement of word recognition skills and does not provide for either the improvement or the development of other reading skills. As with other multisensory strategies, the procedure places a heavy emphasis upon the acquisition of word identification skills from the part to the whole. In so doing, students are forced to learn skills which seem purposeless and rote. As has been suggested in our previous discussions of multisensory strategies, often students either fail to transfer these skills to actual reading situations, or overemphasize their importance.

REFERENCES

Blau, H., and Blau, H. "A Theory of Learning to Read." *Reading Teacher* 22 (1968): 126–129; 144.
Describes the procedure and its rationale, and discusses examples of its use with selected students.

Gearhart, B. R. *Learning Disabilities: Educational Strategies.* St. Louis: C. V. Mosby, 1973, pp. 89–90.
Presents a detailed discussion of steps involved in using the procedure.

Harris, A. J., and Sipay, E. R. *How to Increase Reading Ability*, 6th ed. New York: David McKay, 1975, p. 396.
Discusses the procedure in conjunction with a discussion of various other multisensory approaches.

GILLINGHAM-STILLMAN METHOD

Purpose

The purpose of the Gillingham-Stillman method (Gillingham and Stillman, 1973) is to provide the reader, "disabled" or "potentially disabled," who has a specific language difficulty, with a method for learning to read that is consistent with the evolution of language functions.

Rationale

Gillingham and Stillman (1973) argue that students with specific language disabilities will learn to read successfully only with methods that are consistent with the evolution of language functions. The system they have suggested is based upon the theoretical position and work of Samuel Orton. As suggested in the foreword to Gillingham and Stillman's 1965 text, *Remedial Training for Children with Specific Disabilities in Reading, Spelling, and Penmanship*, their goal was to organize remedial techniques to make them consistent with Orton's (1937) working hypothesis.

According to Gillingham and Stillman, Orton hypothesized that specific language disabilities he observed may have been due to hemispherical dominance in specific areas of the brain. He related certain instances of reading disability to the difficulty students might potentially have when dealing with inconsistencies that result from mixed dominance. Mirror writing and reversals seemed to be evidence of these difficulties. In accordance with this position, that spoken language was acquired via auditory channels and as a reaction to whole-word methods for teaching reading, Orton proposed a "phonetic method" for teaching reading.

The method, as it was developed by Gillingham and Stillman, purports to be new, different, and exclusive. It purports to be new and different in that it provides a "phonetic method" consistent with the evolution of language functions. It purports to be exclusive in that students using it engage in this and only this method. Gillingham and Stillman have claimed that the best teachers for this method are those familiar with traditional reading and spelling instruction. These teachers, it is argued, are cognizant of the need for and utility of Gillingham and Stillman's method.

Intended Audience

The Gillingham-Stillman method is intended for use with students who, due to specific language disabilities, have had or may have difficulty learning to read or spell. These "disabled readers" or "potentially disabled readers" should not include students who show either low mental abilities or sensory deficiencies. The method is intended for use with third graders through sixth graders, but has been adapted for use with older and younger students.

Description of the Procedure

To introduce students to the system, Gillingham and Stillman suggest a narrative entitled "The Growth of Written Language." The narrative is intended to provide a positive mind-set; it traces, with examples, the evolution of communications from spoken language to picture writing to alphabetic writing. The narrative ends with a description of the Gillingham-Stillman method and an explanation to the students that the difficulty they have incurred with reading it is not unique. As Gillingham and Stillman suggest, the latter message might be handled as follows:

> Now I am going to begin with you in an entirely different way. We are going to use the Alphabetic Method. You are going to learn the sounds of the letters, then build them into words. You will find it real fun and it will be nice for you to be attempting something which you can do. There are a great many children, more than you have any idea of, who have had the same kind of trouble that you have. Some of them have grown to be famous men and women. Boys and girls now doing well in college and business were taught to read and write as I am going to teach you. (Gillingham and Stillman, 1973, p. 37)

Thereafter, a sequence of exercises beginning with the learning of letters and letter sounds, then blending sound to words, and finally to sentence and story reading is suggested. Within this framework, the technique will be described in this sequence:

1. Letters
2. Words
3. Sentences and Stories
4. Others

1. Letters

The first principle of the technique is to teach the sounds represented by letters and then build these into words. To this end, each word family is taught by associations involving visual, auditory, and kinesthetic processes.

There are three associative processes involved. The first associative process involves two parts.

a. The teacher shows the student a letter which is said and then repeated by the student
b. With the mastering of the letter name, the sound represented by the letter is said and repeated

The second associative process involves responding with the name of a letter to the sound represented by the letter. That is, the teacher makes the sound represented by the letter and the student names the letter represented.

The third associative process involves learning the letter form. Learning of letter forms takes place in the following manner:

a. The teacher writes and explains the letter form
b. The student traces the teacher's lines, copies them, writes the word from memory, and then writes the word without looking at what is being written

There are several guidelines for the teacher to follow across these associative processes.

a. Letters are always introduced by a key word, such as, *b* would be presented in the context of *boy;* when the *b* card is shown, the pupil would be expected to respond with *boy*
b. Drill cards are used to introduce each letter, provide repetition, and improve the accuracy of sound production
c. Students learn to differentiate vowels and consonants by the manner of their production and through the use of different colored cards, e.g., white for consonants; salmon for vowels
d. The first letters presented to the student should represent clear sounds and non-reversible letter forms
e. An "echo" speech procedure in which the teacher drills the student in reproducing sounds is suggested for students incurring pronunciation difficulties
f. For reinforcement purposes, students who know the name and sound represented by a letter are asked to respond to the names of letters with the sounds they represent
g. In instances where writing takes place, cursive writing is preferred and suggested over manuscript writing

2. Words

After ten letters are well known, blending them into words begins. Drill cards forming a word are placed in front of the student and the student is required to blend the sounds represented by these letters, such as, *h-i-m, t-a-p, a-t, i-f, h-i-p.* It is the teacher's responsibility to devise ways of drilling words effectively. These words, printed on colored cards, are placed in what has been termed the student's "Jewel Case." Time drills are imposed; in some instances, students' growth in accuracy is graphed.

After a few days of sound blending, the student is required to reverse the procedure and analyze words into the component sounds. For example, the teacher might say the word *m-a-p* slowly and have students name and find the cards for each sound. As further reinforcement, the student might write the word. As the student writes the word, each letter is named and then the word is spoken.

Typically not more than one or two additional sounds are introduced each day. When a letter might represent more than one sound, only one of the sounds

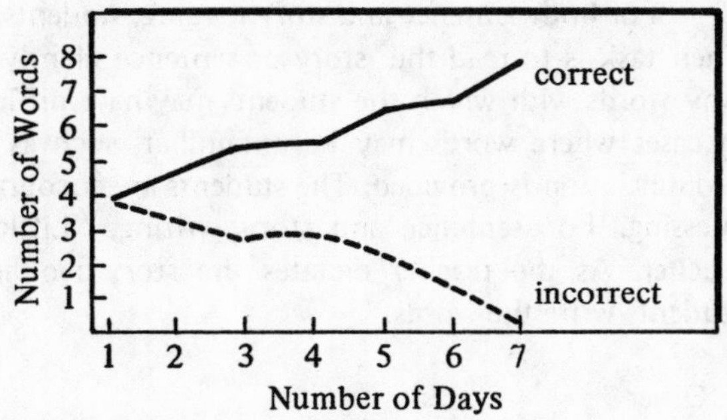

would be introduced. As word families are introduced, the drill card and "Jewel Case" card files are expanded. On a single day, the various activities might be organized as follows:

EXAMPLE OF DAILY LESSONS

(45 minutes to 60 minutes)

Practice in Association I	Selected Word Families
Practice in Association II	Same Selected Word Families
Practice in Association III	Same Selected Word Families (sometimes traced; written to dictation; simultaneous oral spelling)
Drill Words for Reading	
Drill Words for Spelling and Writing	

3. Sentences and Stories

After students can read and write any three-letter "perfectly phonetic" word, sentence and story reading is begun. It begins with simple, highly structured stories, referred to as "Little Stories," which are presented to the student to read and write.

Several of these "Little Stories" are available from Gillingham and Stillman. The following is an example:

Pat sat on the mat.
She had a hat.
The hat was on Pat.
A rat sat on the mat.
Pat ran.
The rat ran.

For both sentence and story reading, students are required to prepare silently. Their task is to read the story or sentence silently until they can read it perfectly. Any words with which the students may have difficulty are either sounded out, or, in cases where words may be unfamiliar, such as "phonetically irregular words," pronunciation is provided. The students are encouraged to be accurate and to avoid guessing. For sentence and story writing, "Little Stories" are dictated by the teacher. As the teacher dictates the story avoiding unnecessary repetitions, the students write the words.

4. Other

As the students' reading skills develop, the teacher may want to use further guidance provided by Gillingham and Stillman.

a. Students learn that polysyllabic words are formed by syllables in the same way monosyllabic words are formed by letters. To this end, students are presented with and asked to combine detached syllables, and are taught to identify the appropriate accent by trying the accent on each syllable
b. Dictionary use is taught for the purpose of identifying the pronunciation of words
c. To deal with a few selected words which are "phonetically irregular," whole-word drill is suggested.
d. Finally, until the student completes a major portion of the phonics program, he or she is discouraged from reading independently.

Gillingham and Stillman suggested that the technique would yield substantial benefits, assuming sufficient time is provided. At a minimum, they suggest the technique requires a commitment of five lessons per week for no less than two years. Eventually, they suggest, the student will be able to return to a regular class; but unless returning students can read their texts and assignments fluently, they should be assisted in reading them.

Cautions and Comments

There appear to be several important similarities and differences between the Gillingham-Stillman technique and the previous multisensory approaches. Both the Gillingham-Stillman and Fernald techniques emphasize constant reinforcement and repetition through the use of visual, auditory, and kinesthetic modalities, both prefer cursive writing to manuscript, and both attempt to develop a positive mind-set in the reader prior to the commencement of remediation. In terms of differences, Gillingham and Stillman insist upon a letter-by-letter, structured, synthetic phonics approach, in contrast to Fernald's concern that students not proceed letter by letter but select their own words to learn, and initially learn through all modalities.

While the Gillingham-Stillman technique purports to yield positive results, there are reasons to caution potential users. First, very few contemporary authorities still accept the theoretical position of Orton as tenable. Secondly, the technique proposed by Gillingham and Stillman assumes that their method is also appropriate for teaching reading. Yet often students who learn by these methods have difficulty when transferring the learning of sounds and words in isolation to actual reading situations. This synthetic letter-by-letter approach, with its emphasis upon word-perfect reading, tends to distort the reading process and to take away from purposeful reading. That is, it places an undue emphasis upon the mechanics rather than reading for meaning. For a further discussion of these points, the reader should refer to the cautions and comments sections of the various strategies presented in Unit 6: Strategies for Improving Word Recognition.

REFERENCES

Chall, J. *Learning to Read: The Great Debate.* New York: McGraw–Hill, 1967, pp. 169–170.
Presents an evaluation and discussion of Orton's notions of reading disability and Orton's suggestions for remedial reading methods.

Gearhart, B. R. *Learning Disabilities: Educational Strategies.* St. Louis: C. V. Mosby, 1973, pp. 103–107.
Presents a detailed discussion of the major aspects of the technique.

Gillingham, A., and Stillman, B. W. *Remedial Training for Children with Specific Disability in Reading, Spelling and Penmanship,* 7th ed. Cambridge, Mass.: Educators Publishing Service, 1973.
Provides the rationale and history, and serves as the manual for the Gillingham-Stillman technique.

Harris, A. J., and Sipay, E. R. *How to Increase Reading Ability,* 6th ed. New York: David McKay, 1975, pp. 369–397.
Discusses briefly the theory and procedure of the technique.

Kaluger, G., and Kolson, C. J. *Reading and Learning Disabilities.* Columbus, Ohio: Charles E. Merrill, 1969, pp. 267–268.
Presents a brief summary and discussion of this and other techniques.

Orton, J. "The Orton-Gillingham Approach." In J. Money, ed., *The Disabled Reader.* Baltimore: Johns Hopkins University Press, 1966, pp. 119–146.
Summarizes Orton's theory and discusses the technique.

Orton, S. *Reading, Writing, and Speech Problems in Children.* New York: W. W. Norton, 1937.
Discusses Orton's theory for specific disabilities in reading.

HEGGE-KIRK-KIRK METHOD

Purpose

The purpose of the Hegge-Kirk-Kirk method (1955) is to provide a systematic synthetic phonic system for "disabled readers" that emphasizes sound blending and kinesthetic experiences in a programmed learning presentation.

Rationale

The Hegge-Kirk-Kirk method was developed by the authors during their work with "mentally retarded students classified as disabled readers." The method is a programmed synthetic phonic system; it emphasizes sound blending and kinesthetic experience. It reflects the influence of Fernald's technique and the work of Marion Monroe (1932). Its presentation follows some of the features of programmed learning: (1) the principle of minimal change; (2) overlearning through repetition and review; (3) prompting and confirmation; (4) teaching one response for each symbol; and (5) providing the student immediate knowledge of success by social reinforcement.

Intended Audience

The Hegge-Kirk-Kirk approach is designed to be used with students who have the following characteristics:

1. The reading status of the student is below the fourth grade
2. The student has a severe specific reading disability
3. The student is educable in sound blending
4. The student has no extreme visual and auditory deficiencies
5. The student is motivated and cooperative

Description of the Procedure

The Hegge-Kirk-Kirk method begins by providing the student auditory training in sound blending, and practice in writing and vocalizing letter sounds. Printed lessons then provide the student with two-or-three-letter words, in which the student sounds each element separately and then blends the sounds into a word. A "grapho-vocal method" supplements these lessons by having the student write words as their components are pronounced and blended.

The discussion of the teaching of the Hegge-Kirk-Kirk approach will focus upon the following:

1. Preparation for the Method
2. Implementing the Method
3. Sentence and Story Reading

1. Preparation for the Method

Preparation for the method involves soliciting the student's cooperation and using an initial training period. The student's cooperation is solicited through a careful explanation of the intent and nature of the procedure to be used. The initial training period exposes the student to the methods used and presents tasks that can and should be readily mastered prior to implementing the procedure. The student is taught some letters and the sounds they represent. The student is shown that words are formed by blending these sounds. An example of the interaction that might occur between student and teacher in this initial period is included here:

TEACHER: Writes *a* on the board. Tells student that it sounds like a baby's cry, *a-a-a*. Then teacher erases letter.

STUDENT: Writes letter from memory and says sound represented by the letter. (This may be done several times.)

TEACHER: Other letters are introduced in similar fashion, and then a word composed of these letters is presented to the student. Teacher asks the student to name the sounds represented by the letters in the word.

STUDENT: Names these sounds one at a time.

TEACHER: Places other words on the board and asks student to blend the sounds to form a word. The teacher explains that knowing the sounds represented by letters allows the student to form many words and that this can help improve reading.

2. Implementing the Method

During the initial training period, the student is expected to have mastered most of the consonants and short vowel sounds and to be capable of blending three sounds into a word. It is at this time the Hegge-Kirk-Kirk method is implemented. It consists of repeated practice in blending specific sounds. Overlearning via repetition is the rule, with an emphasis upon accuracy rather than rate. The student begins with the short *a* sound and proceeds to blend orally long lists of words or word families containing no other vowel sounds, such as *sat, mat, rat,* and *fat.* To this end, Hegge, Kirk, and Kirk provide a total of fifty-five drill exercises and some thiry-seven supplementary exercises. The drill exercises purportedly deal with all the common vowel sounds, consonant sounds, combination sounds, and advanced sounds. The supplementary exercises deal with exceptions to the drills.

Here are some portions of the Hegge-Kirk-Kirk drill and supplementary exercises:

Drill 2					Supplementary Exercise				
		o					*alk*		
hot	pot	not	rot	got	talk	chalk	walk	balk	stalk
sob	rob	mob	fob	bob	stalked				
hop	mop	top	pop	lop			*oe*		
cog	fog	hog	jog	bog	toe	doe	foe	joe	hoe
sod	rod	nod	hod	pod	tiptoe			goes	

3. Sentences and Story Reading

While Hegge, Kirk, and Kirk admitted that the drills in themselves would not teach reading to the student, they argued that the drills were essential in developing correct responses to written symbols, attacking new words, and starting a student in reading. Sentence and story reading, they suggest, must be introduced to supplement the drill material.

It is suggested that sentence reading can be implemented in conjunction with the drills. At the discretion of the teacher, students might be presented sentences composed of the same words being drilled. If these sentences include unknown, "phonetically irregular" words, these words would be taught as whole words.

Story reading poses a different type of problem. Hegge, Kirk, and Kirk suggested that primers and first reading books often are too elementary in content for the age of the intended student. They advised, therefore, the elimination of story reading until the student can read more advanced material. Ideally, the material should be interesting in content and "phonetically consistent." Insofar as transferring the knowledge acquired from sound blending to stories, Hegge, Kirk, and Kirk suggested that teachers should not assume that students can transfer their knowledge of derived sound blending to reading from a story. Instead, teachers should aid the student either by naming "phonetically irregular" words or by blending unknown "phonetically regular" words.

When story reading begins, the drills continue to provide support with the introduction of new sounds and practice in blending larger units. As students move beyond sound blending, the drills and exercises are displaced by word study and reading.

Cautions and Comments

The method proposed by Hegge-Kirk-Kirk has been used for over forty years, and throughout this period it has been purportedly successful with "disabled" readers of normal and subnormal abilities. As a synthetic phonic approach, the method is well organized and articulated. It has several of the same characteristics as programmed learning lessons, including small steps, repetition, review, and feedback. In many ways, the approach resembles the Gillingham-Stillman technique, but does appear to be as flexible to manage.

There are several reasons why the potential user of this approach should be cautioned. In view of contemporary psycholinguistic research and thinking, the approach places undue and inappropriate emphasis upon learning, indeed overlearning, the sounds represented by the letters and sound blending. In this regard, the approach apparently assumes that the"disabled" reader should not and maybe cannot read for meaning until certain word identification skills are acquired. Many authorities (Smith, 1973) would suggest that acquisition and overlearning of these skills may have the reverse effect and hinder reading. For example, students learning these skills may never develop an understanding of what is entailed in purposeful reading. These students may become "word callers" who have a great deal of difficulty understanding what they have read. As Smith (1973) has suggested, reading for meaning is easier and should not be displaced by "reading words." It has the potential, as Smith aptly states, to be an easy way to make learning to read difficult.

REFERENCES

Bond, G. L., and Tinker, M. A. *Reading Difficulties: Their Diagnosis and Correction,* 3rd ed. Englewood Cliffs, N.J.: Prentice-Hall, 1973, pp. 518.
Presents a brief discussion of the procedure and similar techniques.

Hegge, T., Kirk, S., and Kirk, W. *Remedial Reading Drills,* Ann Arbor: George Wehr, 1955.
Presents a detailed description of the procedure, its rationale, utility, and drill exercises.

Kaluger, G., and Kolson, C. J. *Reading and Learning Difficulties.* Columbus Ohio: Charles E. Merrill, 1963, p. 269.
Presents a brief discussion of the procedure and similar techniques.

Kirk, S. A. *Educating Exceptional Children,* 2nd ed. Boston: Houghton Mifflin, 1972, pp. 60–61.
Discusses the theory, method, and development of the procedure.

Monroe, M. *Children Who Cannot Read.* Chicago: University of Chicago Press, 1932.
Describes the Monroe methods, their rationale, and their utility with disabled readers.

Smith, F., ed. *Psycholinguistics and Reading.* New York: Holt, Rinehart and Winston, 1973.
Presents a point of view to reading directly in opposition to this approach.

MONROE METHODS

Purpose

The purpose of the Monroe methods (1932) is to overcome a student's impediments to reading by providing drills and devices which involve motor responses to synthetic word recognition instruction.

Rationale

Monroe proposed drills and devices to reduce the student's errors in reading, to build up discriminations not being made, and to utilize to the fullest discriminations that are being made. She claimed that just as two individuals may think of the same object differently, so different individuals learn to read differently. From this standpoint, she suggested the use of "the possible secondary or vicarious steps in word recognition which are not usually presented in ordinary instruction" (Monroe, 1932, p.111). In accordance with an individual's abilities and needs, methods would be selected requiring motor responses whenever possible. As reasons for stressing motor responses, she suggested that:

1. Motor responses are more easily observed by the teacher and student
2. Motor responses are probably a part of the normal reading process, and movement serves to intensify this process
3. Motor responses reinforce and develop precise discriminations of the auditory and visual features of words
4. Motor responses assist in directing attention to learning

Furthermore, as Monroe noted:

> To the usual child, the emphasis on motor response as outlined here, and the placement of the secondary links in the learning process, may be an unnecessary procedure, detracting from the enjoyment through the mechanical devices for recognition of words. The child who has not learned to read, however, and who for the first time finds that he can succeed in reading simple words and sentences, even if by somewhat laborious methods, finds a new interest and enthusiasm for reading, and a new respect for his own capacities. (p.113)
>
> Reprinted from *Children Who Cannot Read* by Marion Monroe by permission of The University of Chicago Press. Copyright 1932 by the University of Chicago.

Intended Audience

The Monroe methods are intended for those students who deviate to the extent that they have failed or are failing to read by ordinary procedures. Ideally, the methods are intended for use on a one-to-one basis, but can and have been used with small groups.

Description of the Procedure

Monroe's methods have as their ultimate goal the development of the ability to read fluently, "comprehendingly, accurately, pleasurably, and with as little effort as possible" (Monroe, 1932, p. 136). The methods described herein are seen as a means to this end for disabled readers. These methods are intended to be modified to meet the errors or difficulties they attempt to overcome. They address:

1. Faulty Vowels and Consonants
2. Reversals
3. Additions of Sounds
4. Omission of Sounds
5. Substitution of Words
6. Repetition of Words

1. Faulty Vowels and Consonants

Monroe suggested that there are many sources for the type of difficulty when students need help in discriminating speech sounds, in establishing association with letters, and in sequencing these sounds into words. Monroe suggested three steps to this end.

a. The first step is to develop the student's ability to discriminate speech sounds. In this step, students are presented with cards containing pictures of several objects beginning with the same consonant or containing the same vowel. These pictures may be obtained from magazines. Examples of the objects used are:

   b, as in *boy; book*
   e, as in *pen; hen*

   To develop discrimination, the student is presented with cards containing unlike sounds, for example, *m* compared with *s*. The student is instructed to articulate clearly the sound represented by either the letter *s* or *m*, then name the pictured object. If the name of the object begins with the sound the student is asked to articulate, then the student retains the card. As the student proceeds, more difficult discriminations are presented. For example, *s* compared with *sh*. Where the student appears confused, an attempt is made to develop discrimination by articulated movements. To provide variety in the activity, the student is asked to generate words for beginning sounds.

b. The second step involves establishing associations between letters and their most frequent sounds. The suggested procedure involves a sounding-tracing technique. The student traces over a letter written by the teacher, while simultaneously articulating the sound. The procedure is repeated until the student can look at the letter and articulate the sound it represents on sight. Monroe suggested that usually five or six consonant sounds can be learned at one sitting. After the student has retained the associations for five or six consonant sounds, a short vowel sound is presented. The student then is taught to blend the consonants and vowels to form words. From this point, the words learned are listed systematically, traced manually, and reviewed frequently. The student begins to proceed through word family drills. The method was illustrated by Monroe with the following example:

   > The teacher wrote the word to be learned in large handwriting on a piece of paper. She said to the child, "See this word? This word is man. Say man. Now let me see how slowly you can say man, like this, m-a-n. Now I want you to do two things at the same time. Take your pencil and trace over this word while you say m-a-n slowly. Be sure to speak quickly enough and write slowly enough that you will come out just even." (p. 120)
   >
   >

Monroe gave a series of word lists to be learned in this manner. These lists begin with words composed of three sounds, including one short vowel, and end with words containing several syllables. Recall is checked by presenting the students with the words printed on cards. The student is instructed to articulate the separate sounds and to blend them.

As a variation of the tracing method, Monroe proposed substitution or a "sound-dictation" method. The "sound-dictation" method entails the student's writing the words as the teacher dictates the sounds, then re-reading the list.

c. As soon as the student has acquired a vocabulary of a number of words, the next step can be introduced. This step can be implemented concurrently with step (b). The step entails having the students read stories with a controlled phonetic language. "Phonetically irregular" words would be avoided, but if added to the stories, these words would be taught by tracing and by whole-word methods.

2. Reversals

To overcome difficulties incurred as a result of reversals, Monroe made various suggestions for providing cues to direction. The tracing-sounding method described for vowels and consonants was suggested for dealing with many of the more discrete reversals of letters and words. To develop a consistent direction for reading words, it was suggested that the student be instructed to follow, using the sliding motion of a pencil or a finger, the letters within words, then to follow the words within lines and to follow lines on a page. If the student's motor control proves too inaccurate for this approach, then retyping of the selection leaving more space between the lines was suggested. In some cases, Monroe suggested having the students underline, or write the words under each line. In extreme cases, she suggested presenting the students with words on cards, printed in large and raised type. With eyes closed, the student traces the word until it can be differentiated.

3. Addition of Sounds

Monroe claimed that sounds are added to words, such as *tack* and *track*, either due to student confusion of one word with another or as a result of a previous error. To cope with the former case, she suggested auditory and visual drilling to eradicate the confusion. To cope with the latter, no special drill was suggested. Monroe claimed the correction of the previous error was sufficient to eliminate these errors.

4. Omission of Sounds

Monroe suggested that the omission of sounds occurred as a result either of speech defects and discrimination difficulties, or of an overstress on speed of reading. To correct these difficulties, she suggested either speech-training, sound-tracing, training in dividing words into syllables, or encouraging a slower reading rate.

5. Substitution of Words

Monroe expressed differentiated concern for the substitution of words. She suggested that instances of meaningful substitution of words, such as *father* for *dad*, should be overlooked, but meaningless substitutions, such as *day* for *dad*, should be corrected. To cope with the latter, she suggested either moving the student to easier material or increasing the student's reading vocabulary.

6. Repetition of Words

Monroe suggested several methods for dealing with occurrences of repetition of words. In cases where other errors cause the repetition, no specific drill was suggested. She claimed these types of repetition decrease with the treatment of other errors. In cases of habitual repetition, she suggested that the habit be made obvious to the student, by both the teacher and the student reading in unison. In cases where reversals accompany repetitions, manual guidance in the direction of reading was suggested. In cases of repetition which occur as a result of students stalling for time, she suggested no specific method but claimed that this kind of repetition would be eliminated with the acquisition of word analysis skills.

7. Omission of Words

Monroe associated word omission with excessive reading speed. To cope with this type of error, she suggested slowing the reader's rate, either through the use of unison reading or by retyping the stories, leaving increased spacing between the lines of print.

Cautions and Comments

Monroe (1932) claimed that for twenty-seven disabled readers whose reading ability placed them halfway through the first grade, the average gain was 1.3 grades after approximately twenty-six hours of instruction (over an eight-month period) with her methods. In comparison, a control group gained only 0.14 grades. Monroe suggested that her methods were means to an end and not ends in themselves. As she stated:

> Although our methods stressed the mechanics of word-recognition, we utilized the recognition of words, not as an end in itself, but as a means to accomplish the final goal of reading, i.e., the comprehension of meaning. (p. 136)

The question arises: Do the students reach these ends by these means? Monroe claimed they do. As she suggested:

> Re-examinations of children taught by these methods show that after the initial start in reading is made, the children become more and more

> like normal readers. The secondary links, while utilized extensively by the children at first, become less in evidence and seem to disappear. Speed of reading develops gradually without specific pressure. Words are grouped into phrases and larger thought units. After remedial training, reading takes on the characteristics of normal performance until the child meets a strange, unfamiliar, or forgotten word. The mechanical links thereupon immediately become evident as the child attacks the word. Incipient tracing or articulary movements appear until the word is recognized and the child proceeds with the reading. Thus, it appears that the child ultimately builds up an organization of responses which is very similar to the usual reading performance of unselected children, although the underlying steps in building the organization are somewhat different. (p. 114)
>
>

Inasmuch as Monroe's methods are similar to those suggested by the Gillingham-Stillman and Hegge-Kirk-Kirk procedures, many of the criticisms suggested previously are again relevant. While the procedures suggested by Monroe are less insensitive to individual differences and do not divorce word recognition from comprehension, these procedures do seem to place undue emphasis upon a synthetic-letter and word-by-word type of reading.

REFERENCES

Bond, G. L., and Tinker, M. A. *Reading Difficulties: Their Diagnosis and Correction,* 3rd ed. Englewood Cliffs, N.J.: Prentice-Hall, 1973, pp. 501–504.
Presents a discussion and evaluation of Monroe's methods.

Chall, J. *Learning to Read: The Great Debate.* New York: McGraw-Hill, 1967, pp. 166–168.
Presents a discussion of Monroe's methods and research on the disabled reader.

Monroe, M. *Children Who Cannot Read.* Chicago: University of Chicago Press, 1932.
Describes the methods, their rationale, their utility, and potential use with disabled readers.

8

Practices for Individualizing Reading

UNIT OVERVIEW

The Unit and Its Theme

Individualized reading, which centers on the child and not on the material, seeks to counteract some of the disadvantages of those approaches which do not account for individual differences in each learner. It is a major premise of practices for individualizing reading that the development of the individual is more important than the materials, the sequence of skills or activities, or any other mandates which might homogenize students. The teacher's task becomes to work with each student in an intensive one-to-one situation and to tailor reading programs to the specific needs of those individuals. The task demands that teachers have the knowledge and skill required to plan, implement, direct, and evaluate reading programs.

The Practices

Three practices designed to aid classroom teachers in individualizing their reading program are discussed in this unit. Unlike many of the practices discussed in previous units, which are very specific in design, the practices discussed here are global in nature.

To provide a preview of this unit, a brief summary of the practices follows.

Individualized Reading

Individualized reading is a reading system based upon self-interest, self-selection, and self-pacing. It is appropriate for use at all levels, and it attempts to capitalize upon the notion that students should assume some responsibility for their own learning.

Learning Stations and Centers

Learning centers are designed to create an alternative classroom environment which combines the structure of traditional classrooms and the personalization of open education. Learning centers, which may be used throughout the grades for reading instruction, provide opportunities for increased self-direction and interaction by students.

Criterion-Referenced Management Systems

Used to focus instruction on specific skill behaviors, criterion-referenced management systems provide the means for teachers to begin to individualize instruction. Criterion-referenced management systems provide the teacher with specific information concerning students' skill mastery at various stages of reading acquisition.

Utilization

Although these practices may provide the general framework within which teachers may begin to individualize reading, they do not take into account the intangibles of dealing with one-to-one instructional situations, the complexities involved in moving from whole-group to individualized instruction, the economics of planning a different program for each student, and whether or not the teacher has an adequate background in teaching reading.

INDIVIDUALIZED READING

Purpose

Based upon the notion of seeking, self-selection, and self-pacing, individualized reading is designed to:

1. Focus reading instruction on the individual needs of each child
2. Aid teachers in guiding children toward assuming responsibility and initiative for their own growth in reading

Rationale

As with any reading method, individualized reading is designed to develop a reader's abilities and interests. However, the basic premise in individualized reading differs greatly from that in other methods. Olson (1949) suggested three major principles which have become the foundation of individualized reading—seeking, self-selection, and self-pacing. Olson explained that students are continually exploring their own environment in search of experiences that fit with their growth and needs. Applied to reading, this means that the most conducive environment for reading growth would be one in which students are surrounded by materials to explore and select from and to read at their own pace. Such exploration is done in accordance with students' own needs and interests. In terms of actual reading instruction, the procedure that has evolved from this point of view was summarized briefly by Smith (1963) as follows:

> Each child selects a book that he wants to read. During the individual conference period, the teacher sits in some particular spot in the room as each child comes and reads to her. As he does so, she notes his individual needs and gives him appropriate help. Finally, she writes what the child is reading, his needs, and strengths on his record card. Then another individual conference is held and so on. If several children need help on the same skills, they may be called together in a group for such help. (p. 142)

Intended Audience

Although individualized reading has been more widely used in the elementary grades, the technique readily lends itself to teaching in the content areas, particularly where a multiple-textbook approach is employed to expose students to various ideas and opinions.

Description of the Procedure

An individualized reading program is heavily dependent upon the following components:

1. Self-selection
2. Ample supply of reading material
3. Student-teacher conference
4. Flexible needs grouping
5. Sharing books

Self-Selection

Possibly the most basic ingredient in the individualized reading program is that every student be taught reading with materials that the student chooses. As Veatch (1978) suggests, the student is taught to select reading material based on two criteria:

a. I like it.

b. I can read it.

Obviously, an important teacher function is to expose students constantly to the variety of material available for reading. Through brief, enticing descriptions of these materials, the teacher can encourage the student to select the most desirable and motivating material. This, in essence, is the first responsibility of the teacher in planning—to make sure each student is given suitable material during the reading program.

2. Ample Supply of Reading Material

Essential to a program of self-selection is an ample supply of reading material for the student. A variety of material is needed if a student is to select a book he or she can handle with comfort. Veatch (1978) recommended that in order to maintain an adequate supply of reading material in the classroom, there should be available at least three to five titles per student.

Books are needed on many grade levels, since the range of ability in a classroom is wide. Typically, the range of difficulty should extend from one or two grade levels below the slowest reader to one or two grades above the best reader in the class. Thus, for example, in a typical first grade class, the teacher would select books for students ranging from picture books of the earliest prereading level to those books of at least fifth-grade difficulty.

Additionally, even though bright readers can effectively deal with materials of greater difficulty than average readers, their interests may be similar. Hence, a variety of books dealing with the same topic on different levels of difficulty is necessary.

There are many possible sources available for a teacher who is trying to gather three to five titles for each student in the class. The school librarian can be an invaluable aid and a tremendous source of information concerning books. Public libraries and bookmobiles provide other sources of reading material for the classroom. Book fairs also can be a means of securing additional materials for the students.

Paperback books are another source for stocking the classroom library, since they are relatively inexpensive when compared to the price of hardbacks. Book clubs, such as those of Scholastic Book Services, often provide discount rates for paperbacks. Often neglected, but still excellent sources of reading materials, are magazines and newspapers. Again, they are relatively inexpensive, and a teacher can request that the students bring in old magazines or newspapers from home to maintain an adequate supply.

Finally, abandoned or old sets of basal readers can be used to supplement the book supply. Basal readers do have stories which attract children; the individual story selections can be separated into small books for distribution as "mini-books." Teachers of different grade levels can exchange a certain number of basal readers among themselves.

3. Student-Teacher Conference

Central to the individualized reading program are the individual sessions a student has with the teacher. These individual conferences essentially determine the character of the reading program, since it is during these conferences that the student receives important personal direction in reading activity. The teacher needs to have specific purposes in mind and the ability to analyze and understand the reading performance of each student. This is essential in order to conduct a speedy, but thorough, conference and in order to insure that each student gets the necessary amount of individual attention and instruction that will provide for optimum growth.

A teacher does not check on everything a child reads, but rather, concentrates on what the child has selected and prepared for presentation. Veatch (1978) described four areas which should be explored in the conference session:

1. The mechanical aspects of the student's reading ability
2. The student's ability to read critically
3. The student's personal involvement
4. The ability to hold an audience while reading aloud

In the area of mechanical skills, the teacher might ascertain the student's ability to use word attack skills when encountering words that present difficulty. When reading critically, the student should be able to get the overall sense of the story, as well as be able to delve into the author's purposes. Knowing why a certain book is chosen is considered important for the student, not only for the student's own personal development, but also for gaining the ability to recommend the book to others in the class. Personal involvement with characters in the book also should be explored. Finally, the area of oral reading with expression should be explored.

Essential to the individual conference are the records the teacher keeps on each student. It is with these annotations that the teacher can guide the student in reading and also plan for grouping activities. The following is an example of such a record:

Juan	8.5 Age	2.5 Rdg. Ach.
9/5 Horton Hatches the Egg (p. 21, oral) Saw value of commitment. Group: checking organization of details Ind. Assign.: Vocabulary exercises		

From such an annotative record, the teacher can plan the next day's reading activities for the student. For example, the student Juan might work in a group to improve his skill in reading for details. Additionally, he will work on his own with vocabulary activities or the teacher can wait until several children have the same skill need and group them together to work on that area.

4. Flexible Needs Grouping

Groups are formed based upon the observations and diagnoses teachers have made during individual conferences and other observations made during school day. When the teacher sees that at least two students have the same need, a group can be formed.

It is to be emphasized that groups should be formed in an individualized program when at least two students need to know something or do something that the others in class do not need to know or do. These groups are flexible in the sense that they are formed only temporarily to fulfill a need and then are disbanded.

This is contrary to the usual practice of grouping, which is organized on the basis of low, middle, and high reading abilities. This conventional grouping plan is usually indefinite and allows for little flexibility in instruction. Additionally, such grouping allows for the negative aspects of peer pressure and labeling—the low group (e.g., "the Buzzards") become "dummies," and everyone knows it!

Groups may be formed easily when the teacher keeps good records of the individual conferences. By looking over these records, the teacher can readily see those students who are having common difficulties. For instance, the teacher can see that Juan, the student mentioned in the sample record, is only one of five students who are having difficulty with organizing their ideas. Thus, the teacher can save valuable time by grouping the five together. Instead of spending time teaching each student individually, time is efficiently used by helping all of them with the same thing at the same time.

Groups may also be formed for other purposes, some of which may be highly specific. Interest groups may be organized around a common concern. On the other hand, a few students can be grouped together for the specific purposes of finding more challenging reading material or for help in selecting a book at their reading level.

5. Sharing Books

Individualized reading provides students with an opportunity to share their reading experiences. In common practice, the sharing of books is accomplished through written reports which, unless creatively used, become tedious. As an alternative, teachers might give students a variety of ways to share books. These sharing activities might range from simple reflection on the content of the book to a dramatic presentation of an inspiring part of the book. Role playing, pantomiming, movie scripts, advertisements, radio scripts, posters, and puppetry are suggested alternatives from which the children might select.

Cautions and Comments

Individualized reading presents the teacher with a viable alternative to other approaches, by emphasizing personal involvement and decision making on the part of the student. However, there are some major deterrents to its use.

Since individualized reading is predicated upon the idea of self-selection, and self-selection from an ample supply of books, these two factors may militate against the success of the program. For example, the lack of a large number of appropriate titles from which to choose may limit the self-selective process, and students may not find a title which matches both their interests and their reading abilities.

A problem that seems to arise is the pressure to complete as many individual conferences as possible in each day. Ideally, the teacher will not neglect anyone, even the brightest of readers. In reality, overly long conferences with some students will result in less available time for the other students. Thus, some students may not get the individual attention necessary to progress adequately in reading.

Similarly, the success of an individualized reading program is in part dependent upon the vitality of the teacher-student conferences and sharing experiences. To ensure student involvement, both student conferences and sharing experiences will need to be meaningful and varied according to individual reading experiences.

Finally, individualized reading represents a viable alternative for the classroom teacher. Like most approaches, it demands that teachers possess an adequate understanding of the reading process and the reading curriculum. Like an individualized reading practice, it demands extensive teacher preparation and record-keeping.

Check appendix for the following:
Suggestions for individualized contracts.

REFERENCES

Blakely, W. P., and McKay, B. "Individualized Reading as Part of an Eclectic Reading Program." In W. H. Miller, ed., *Elementary Reading Today: Selected Articles.* New York: Holt, Rinehart and Winston, 1972, pp. 111–120.
Presents the results of an investigation which lends credibility to individualized reading procedures.

Fader, D. N., and McNeil, E. B. *Hooked on Books: Program and Proof.* New York: Berkley, 1968.
Describes the rationale for, and the implementation of, a saturated book program in an inner-city secondary school.

Groff, P. "Helping Teachers Begin Individualized Reading." In W. H. Miller, *Elementary Reading Today: Selected Articles.* New York: Holt, Rinehart and Winston, 1972, pp. 101–106.
Reviews twelve basic questions and points of concern when planning and initiating a program of individualized reading.

Hunt, L. "Effect of Self-Selection, Interest, and Motivation upon Independent, Instructional, and Frustration Levels." *The Reading Teacher* 24 (1970): 146–151.
Examines the effect of major tenets of individualized reading on the traditional concepts of reading levels.

Olson, W. C. *Child Development.* Boston: D. C. Heath, 1949.
Presents the basic principles of individualized reading.

Olson, W. C. "Seeking, Self-Selection, and Pacing in the Use of Books by Children." In *The Packet.* Boston: D. C. Heath, Spring 1952, pp. 3–10.
Provides an overview of the application of Olson's principles to individualized reading.

Sartain, H. W. "Advantages and Disadvantages of Individualized Reading." In L. A. Harris, and C. B. Smith, eds., *Individualizing Reading Instruction: A Reader.* New York: Holt, Rinehart and Winston, 1972, pp. 86–96.
Provides the pros and cons of an individualized reading program.

Smith, N. B. *Reading Instruction for Today's Children.* Englewood Cliffs, N.J.: Prentice-Hall, 1963, pp. 129–162.
Traces the historical development of individualized reading and presents examples of its use.

Veatch, J. *Reading in the Elementary School* 2nd ed. New York: John Wiley and Sons, 1978.
Provides the basic plans from which to establish an individualized reading program with particular emphasis on classroom management.

Wilson, R. C., and James, H. J. *Individualized Reading: A Practical Approach.* Dubuque, Iowa: Kendall/Hunt, 1972.
Describes the essential features of an individualized reading program and explains the processes involved.

LEARNING STATIONS AND CENTERS

Purpose

The purpose of learning stations and centers is to:

1. Create a classroom environment conducive to individualizing reading instruction
2. Increase the opportunities for students to be involved in self-directed learning activities

Rationale

Learning stations and centers represent a rather recent attempt at individualizing instruction, reflecting contemporary attitudes toward accountability and open education. Learning stations and centers reflect a compromise between the rigidity of the traditionally structured classroom and the disenchantment resulting from noisy and undirected open classrooms. They also reflect certain political and social pressures which prompted their advent. As Gilstrap and Martin suggest:

> Although the learning center strategy appears to be a natural outgrowth of the continued search for ways to individualize instruction, which has been supported through research and practice, the search has been intensified by the recent social and economic pressures on public school educators to be more accountable for their work with students. (Gilstrap and Martin, 1975, p. 77)

The term learning center is a rather loose term for an area in either the classroom or the school where students may have access to learning materials and activities. These materials and activities are directed toward providing specific learning opportunities with defined objectives and self-management procedures.

Typically, the classroom employing learning centers differs in a number of ways from the conventional classroom. The classroom becomes a decentralized learning laboratory, physically divided into various areas, or centers, instead of having the chalkboard and teacher's desk at the front serve as the focal point of learning. The students, working independently or in small groups, carry out their own learning activities with the aid and guidance of the teacher. The time involved in whole-group instruction also is significantly reduced (Hanson, 1972).

Intended Audience

Learning centers may be used throughout the grades for reading instruction. Although they are commonly associated with the elementary and middle schools, they are also appropriate for reading instruction in secondary schools.

Description of the Procedure

Learning centers can play a significant role in helping students learn to read. They can be used effectively with almost any reading system, by providing both the incentive and the materials to practice reading and the developmental skill activities necessary for independence in reading.

A discussion of learning centers and how to employ that strategy in the classroom revolves around three areas:

1. Classroom organization
2. Student and teacher responsibilities
3. Integrating centers into the reading program

1. Classroom Organization

Major differences can exist in the way a classroom is organized and in which centers are used. Central to the organization are the goals of instruction and the needs of the students. Once these areas have been considered, decisions can be made to obtain maximum effectiveness from the centers.

One decision which must be considered is whether the centers are to be used as the primary vehicle of instruction or as a supplement to the regular instruction program. The mode of instruction has a bearing on how the classroom is arranged. For example, if centers are used as supplementary, then they probably will be limited in number and are best placed around the classroom, leaving the central area of the classroom open for whole-group instruction. On the other hand, if centers are the primary mode of instruction, the number of centers will be larger and the need for a central area for whole-group instruction is not as imperative.

Another decision concerning classroom organization that must be considered is the type, number, and arrangement of learning centers. Once the teacher has decided whether centers will be primary or supplementary in scope, the variety of centers used in the classroom is limited only by the imagination of that teacher.

Obviously, the total room arrangement needs careful examination. The use of centers requires that the classroom be arranged into areas. These areas might include an area for teacher-directed group activities and areas for independent and follow-up work. Around the classroom, independent centers might be located on bulletin boards, chalkboards, connected desks, tops of cabinets, even the floor. A possible room arrangement which might be used and several examples of learning center structure are shown in Figures 8-1 and 8-2.

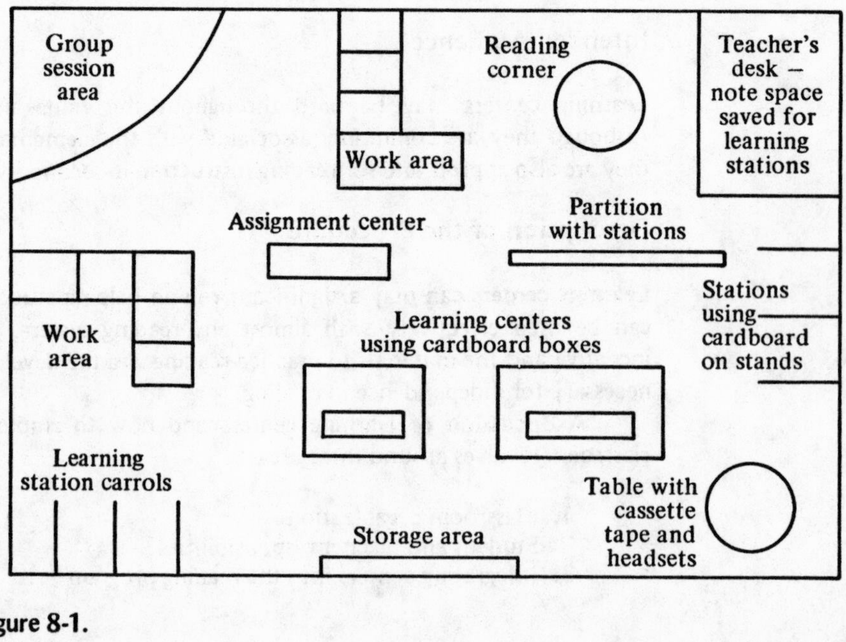

Figure 8-1.

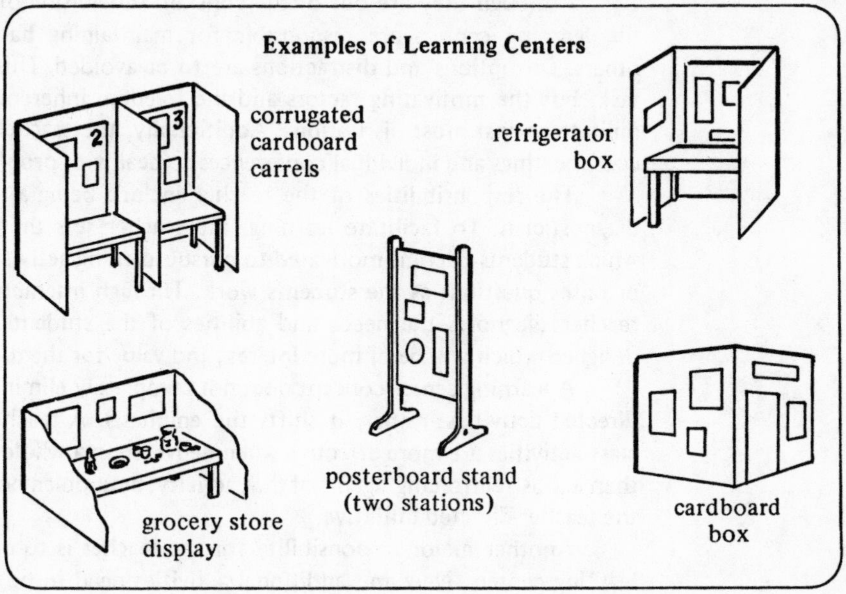

Figure 8-2.

Allen (1976) recommends that centers be organized around three major themes:

a. *Self-expression* activities for personal communication
b. *Language study* activities for comprehending how language works, particularly for reading and writing
c. *Language-influence* activities which bring learners in contact with the ideas and language of others

Centers organized around self-expression activities would include opportunities for oral expression, creative writing and dramatics, art expression, and musical expression. Language study centers would be organized to include games for reviewing language skills, dictation experiences, writing mechanics and study skills. Finally, centers organized around language-influence activities would provide opportunities for students to view films and filmstrips, to use puppets as story characters, to listen to stories and music, to browse through books, and to have reading instruction.

2. Student and Teacher Responsibilities

Students may work in individual, paired, or small-group instructional situations at the centers. They are responsible for getting involved in their work, planning their time accordingly, and asking for help when needed. Students are permitted to talk or work with their friends and to enjoy some free time when their work is finished.

Although they are out of the constant supervision of the teacher, students in the learning centers are responsible for maintaining harmonious relations with others. Disruptions and distractions are to be avoided. This may seem a formidable task, but the motivating factors and the freedom inherent in the center approach militate against most disruptions. Additionally, the teacher can employ the use of class meetings and individual conferences to deal with problems of that type.

The responsibilities of the teacher include being a learning facilitator and a diagnostician. To facilitate learning, the teacher sets the psychological climate in which students become motivated to pursue learning activities and offers suggestions or raises questions as the students work. Through interaction and observation, the teacher diagnoses the needs and abilities of the students. Activities can then be designed which will be of more interest and value for them.

A learning center concept does not completely eliminate the need for teacher-directed activities; rather, it shifts the emphasis. A teacher may find that certain class activities are more effective when delivered in a whole-group situation. Centers then act as reinforcing agents of that activity, by supplementing and complementing the teacher-directed initiative.

Another major responsibility for the teacher is to develop and maintain the learning centers. New and additional activities need to be added continually to the centers. Additionally, some centers need to be replaced or rotated to provide a wide variety of experiences for the students. Although it will take considerable effort and creativity by the teacher, the richer the learning environment is in opportunities and materials, the better the students will learn.

Before initiating learning centers, the teacher is also responsible for communicating the intent of the learning center approach and for maintaining a stable, calm environment conducive to learning. Students must be made aware of their responsibilities to themselves as learners and to others in the class attempting to learn. The ground rules can be laid in group meetings and reinforced in individual conferences. Upon beginning this approach, teachers need to start slowly and build slowly, as children become accustomed to working on their own.

Finally, the teacher is responsible for establishing methods of scheduling and assigning learning center activities. Work should be scheduled at the centers in accordance with their intended purposes. For example, if learning centers were to be used mainly for reinforcement, this schedule might be used.

8:30–8:45	Following whole class discussions, students are assigned either to a teacher-directed group activity or to independent learning center activities.
8:45–9:15	Teacher guides the reading of a selection with one group. At learning centers, other students proceed with follow-up activities from work of the previous day.

9:15–10:00 Upon completion of the selection, groups are assigned to centers to extend and reinforce understandings from the selection. Teacher supervises the work at all centers.

For purposes of assigning and organizing activities at the learning centers, teachers need a mechanism for distributing and gathering the students' learning center work. To initiate learning center activities, students might be given schedule sheets and/or assigned "mailboxes," such as milk cartons, in which they may both locate and return their assignments. A numbering system could be used to assign students to specific learning center sites; these assignment sheets could serve as a record or to evaluate the work done at the centers.

3. Integrating Centers into the Reading Program

In the classroom organized around learning centers, centers can be integrated or organized around some presently or previously existing programs. For example, centers can be integrated with the basal reader series by providing opportunities for individualized practice. Using their diagnostic abilities, teachers can identify areas where additional practice is warranted and prescribe activities for students to do in the center. To augment the basal approach, extension enrichment, or follow-up activities can be developed and situated in the centers.

Formatively, the language experience approach can readily work concurrently with a learning center approach. For example, a reading center could expose students to what others have written, while a writing center could provide students with the opportunity for self-expression by creating their own story. A listening center could expose the student to the thoughts and words of others.

To these several ends, learning centers should be self-administrative. They should provide a purpose, good directions, and evaluation to ensure that students are involved not only in learning, but in learning about learning. Sometimes, especially with poorer readers, the use of tape recorders and visuals may substitute for written directions. The following example may illustrate this idea.

Purpose: As we continue with our unit on "The World of Sports," we need to become aware of the equipment used in various sports. The stories you have read mention different equipment. Match the sports equipment words correctly with the sports of baseball, hockey, golf, and basketball.

Directions

1. Take word cards from the pocket.
2. Read the words and place them in the large pocket that best describes the sport.
3. If some words are new to you, check the stories you have just read on this sport and maybe a dictionary.

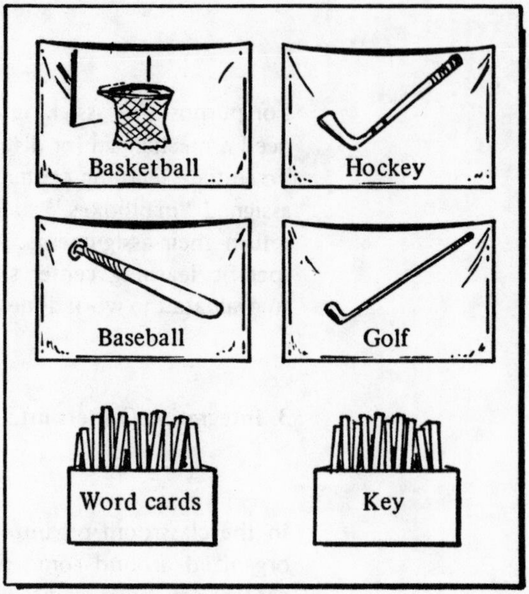

Evaluation

1. Check your products with the key.
2. Put all word cards and key cards back in right pockets.

Follow-up Activity: Write up an advertisement about the equipment from one of the sports, using as many of the products as possible. Compare your advertisement with others in the local newspaper.

Cautions and Comments

Learning centers can aid a teacher in individualizing the classroom by providing opportunities for students to work in an informal atmosphere on specific activities designed to meet their needs and interests. Additionally, learning centers provide opportunities for the development of self-direction and self-awareness, and the enhancement of students' self concepts.

However, the decentralization of the classroom under the centers approach does present the teacher with a few management problems. Foremost among these problems is the noise level of the classroom. The busy hum natural to learning centers can become an incessant clamor. On the other hand, trying to enforce a rule of silence in the centers may stifle interaction and informality in learning.

Management problems could also arise from the constant movement from center to center as students endeavor to complete their activities. It is essential for the teacher to communicate to students the necessity of settling into groups to do their work. Centers must be well stocked and constantly replenished with new learning activities designed to involve students in the work. To be meaningful, learning activities should not just be "busy work." Students should understand why they are doing what they are doing.

Another management problem may result from not providing help to students when they need it. If more than one student needs help at a time, grumbling, or, even worse, disruption, could result while they await the teacher's help. Students are many times impatient when they seek assistance; yet they must learn to wait their turn and, perhaps, be taught to go on to an alternate task while waiting. Also, if too many students are demanding assistance, the assigned work may not be at the right level of difficulty or in the correct amount. Better materials may be the answer.

Since learning centers aid in individualizing instruction, it becomes incumbent upon teachers to develop and maintain efficient methods of record-keeping. Without such a system, it will become impossible to prescribe the kinds of meaningful activities necessary for students to develop in reading.

REFERENCES

Allen, R. V. *Language Experiences in Communication.* Boston: Houghton Mifflin, 1976, pp. 66–74.
Discusses the role of learning centers as part of an overall language laboratory organization designed to promote language learning in all curricular areas.

Allen, R. V., and Allen, C. *Language Experience Activities.* Boston: Houghton Mifflin, 1976.
Presents various learning centers which can be used as part of an overall language laboratory organization.

Gilstrap, L. R., and Martin, W. R. *Current Strategies for Teachers.* Pacific Palisades, Calif.: Goodyear, 1975, pp. 77–84.
Provides suggestions and checklists for setting up learning centers.

Hanson, R. A. "Creating a Responsive Classroom Reading Environment with Learning Centers." In L. A. Harris and C. B. Smith, eds., *Individualizing Reading Instruction: A Reader.* New York: Holt, Rinehart and Winston, 1972, pp. 122–129.
Concerns the role of learning centers in the classroom environment with specific emphasis on the reading program.

Kaplan, S. *Change for Children.* Pacific Palisades, Calif.: Goodyear, 1973.
Ideas, illustrations, and activities for learning centers and room arrangements.

Marshall, K. *Opening Your Class with Learning Stations.* Palo Alto, Calif.: Education Today, 1975.
Presents practical suggestions for developing and implementing a learning stations approach in the classroom.

Vacca, R. T., and Vacca, J. L. "Consider a Stations Approach to Middle School Reading Instruction." *The Reading Teacher* 28 (1974): 18–21.
Offers a rationale and suggestions for the use and implementation of learning centers in a middle-school reading class.

Veatch, J. *Reading in the Elementary School,* 2nd ed. New York: John Wiles and Sons, 1978, pp. 98–141.
Discusses the use of a variety of learning centers to augment independent work during the reading period in an individualized program.

Wilson, R. C., and James, H. J. *Individualized Reading: A Practical Approach.* Dubuque, Iowa: Kendall-Hunt, 1972, pp. 45–52.
Describes how learning centers may be utilized in an individualized reading program.

CRITERION-REFERENCED MANAGEMENT SYSTEMS

Purpose

The purpose of criterion-referenced instruction is to:

1. Provide focused instruction on specific skill behaviors by describing and prescribing an individual's mastery of specific skills
2. Aid teachers in individualizing their reading programs by providing the means by which to differentiate those students who have mastered program objectives from those who have not

Rationale

The term criterion-referenced management systems is used to describe the plethora of commercially-made and teacher-made systems that share these components: (1) a sequentially ordered set of objectives for reading skills monitored by such systems; (2) tests composed of items or subtests designed to measure these objectives; (3) prescribed mastery levels for determining either adequate or inadequate skill attainment; (4) a cross-referenced file of exercises which teachers can use with students toward the attainment of skill mastery; and (5) reports which specify individual and group performance by skills and mastery levels. The terms skill management systems, objective-based reading instruction, and subskills approach are often used interchangeably to describe what has been deemed criterion-referenced management systems.

Advocates of criterion-referenced management systems argue that there is both pragmatic and theoretical support for their hierarchical skills management position. As Samuels (1976) suggests:

> The subskill approach . . . attempts to reduce the number of students who will experience difficulty in reading by teaching skills before the problem appears. (pp. 173–174)

As Smith, Otto and Hansen (1978) suggest:

> We need skills. Teachers need them to systematize instruction and to teach efficiently. Readers need them to approach the complex task of reading efficiently and effectively. (p. 44)

It would seem that among advocates of such approaches, criterion-referenced management systems afford both useful and efficient individualized learning experiences. In an era of accountability, criterion-referenced management systems are viewed as a procedure by which instruction can be systematized and progress toward goals monitored by parents, administrators, and legislators.

Intended Audience

Although criterion-referenced instruction has been used more extensively in the elementary grades, it is also used throughout the grades to provide evaluation and instruction for students purported to need specific skill reinforcement.

Description of the Procedure

The key to individualizing instruction using criterion-referenced systems lies in an effective management system. Typically, a management system for a criterion-referenced system consists of the following components:

1. Program objectives
2. Record-keeping system
3. Cross-referencing of materials

1. Program Objectives

A basic ingredient of criterion-referenced instruction is the program objectives, usually stated in behavioral terms. Such behavioral objectives define performance standards, the basis of criterion-referenced instruction. It is against these performance standards, or criteria, that an individual's performance, or mastery, is evaluated. It is toward these performance level standards that instruction is prescribed.

In organizing for instruction in the individualized program, behavioral objectives function to break the broad content of reading into manageable parts or skill areas. Behavioral objectives purportedly help set clear purposes for both the student and the teacher as to why a particular task is being performed.

2. Record-keeping System

Essential to criterion-referenced instruction is keeping accurate records of the objectives which have and have not been mastered by the students. Such information is used for sorting students into flexible skills groups based on common instructional needs.

From this basic information, the teacher can construct individual folders and/or classroom charts as aids for individualizing instruction. The individual folders are simply file folders keyed to the program objectives stated for that particular grade level of the total school reading program. Next to each objective, space might be provided to indicate criterion-level performance and to specify whether mastery has been attained. Constructed in this way, the folders often follow a student through the elementary school years to provide a continuous record of progress.

Classroom charts are sometimes used to ascertain the progress of a total class of students in their attainment of particular objectives. Student names might be listed on one side of the chart and program objectives listed across the top. In this way, a grid is obtained for checking off students who have attained each objective. Figure 8-3 provides an example of a classroom chart.

Comprehension Objectives – Grade One						
NAME	1	2	3	4	5	6

Figure 8-3 Classroom Chart.

3. Cross-Referencing of Materials

Within the framework of criterion-referenced instruction, the teacher's task is to fit the specifics of the materials into the specific exercises students need to do in order to reach mastery of their program objectives. Once the objective has been specified, the teacher must gather and identify reading passages, workbook exercises, games, and activities which will aid the student in attaining mastery of that objective. To this end, criterion-referenced systems will usually provide cross-indexes of published reading.

Cautions and Comments

As Gerald Duffy (1978) recently pointed out:

> A controversy surrounds the use of objective-based reading instruction. Proponents point to promising research results and to the help teachers receive from its focus on task analysis, subskills, specific pretesting for diagnosis, and systematic monitoring for pupil progress. Critics, on the other hand, point to the weaknesses that result when objective-based instruction is carried to extremes to the abuses evident in hasty or poorly conceived implementation. (p. 519)

The advantages of criterion-referenced management systems are obvious. They afford a sytematic procedure for monitoring, prescribing, and measuring mastery of reading skills and subskills. They allow teachers, administrators, legislators, and parents to operate with clearly established guidelines.

To the layperson, the shortcomings of criterion-referenced management systems are less obvious, but substantial. Johnson and Pearson (1975), for example, have suggested six major shortcomings. As they stated:

> There are at least six things that bother us about skill monitoring systems: 1) their psycholinguistic naivete, 2) their "assembly-line" underpinnings, 3) their concern for skill at the expense of interest, 4) their advocacy of sequencing separable reading skills, 5) the validity of their assessment instruments, and 6) the very notion of mastery itself. (p. 758)

It is their argument that criterion-referenced management systems are theoretically naive, practically inappropriate, and minimally beneficial. They argue that criterion referenced management systems inappropriately and inaccurately purport to define, measure, and monitor educational accountability in reading. Furthermore, in so doing criterion-referenced systems often misdirect attention away from the goal of learning to read for meaning and enjoyment.

REFERENCES

Barbe, W. B. *Educator's Guide to Personalized Reading.* Englewood Cliffs, N.J.: Prentice-Hall, 1961.
Presents highly detailed plans for implementing an individualized reading program, along with a model for a skill checklist.

Coulson, J., and Cogswell, J. F. "Effects of Individualized Instruction on Testing." *Journal of Educational Measurement* 2 (1965): 59–64.
Presents some initial research on the effects of criterion-referenced testing in an attempt to individualize instruction.

Duffy, G. G. "Maintaining a Balance in Objective-Based Reading Instruction." *The Reading Teacher* 31, no. 5 (1978) 519–523.
Discusses some of the pitfalls and solutions involved in implementing a skills management system.

Guszak, F. J. *Diagnostic Reading Instruction in the Elementary School.* New York: Harper & Row, 1978.
Presents the concept of the diagnostic reading teacher—one who uses criterion-referenced instruction as the basis for the teaching of reading.

Johnson, D. D., and Pearson, P. D. "Skills Management Systems: A Critique." *The Reading Teacher* 28, no. 8 (1975): 757–764.
Critically reviews the use of skills management systems in the teaching of reading.

Kibler, R. J., Barker, L. L., and Miles, D. T. *Objectives for Instruction and Evaluation.* Boston: Allyn and Bacon, 1974.
Develops a conceptual framework for behavioral objectives and aids the reader in organizing subject matter according to a behavioral objective perspective.

Lawrence, P. S., and Simmons, B. M. "Criteria for Reading Management Systems." *The Reading Teacher* 32, no. 3 (1978): 332–336.
Reviews factors to be considered in the initiation of a criterion-referenced management system.

Mager, R. F. *Preparing Instructional Objectives.* Palo Alto, Calif.: Fearon, 1962.
Provides a basic programmed handbook for the preparation and construction of behavioral objectives.

Otto, W. "Evaluating Instruments for Assessing Needs and Growth in Reading." In W. H. MacGinitie, ed., *Assessment Problems in Reading.* Newark: International Reading Association, 1973, pp. 14–20.
Reviews the basic approaches of assessment and their limitations in measuring student growth.

Otto, W., Chester, R., McNeil, J., and Meyers, S. *Focused Reading Instruction.* Reading, Mass.: Addison-Wesley, 1974.
Presents a basic approach to focusing reading instruction through the use of behavioral objectives and criterion-referenced instruction.

Otto, W., Rude, R., and Spiegel, D. L. *How to Teach Reading.* Reading, Mass.: Addison-Wesley, 1979.
Describes skills-management systems: their characteristics and application.

Rude, R. T. "Objective-Based Reading Systems: An Evaluation." *The Reading Teacher* 28 (1974): 169–175.
Reviews six published criterion-referenced programs and suggests a format for evaluating other programs.

Samuels, S. J. "Hierarchical Subskills in the Reading Acquisition Process." In J. T. Guthrie, ed., *Aspects of Reading Acquisition.* Baltimore: Johns Hopkins University Press, 1976, pp. 162–179.
Discusses the advantages, disadvantages and problems associated with skill hierarchies.

Smith, R. J., Otto, W., and Hansen, L. *The School Reading Program.* Boston: Houghton Mifflin, 1978, pp. 38–63.
Provides a discussion of skills management systems, including a response to criticisms.

Thompson, R. A., and Dziuban, C. D. "Criterion-Referenced Reading Tests in Perspective." *The Reading Teacher* 27 (1973): 292–294.
Concerns the nature of criterion-referenced testing and the cautions inherent in such an approach.

Wormer, F. B. "What Is Criterion-Referenced Measurement?" in W. E. Blanton, R. Farr, and J. J. Tuinman, eds., *Measuring Reading Performance.* Newark: International Reading Association, 1974, pp. 34–43.
Provides a definition of criterion-referenced measurement and compares it to standardized testing.

PART 2

Diagnostic Use of Selected Teaching Strategies

OVERVIEW

In the previous units, various teaching strategies have been suggested as a means of directing learning in various settings. In the present section, the diagnostic use of teaching strategies is presented. Thus, there is a change in intent, emphasis, and format.

In terms of intent and emphasis, without attempting to separate diagnosis from learning, Part Two attempts to make explicit the various diagnostic purposes selected teaching strategies can serve. In so doing, it connects diagnosis and learning, rather than separates them, and provides the reader with an opportunity to examine the potential utility of a strategy within the framework of analyzing the students' responses. Two points should be emphasized about this section. First, Part Two restricts itself to the diagnostic use of selected teaching strategies, rather than the traditional formal and informal diagnostic procedures such as cloze and the informal reading inventory. Second, with this in mind the unit should be reviewed in conjunction with the strategies and practices described in Part One. That is, the presentation of the diagnostic use of selected teaching strategies is intended to extend beyond Unit One.

The inclusion of a strategy within this selection should not be deemed a sign of the endorsement of strategies by the authors of this book. Also, the reader should note that the specific suggestions for the diagnostic use of each strategy extend beyond the rationale and description of procedures afforded by the original authors/advocates of these same strategies. It is possible that the original authors/advocates would disagree with these suggested uses.

The format begins with a discussion of the general diagnostic purposes teaching strategies serve, and proceeds with a description of the diagnostic analyses of the responses of students to teaching strategies.

General Diagnostic Uses of Teaching Strategies

The use of diagnostic teaching strategies affords:

1. Analyses of the abilities, attitudes, and behavior of students within the context of "real" learning situations

2. Systematic assessment of the suitability of selected teaching strategies or their modifications for students

To these ends, teaching strategies can be used diagnostically in either a formal or informal sense. Formally, teachers might prepare selected teaching strategies and use them much as they might use a diagnostic battery of tests. For example, teachers might implement either a series of miniature sample lessons that involve variations of a single teaching strategy, or a variety of different teaching strategies. Informally, within the context of daily classroom activities, teachers might analyze student performance and assess the suitability of teaching strategies. This would involve observing the strengths and weaknesses of students during implementation of selected teaching strategies. Such evaluations yield valuable information about the efficacy with which selected teaching strategies meet the needs of students.

Obviously, if teachers are to use teaching strategies for these purposes, they must remain alert to students' needs and be aware of ways to either select or adapt strategies to meet these needs. In so doing, teachers must understand the intent of the various teaching strategies and their modifications.

The strategies selected for discussion include lesson frameworks and strategies for improving comprehension, strategies for content area reading and the improvement of study skills, strategies and practices for teaching reading as a language experience, and strategies for recreational reading.

LESSON FRAMEWORKS AND STRATEGIES FOR IMPROVING COMPREHENSION

Lesson frameworks and strategies for improving comprehension were presented in Unit One. Diagnostically, they might afford: (1) an analysis of students' reading abilities in the context of these strategies, and (2) a determination of the effectiveness and suitability of the strategies themselves. Specifically, they provide an opportunity to analyze a student's:

1. Reading behavior, including an examination of the student's purposes for reading, ability to read to verify purposes, ability to evaluate and to generate further purposes for reading
2. Reading products, including the student's recall of details, main ideas, inferences, and organization of information into a meaningful interpretation
3. Skimming, previewing, scanning, rate-of-reading, and word-recognition skills
4. Reading-related skills, including vocabulary, oral reading, use of reference skills, and study skills such as outlining, classifying, summarizing, and using reference material

5. Readiness for a strategy, and the general efficacy of each strategy, by contrasting student responsiveness and abilities across the various frameworks and strategies. (For example, by comparing a student's responsiveness to a Directed Reading Activity and a Directed Reading-Thinking Activity, the student's readiness for and the efficacy of either a teacher-directed approach or a student-centered approach can be determined)
6. Differential abilities across material varying in difficulty, length, content, and type
7. Differential abilities across segments of a single selection
8. Differential abilities across reading, viewing, and listening modes

Illustrations

The following examples illustrate the use of selected strategies for these purposes. Illustration One describes the diagnostic use of the Directed Reading-Thinking Activity. Illustration Two describes the diagnostic use of the Guided Reading Procedure (GRP). Illustration Three provides a comparative analysis of the diagnostic use of the Directed Reading Activity, the Directed Reading-Thinking Activity, and the ReQuest procedure. Illustration Four describes a comparative analysis of the diagnostic use of the Directed Reading-Thinking Activity across reading, listening, and visual modes.

Illustration One

Using the Directed Reading-Thinking Activity Diagnostically. Sherry, Michael and Tony were sixteen-year-old ninth graders who were having difficulty reading in material intended for their grade level. Their performances during a Directed Reading-Thinking Activity were examined with respect to the following reading behaviors: (1) purpose-setting (predictive) capabilities and subsequent modification/confirmation of predictions with the discovery of further information; (2) motivation to pursue predictions; (3) use of experiential background; (4) comprehension skills involvement, such as ability to recall details, make inferences, and derive a main idea; and (5) word identification skills through contextual use.

They were asked to read silently a passage on weather forecasting excerpted from a science text. The material was selected because of the emphasis upon this type of reading in their high school curriculum. They were directed to stop at various points and to comment upon their previous predictions and predict forthcoming information. Then they were asked several comprehension questions and vocabulary questions, and asked to read sections of the passage orally.

They were fairly successful with the technique. They were able to make predictions based upon the available information, and to bring their own experiential base to the process; however, their subsequent confirmations and modifications of predictions were made independently of the text, and they had to be redirected to the material to confirm or refute statements. Questioning at the end of the passage revealed a good grasp of the main idea, of supporting details, and of inferences. Sherry's oral rereading, ninety-seven words in length, contained only one miscue, in which she changed a verb from active to passive voice. It is interesting to note that she was able to use context to figure out the meaning of "meteorologist." The other students read equally well.

Conclusions: The students were able to bring their experiential background to the task, process the textual information, and acquire an understanding from what they had read. Motivation for continued reading, however, did not appear to be internalized. Instead, it seemed that the three students needed some encouragement to make predictions through the text. Obviously, if this strategy were to be used successfully with them, adjustments would need to be made to avoid these lags. Possibly, interactions within a different group setting or changing the nature of the purpose-setting activity might prove beneficial. In other areas, it would seem that the students should receive encouragement. In particular, they should receive continued support in their ability to read for meaning and to use context. With some modifications, then, the Directed Reading-Thinking Activity might prove suitable for encouraging and monitoring their reading comprehension of these materials.

Illustration Two

Using the Guided Reading Procedure (GRP) diagnostically. The Guided Reading Procedure was used with six fifth graders to evaluate their ability to recall main ideas, details, and sequence through unaided recall and guided rereading. The Guided Reading Procedure was selected as a medium through which the students' capabilities in developing an organizational structure for information might be viewed.

An informational passage, approximately 500 words in length, was selected. It was selected for its historical ordering of information and for its match with the students' reading levels. The material was considered to be reasonably difficult, moderately interesting, and simply organized.

The students were asked to read the story once silently and then to recall verbally everything they possibly could. This was intended to give an indication of the skills used in dealing with a body of information without external direction. Their responses were recorded for them to use for future reference. They then were asked to reread the text and make any additions and/or changes in their recalls. The information was then organized into a simple outline.

The students read the material intently, at an appropriate rate with few hesitations. Their initial recall of the selection was very sketchy and general; each student recalled only isolated pieces of information. Upon rereading the selection, they were able to confirm their choices and add some details to their recall. When asked to organize their material, three students were able to mention outlining as an organizational aid, but none could correctly sequence the information without the addition of irrelevant details. At no point did the students demonstrate a grasp of either the main ideas or the theme of the text. They did seem enthusiastic, however, about the tasks they were asked to perform.

Conclusions: If we can assume that the students' performance on this task was typical, it seems they have difficulty organizing and recalling what they have read. It is possible that classroom activities in which a student is asked to "read this and answer questions at the end" might be inappropriate for them. They may lack the ability to set their own purposes for reading, be motivated to read a passage on their own, and possess the organizational skills to do so. If experiential background is a factor, they may profit from discussions and experiences through which topics can be explored. At present, it would seem that they could all profit from instructional methods and interesting materials that would prompt them to set, focus, and organize their purposes and information-gathering abilities.

Illustration Three

Comparing the use of the Directed Reading Activity, the Directed Reading-Thinking Activity, and the ReQuest Procedure with an individual. (The procedure could be adapted for use with a group of students.) Jacob was a sixth grader who seemed rather uninterested in reading for meaning. To learn more about Jacob's reading behavior and to assess the suitability of different teaching strategies, the following analyses were made from Jacob's responses to miniature sample lessons using the Directed Reading Activity, the Directed Reading-Thinking Activity, and the ReQuest procedure.

Directed Reading Activity. As described in Unit One, the Directed Reading Activity (DRA) is an instructional technique in which the instructor introduces the story and selected vocabulary, establishes the student's purposes for reading, and, after the reading, questions the student.

Jacob was given a verbal introduction to the material, and then was asked to identify selected vocabulary words presented prior to reading, ultimately using these words in sentences of his own composition. Jacob read the story silently, then related as much of it as he could recall, and answered questions on the material. He was asked to verify through oral rereading some of his responses in the text. For this purpose, the first half of a story was selected. The selection was a detective story chosen from Jacob's school reading program because of the story's appeal.

The introduction of vocabulary seemed to be of limited value, since Jacob was already familiar with the words. Jacob read the selection slowly, but with few hesitations. His recall was comprehensive, he answered questions accurately, and he was able to skim to verify the information. However, Jacob's involvement in the activity appeared perfunctory. He seemed uninterested and appeared to lack intrinsic motivation.

Directed Reading-Thinking Activity. This Directed Reading-Thinking Activity was used to assess how Jacob would react to the second half of the above-mentioned story. With the Directed Reading-Thinking Activity, the teacher has the student read sections of a passage and make predictions about what will occur next. Unlike the Directed Reading Activity, there is no prior introduction of vocabulary and students set their own purposes for reading.

Initially, Jacob appeared very involved in the activity, but as it proceeded, he seemed unwilling to alter predictions and to await guidelines and directions. It appeared that Jacob would rather rely on established guidelines and purposes than generate his own.

The ReQuest Procedure. This approach was used to determine Jacob's comprehension and responsiveness to the role reversal situation of this strategy. For this purpose, the ReQuest procedure consisted of allowing Jacob to be the teacher. An article dealing with Alaska was taken from a science text and used in the task. The material was of medium appeal and written at a reasonable level of difficulty. Jacob and the teacher each read the first sentence from the selection and proceeded to question each other. A total of five sentences were treated in this manner.

Jacob readily understood the task and seemed highly motivated. He asked and could answer a variety of types of questions including questions dealing with explicit and implicit detail and relationships, sequence, cause-effect, probable outcomes, and inference. When asked to suggest a prediction about what might follow, he offered several. During the use of this strategy, it seemed that Jacob was willing to become more actively involved in his reading. That is, he appeared to generate his own purposes for reading and be interested in relating the text to his own background of experiences.

Conclusions: Based upon Jacob's differential success with the three strategies, the use of the ReQuest procedure is suggested and also possibly the use of Group Directed Reading-Thinking Activities. While Jacob possesses the capability to read for meaning, he seems to lack the internal motivation to do so. Jacob needs to become more involved in reading for meaning and pleasure and less concerned about correctness. To this end, he might be made more aware of reading for meaning and given more responsibility for his own learning.

Illustration Four

Comparing the use of the Directed Reading-Thinking Activity across a reading mode, a listening mode, and a visual mode. Rosa and Peter were beginning readers in their second semester of the first grade. To learn more about their reading performance and to assess their instructional needs, an analysis was made of their responses to the above-mentioned variations of the Directed Reading-Thinking Activity.

Directed Reading-Thinking Activity: Reading Mode. In this activity, Rosa and Peter were directed to read a story and, at appropriate points in the story, make predictions about what was likely to happen on the basis of the events so far. They read two stories selected from their reading series. Their responses throughout this activity were hesitant. They would set purposes and make predictions only after much encouragement, and even then their purposes were specific rather than general. It appeared they were unable to relate personal experiences to those in the stories. Rosa seemed to be afraid to take chances on predicting, for fear her predictions would be incorrect or would not please the examiner. When she ventured a prediction which seemed correct, she was reluctant to try other alternatives. Peter seemed unwilling to suggest even a single prediction.

Directed Reading-Thinking Activity: Listening Mode. Using the procedure in this fashion allows appraisal of purpose-setting behavior and comprehension outside the context of their reading. Using this procedure, the teacher read the title and asked Rosa and Peter to look at the page to determine what the story might be about or what might happen. At first, both Rosa and Peter were very reluctant to raise any kind of questions or to make any predictions. As the story progressed, they were encouraged to raise questions and to check their answers upon hearing the story and viewing the pictures. Rosa made predictions as to who the characters were and what they might be doing. Peter was still quite reticent and only gave one or two predictions. He seemed unable to apply his own experiences and relied entirely upon the pictures to make predictions while using the text to confirm them. For instance, upon viewing a new picture, he would name the people and activity, and would confirm his predictions by listening to the text. At no time did he attempt to read any of the text for himself. Upon hearing the text, he would comment on the validity of his predictions, and he did not wish to guess what would come next until seeing a new picture. As the activity progressed, Rosa became more interested in the story. She had to be discouraged from turning the page too quickly. As her interest grew, her predictions were more frequent although still specific; that is, within the range of specific events. As Rosa's interest grew, so Peter also became more involved. Many of Rosa's early predictions proved to be inaccurate, although all were reasonable. She did not seem at all discouraged by these errors and freely corrected her predictions. She did not seem to hold any of her predictions unalterable although they might have seemed correct. She rather unhesitatingly generated several predictions throughout the selection. Peter, on the other hand, did not generate as many predictions as Rosa, but many more than he had ever done before. They both commented that they had not previously used this activity and usually relied on the teacher to correct their ideas.

Directed Reading-Thinking Activity: Visual Mode. In this activity, Rosa and Peter were asked to interact with three types of exercises:

1. Picture jigsaw, in which increasing amounts of a final pattern were displayed; Rosa and Peter were asked to make predictions on final pictures
2. Cartoon story, in which sequential frames of a pictorial story were shown; they were asked to make predictions as to possible story-endings
3. Single picture frame, in which a single picture of an event was shown and the students asked to conjecture as to what had pre-ceeded the action and what might follow

On all exercises, Rosa and Peter responded enthusiastically and were able successfully to implement behaviors analogous to those involved in reading: purpose-setting, use of experiential framework, use of several comprehension skills, and risk-taking. On the first exercise, both Rosa and Peter were able to make several predictions about potential final pictures, to modify their predictions in the light of further information, and to bring their prior experience and the text to bear upon their predictions. On the second exercise, they were able to make several predictions about a logical story, using similar behaviors to those cited for the first exercise. On the third exercise, both Rosa and Peter used these same skills to offer a number of different, plausible suggestions for events preceding and following the action.

Conclusions: In the reading situation, both Rosa and Peter appear hesitant to participate in activities that require prediction, purpose setting, and involvement. When they make predictions, they tend to hold to them. They seem to lack motivation and are reluctant to trust their own judgment. Rosa's responses are quite different, outside a reading mode. In a viewing and listening situation, she readily makes predictions and seems highly motivated. Peter's responses are quite different outside either a reading or listening mode. It would appear that Rosa's confidence and reading-thinking abilities would improve if she were given Directed Reading-Thinking Activities using viewing and listening modes. It would seem that Peter could profit from the viewing mode. For purposes of improving their purpose-setting behaviors within these contexts, both Rosa and Peter should be encouraged to make multiple predictions of both a specific and general nature, without being concerned about their correctness. If possible, activities in which there are no correct responses should be used. In general, it would appear that both students need to become involved in reading for meaning. Maybe high-interest material which involves reading and doing (e.g., directions, menus) would prove beneficial.

STRATEGIES FOR TEACHING READING AS A LANGUAGE EXPERIENCE

Strategies for teaching reading as a language experience were described in Unit Three. This description of diagnostic use of these strategies is intended to be relevant to each of them and to the general use of the language experience approach. Of necessity, therefore, this section is nonspecific to the different strategies. Its main focus is upon the kind of activity necessary to meet and expand the student's language capabilities. It focuses upon four aspects involved in the dictated-story strategy for teaching reading as a language experience. These aspects are language generation, language expression, language production, and language study. Language generation refers to the motivation for sharing and describing experiences by the student. Language expression refers to the structure or nature of expression rendered by the student. Language production refers to the production of a record of the student's expression. Language study refers to the reading and reading-related activities that follow the generation, expression, and production of a dictated story.

Language generation refers to the motivation or stimulus activity used to create student interest in sharing and describing experiences. Student responsiveness varies with interest in a topic and students' motivation for sharing. The question arises: what is needed to stimulate expression? Expression may be stimulated through the use of a picture, a concrete object, dramatization, puppets, manipulative activity, a field experience, or a discussion. Activities can range from the concrete to the vicarious, depending upon the motivation and background of the student for a particular topic.

Language expression refers to the nature and structure of the expression rendered by the student. Based upon the students' capabilities and the topic under consideration, it may be appropriate to expect students to describe and relate their ideas in either words, phrases, a sentence, sentences, or a story. A decision will need to be made as to which should be sought and expected.

Language production refers to producing a record of the student's expression. After the student's ideas have been expressed, a decision must be made about recording these ideas. This should be based upon the student's capabilities, and the purpose which the language activities and the record will serve. Language production can range from a record of part of the student's dictation to a record of the student's entire dictation. To avoid the potential tedium of this activity, both the teacher and student might record segments of a single dictated story. In some cases, the student's purposes can be best served with the task of writing one or two words.

Language study refers to the activities which follow the student's generation and expression of ideas. Usually these activities involve rereading the student's written record and other reading-related actions. For the purpose of rereading, a decision must be made as to when and how much a student is capable of reading. It is possible that students may be able to read a record of their ideas with little or no assistance. In other cases, the teacher may need to read it to the student several times or along with the student before the student is ready to read even a few sentences or even a few words. In terms of reading-related activities, a decision must be made as to the nature of the activities. A student's needs may be best met through comprehension, or through vocabulary-related or other activities.

Illustration

To illustrate the diagnostic use of strategies to teach reading as a language experience, the following example with a single student is offered. The strategy would need to be modified slightly for use with a group.

Scott was a seven-year-old with limited interest and ability in reading. He seemed unable to read material at a low first-grade level and was reported to be unable to recognize many words. To assess Scott's reading and reading-related abilities, his responsiveness to various activities was examined. Specifically, Scott's responsiveness in language generation, language expression, language production, and language-study activities was examined. In addition, his differential responsiveness to selected print awareness activities and book-handling abilities was determined.

Task One. Language Generation, Language Expression, Language Production, and Language Study

As a language generation activity, Scott was asked to describe a caterpillar presented to him in a jar. During this activity, Scott seemed most attentive and interested. He described the caterpillar in rich detail. He was then asked to tell a story about the caterpillar; he did so with enthusiasm. He gave complete sentences and a cohesive story. The story was then written for Scott while he watched. At this point, his interest seemed to dwindle. He even seemed distracted when asked to write selected words. He gave his story a title but seemed uninterested in rereading the story. The story was read to Scott; then Scott was asked to read along. He responded without much enthusiasm, but showed that he could read along. When asked to read the story by himself, Scott faltered on approximately ten percent of the words. He seemed overly concerned about "sounding out" the words, rather than reading for meaning. Through follow-up activities, Scott's comprehension and use of context were further assessed. Scott accurately answered questions dealing with main idea and supporting details, with cause-effect, and with predicting outcomes. When given an oral cloze activity, he could accurately fill in the blanks. His responses are scored on the following scale.

LANGUAGE EXPERIENCE ACTIVITY NEEDS

Language generation

Concrete experience — Vicarious experience

//—x——————————————————————//

Describe: Concrete activities and directed discussion needed

Language expression

words — phrases — sentence — sentences — story

//———————————————————x————//

Describe: Capable of generating connected sentences and a story

Language production

teacher writes — teacher and pupil write — pupil writes

//———x————————————————————//

Describe: Inattentive, needs teacher direction

Language study

teacher reads	teacher and pupil read	pupil reads
//	x	//

Describe: After teacher reads, can read along

Related activities: (Comprehension, identifying important words, context clues) Specify: good comprehension, asked and answered questions, good oral cloze

Specific language abilities

	Many	*Some*	*Little*	*None*
Spontaneous ideas	x			
Variety of ideas		x		
Originality of ideas		x		
Specificity of ideas	x			
Completeness of sentences		x		
Connections between sentences		x		
Variety of sentences				x
Richness of sentences				x
Variety of phrases				x
Variety of vocabulary				x

Conclusions: The language experience lesson suggested that with appropriate adaptations the strategy could be used effectively with Scott. In terms of language generation and expression activities, Scott responded with interest to concrete experiences. He was able to express his thoughts orally, to observe details such as likenesses and differences, and to express his thoughts in a logical manner. In terms of language production, Scott tended to be inattentive. For this reason and based upon his present abilities, Scott might profit from language production activities in which a portion of his dictation was recorded by the teacher and a portion by the student. In terms of language study, he should be afforded an opportunity to have the story or sentences read back to him several times prior to his own reading of these materials. Related word and language study, including oral cloze and comprehension, would seem appropriate to help extend and reinforce Scott's acquisition of reading skills. Given his general inattentiveness, sessions should be brief and free of distractions, and should afford varied teacher-pupil interactions.

Task Two. Print Awareness

To determine Scott's general awareness of print, he was given two sets of print awareness activities.

In the first set of activities, Scott was asked to identify words "in" and "out of" a familiar context. Product labels or trademarks supplied the familiar context, such as "Coca Cola" and "Kentucky Fried Chicken." To assess whether Scott recognized the purpose of the labels, he was shown the products and asked to identify the portion of the labels which named the product. The labels were then presented for identification apart from their packages. Scott performed well on all of these tasks. He seemed aware of the function and meaning of print. Next, he was shown the words isolated from the label for identification purposes, both in the commercial and the standard printed forms of the labels. Scott would recognize most of these words when they were presented in the commercial print form, but not when presented in the standard print form. It was obvious that Scott had not transferred his knowledge of print in his environment to the more standard form of print as commonly seen in books. His level of responses are shown on the following scale.

	Many	Some	Little	None
Recognizes purposes of labels on packets	x			
Recognizes puposes of print on labels	x			
Recognizes meaning of print detached from label	x			
Recognizes print in standard label form				x

In the second print awareness activity, Scott worked with a simple recipe. He was shown four directions with identical three-word stems. "Put in the _________." Only the ingredient word for each direction differed. In the context of the recipe, Scott learned the three-word stem and the ingredients. He could read the directions by himself and read the label on each ingredient.

Conclusions: It was apparent that Scott was familiar with print in his environment, but had yet to transfer this knowledge to reading standard print. When given a reason to read, such as following a recipe, Scott quickly became familiar with the print, regardless of its graphic form. If he is given meaningful print experiences, it would seem that Scott can and will read. This fact should be capitalized upon for improving Scott's general and specific reading ability.

Task Three. Bookhandling Knowledge

To determine bookhandling behavior, Scott was given the following tasks. He was asked to identify a book on display and to tell what might be done with it. He was asked to describe what was inside a book and then told to show where the book actually began. To assess Scott's knowledge about pages, he was asked to show a page, and to indicate the first and last page in a book as well as the top and bottom of the page. To assess Scott's knowledge of the purpose of print, he was asked to explain what the print on the page tells and to identify where the print began and ended on the page. He was then asked to identify the first and last word on the page and to show how the page would be read. To assess his knowledge of words, he was asked to point to any word, to look for matching words, to find words that began the same way, to locate words that ended the same way, and to tell what was indicated by words beginning with capitals. Finally, he was asked to show and to explain the purposes of the pictures in the book.

Conclusions: Scott's responses to these tasks indicated familiarity with the purpose of a book and with the function of pages and print, and an understanding of the left-to-right and top-to-bottom conventions of the printed page. Scott was able to identify a word and match words but did have difficulty understanding the function of capitals and letters. It seems likely that as Scott dictates, reads, and writes his own experience stories, a better understanding of the latter will be gained.

STRATEGIES FOR CONTENT AREA READING AND THE IMPROVEMENT OF STUDY SKILLS

Strategies for content area reading and the improvement of study skills were described and discussed in Unit Two. Their use diagnostically can serve several purposes. These strategies can afford an analysis of students' general comprehension abilities, study techniques, and notetaking abilities. They can provide for an examination of the suitability of selected strategies for improving these abilities.

Illustration

The following example illustrates how study skills and content area reading skills can be assessed informally and through the use of selected strategies discussed in Unit Two. The example includes an informal assessment of study skills and an assessment of selected skills through the use of a structured overview and study guides. The students for whom these assessments were made were having difficulty reading and studying content area reading material.

Informal Individual Assessment of Study Skills (This procedure could be readily adapted for use in a group situation.)

A student, Thomas, was given an assignment to read pages 301 to 305 in his history textbook. He was given a paper and pencil and told that he would be given a test on the material.

Thomas read to page 303, but did not read pages 304 and 305. Thomas failed to use a provided overview for the selection, survey technique, the questions at the end of the section, or the notes, but he did refer to the picture and graphic aids. When given a test on the material, Thomas failed to read the test directions; he proceeded to circle an answer rather than underline possible answers. His performance seemed mediocre. When Thomas was halfway through the test, he was permitted to return to his textbook to help him find the answers and to recheck other answers. He did not use the book until he had started the next-to-the-last question. This was a question about Orville Wright. Thomas scanned the selection and then went to the index to look up "Orville." He then was instructed to look for "Wright." He found the page number but still could not find the answer. Next, Thomas was directed to suggest and use selected references to learn more about the topic. He offered to use these: the dictionary to learn more about the meaning of a word; encyclopedias to learn more about the topic; and an atlas to locate places mentioned in the text. When told to describe and refer to these reference sources, it was apparent that he was familiar with them and could use them profitably. When asked how often he used this material, he said, "Rarely."

From an analysis of his performance, it seems Thomas makes limited and ineffective use of study skills. He scans, uses visual aids, and knows about the use of an index; however, he does not preview , vary reading rate, take notes, outlines, or follow written directions. To help Thomas study more efficiently and effectively, the SQ3R method of study or a modification might be used. The five steps of SQ3R should result in Thomas' fixing important points in his memory. A modification of SQ3R might emphasize the value of prereading material—skimming through the pages to be read, reading headings and subheading, summarizing paragraphs, or formulating questions to guide reading. In addition, Thomas should be shown and given opportunities to improve his organizing, outlining, summarizing, note-taking, and test-taking skills. To guide his reading, he might be encouraged to ask himself the following question. Prior to reading, he might ask: What do I already know about this subject? After and during reading, he might ask: What do I now know about this subject? What else do I want or need to know? How might I use this information?

Structured Overview and Study Guide

A structured overview and study guide were used to assess the study skills and content area reading skills of selected high school sophomores and to determine the suitability of these strategies for use with those students.

A structured overview was used to introduce the students to the major ideas represented in a selection from their science textbook. They were able to understand the overview with a minimum of discussion and seemed well-prepared for the selection.

The students then were given a combination reading-reasoning study guide to fill out as they read the passage. The combination of these two types of study guides was used to determine the students' ability to perceive cause-effect patterns in a selection and to classify causes into categories. It also served to assess the suitability of this technique for use with the students as an aid to developing reading and study skills. The reading guide consisted of matching causes with effects. The reasoning portion of the guide consisted of listing causes under various categories. Several of the students were unable to grasp the relationship between cause and effect and had difficulty with the reading guide. These same students were unable to categorize the causes correctly.

Conclusions: The students seemed to profit from the use of a structured overview as a prereading mechanism. Through the use of the overview, they seemed interested and established purposes for reading. As the lesson proceeded, however, several students seemed to have difficulty with the reading-thinking skills necessary to cope with a reading-reasoning study guide. They were unable to either determine cause-effect relations or to categorize causes. Furthermore, they seemed uninterested in doing so. It is possible that either the guides detracted from reading the text or the students need to explore cause-effect and other relationships through discussion of topics within the realm of their experiences. For example, once an understanding of these relationships is developed with familiar material, the students might be given similar activities through which to apply these understandings to their reading. To this end, they might be encouraged to develop their own study guide for the material being read.

RECREATIONAL READING

A recreational reading strategy was described in Unit Four. Diagnostic use of a recreational reading strategy involves studying the students' recreational reading behavior and preferences. On an informal basis, studying recreational reading behavior can afford information on how students locate material; on what students read; on how students read; and on why students read what they read. Formally, recreational reading behavior can be studied for these same purposes, in addition to the purpose of answers to the following questions: What other materials might students read? How might students improve their ability to locate material? How might students increase their reading enjoyment?

Illustration

The following two examples illustrate a slightly formal assessment of recreational reading behavior. The first example describes an assessment of the recreational reading behavior of an advanced high school student. The second illustration describes behavior of several fifth graders.

Illustration One

Ralph was an advanced high school student who claimed that he read some magazines and scanned the newspaper, but did not do much recreational reading.

In order to assess Ralph's recreational reading behavior, a somewhat formal assessment was planned. Three types of material were selected for this purpose: fictional material, periodicals (magazines and newspapers), and nonfictional material. Twenty to thirty items on a broad range of subjects in each area were presented to Ralph. He was asked to choose the item he preferred; to explain why he chose it; to make two other choices in each area; and to identify what he would definitely not choose to read. In all three areas, he had read some books and was familiar with others. For those that were unfamiliar to him, he was given a brief description.

Fictional books were presented first. Ralph quickly selected a book containing Mark Twain stories, choosing the book because, "I know he's entertaining." Ralph suggested that he enjoyed Twain's characters and stories. His next selection was *The Choirboys* by Joseph Wambaugh because someone had recommended it. *Siddhartha* was Ralph's third choice because it was "thin." *In One Car,* a book containing "1,000 funny stories," Ralph suggested he would not read.

Next, Ralph was presented a variety of periodicals. From the magazines presented, he selected *Réalitiés,* a French magazine translated into English which he had never seen before. He claimed he enjoyed magazines with interesting and different articles. His other choices were an engineering journal and *Smithsonian.* He showed no interest whatsoever in any of the popular magazines, such as *Sports Illustrated.*

Of the nonfictional books presented, Ralph chose *The Essential Lenny Bruce* because of a strong interest in Lenny Bruce's humor. He had read and enjoyed *Bury My Heart at Wounded Knee* and said he would like to read *Passages,* but suggested that he did not usually like self-awareness books. In terms of reference material, he showed no interest in the *Guinness Book of World Records,* in *The World Almanac,* or in encyclopedias. Ralph said that he had access to these materials but rarely used them unless it was required. He did show an interest in one specific reference book dealing with opera; Ralph stated that he wished he owned such a book.

Conclusions: Ralph based his selection of books on several things: his familiarity with the style of the author, the book's novelty, personal interest in the book, the recommendations of others, and the book's size. Ralph expressed strong likes and dislikes, spontaneously explaining the reasons for his choices. His choices reflected well-developed interests in selected areas, such as opera. Given appropriate material, Ralph's recreational reading could be extended within his areas of interest and perhaps to other areas. To this end, Ralph should be given regular opportunities to review and select reading material. The teacher might suggest that Ralph read published book reviews, join a book club, visit bookstores, or join a library. Ralph should adopt a daily recreational reading schedule, plan regular library visits, and subscribe to one or two magazines. Finally, Ralph's concept about his recreational reading behavior seems unwarranted. Ralph should realize that while he may not be an avid reader, he does read sufficiently and does seem to enjoy reading. He should feel better about his acquired habits and interests.

Illustration Two

Except for some occasional newspaper reading, Pat, Sandon, Monique, and Nadine were ten-year-olds who did very little reading apart from what was required.

An informal assessment of their recreational reading was conducted to assess their interests, their methods of selecting books, and their behavior while reading for pleasure. To this end, they were presented three tasks. The first was to select from a variety of books and magazines those they would prefer to read and those they would prefer not to read. The second task was to go through a basal reader and select stories or poems that interested them. The final task was to go through the newspaper in the same manner that they did at home.

In the first task, that of choosing books and magazines that they liked or disliked, they seemed reasonably sure of what they did not care to read: they immediately rejected two books on football and one about a dog. They mentioned an interest in *Black Beauty*, due to a recent television viewing of this story. Individually, they chose books on automobiles, gymnastics, mystery stories, cartoon-type paperbacks, and comics. When asked to read orally short segments of their choice from these selections, each read with obvious interest and understanding. In the second task, they each browsed through a basal reader and chose a story they would enjoy. Again, they could read this without any difficulty. Throughout this session, they talked enthusiastically about their interests, especially of cars, horses, and gymnastics.

In the final task, the students were asked to recreate their normal newspaper-reading habits with the morning paper. The students looked through the newspaper from front to back, skimming headlines, stopping once to read about a truck crash. Sandon explained he collected interesting articles from the paper, especially any dealing with cars. Sandon, Nadine, and Pat expressed interest in the comic section and listed as favorites those comics with a mininum of print. In terms of other sections of the paper, all students said that they referred to the weather forecast, the television schedule, and sometimes the advertisements. The students could answer questions about what they had read in the various sections of the newspaper.

Conclusions: The students' reading interests seem restricted to selected topics and to certain types of stories. They expressed an interest in fiction and nonfiction dealing with automobiles, horses, and gymnastics. To foster their enjoyment of reading, they might be given an opportunity to select from several books and magazines dealing with these topics. A librarian might be consulted for these purposes. To encourage the students to read this and other material, they might be introduced to new books through posters, discussions, listening experiences, films, or filmstrips. Sandon's interest in newspaper reading should continue to be encouraged and might be extended to other magazines. To this end, he might sample magazines and books from bookstores and the library. The other children should be encouraged to follow up their interests in similar ways.

FINAL COMMENTS

The diagnostic use of teaching strategies as described herein is intended neither to be exhaustive nor to represent exemplars. Rather, it is hoped that these examples will suggest other possibilities and ways most teaching can become formally and informally diagnostic.

PART 3

Strategies for Examining Teacher Effectiveness

OVERVIEW

With concern for educational accountability growing, interest has increased in improving the effectiveness of the teaching of reading. To this end, Part Three describes a number of different strategies for examining teacher effectiveness. Specifically, it describes strategies teachers and supervisors might use to analyze and appraise the teaching of reading and aspects of the reading program. This section includes a description of the following:

1. **Systematic observation methods**
2. **Self-appraisal methods**
3. **Needs assessment methods**

SYSTEMATIC OBSERVATION METHODS

Systematic observation procedures identify, classify, quantify, and analyze specific classroom behaviors and interactions. They serve as tools for obtaining data that can be used to compare intentions with actions. Basic to the use of systematic observation procedures is the notion that teachers should be aware and in control of their teaching strategies. As Ober, Bentley, and Miller (1971) suggest:

> . . . perhaps the key to using systematic observation procedure is that through the assaying process—identifying and classifying— inconsistencies in behavior and perceptions can be alleviated. (p. 16)

Toward improving teacher performance, various systematic observation methods have been advocated, all of which purport to afford teachers and supervisors a means of systematically defining, analyzing, and improving instruction (Durkin, 1979; Flanders, 1970; Medley and Mitzel, 1948; Simon and Boyer, 1970; Withall, 1949). These methods involve objective recording and analysis of teachers' and pupils' behaviors within instructional settings.

Among the scales developed for systematic observation procedures is the Reading Instruction Observation Scale (Tierney, 1976), which analyzes teacher and pupil behavior, along with the pattern, activity, and materials of reading instruction. The various aspects of this scale will be described, as an example of an observational scale.

Reading Instruction Observation Scale

The Reading Instruction Observation Scale affords an analysis of teacher and pupil behavior and an examination of the organizational pattern, activities, and materials of reading instruction.

Analysis of Teacher and Pupil Behavior

To analyze cognitive and affective aspects of teacher and pupil behavior, the Reading Instruction Observation Scale incorporates thirteen categories of behavior. Two criteria were used to select these categories. Behaviors were relevant to reading instruction and were separate from each other.

To use the scale effectively, teachers will find it helpful to keep the nature and purpose of the scale in mind. It is suggested that teachers be familiar with the behaviors analyzed, the method of tabulation, and the intended interpretation.

To record behaviors, an outside observer familiar with the scale and method of behavior tabulation is essential. It is suggested that an observer can acquire this familiarity after an hour of study and practice with the scale. Once the observer is familiar with the scale, the observational procedures involve following the teacher, and categorizing and tallying the teacher's behavior and the behavior of the students with whom the teacher interacts.

READING INSTRUCTION OBSERVATION SCALE CHECKSHEET

Pattern:

1. Whole class . . . .
2. Group . . . . No. of Groups . . . . Teacher works with (Group No.) . . . .

3. Individualized . . . . No. of individual teacher contacts . . . . No. of students involved in individualized activities . . . .

Activities:

Word-attack skills . . . . comprehension skills . . . . vocabulary activities . . . . listening skills . . . . oral reading . . . . directed silent reading . . . . free reading . . . . other activities (please specify) . . . . study skills . . . .

Materials:

Basic series . . . . workbooks . . . . worksheets . . . . supplementary books . . . . periodicals . . . newspapers . . . . supplementary series . . . . audiovisual aids (please specify) . . . . other materials (please specify) . . . .

Teacher	1	2	3	4	5	6	7	8	9	10	11	12	13	14	15	16	17	18	19	20
Directions																				
Initiates																				
Corrective																				
Criticism																				
Cognitive Mem.																				
Converg. Think.																				
Evaluat. Think.																				
Diverg. Think.																				
Narrow																				
Accepts																				
Praise or Encour.																				
Student																				
Response																				
Initiates																				
Oral Read.																				
Silent Read.																				
Activity																				
Nonfunctional																				
Confus. or Irrel.																				

Seating Plan (Note seating arrangement and student arrangement.)

Behaviors are categorized every time the behavior changes and every five seconds for any behavior that lasts longer than five seconds. The sequence of behavior is not noted. The minimum suggested observational period is twenty-five minutes. For tabulation purposes, Reading Instruction Observation Scale checksheets are used. A copy of a checksheet is shown.

For the purpose of analysis, a percentage is tabulated for each category of behavior. Each percentage represents the frequency of a behavior in proportion to the tallies for all behaviors.

A summary of the categories of behavior with a brief description of each may be helpful.

TEACHER BEHAVIORS

1. Directions: statements, commands, or orders to which a student is expected to comply
2. Initiates information or opinion: all statements regarding content or process which give information or opinion; included in this category are theoretical questions and demonstrations
3. Corrective feedback and criticism: statements that are designed to indicate the appropriateness of behavior in a way that enables the student to see that a certain behavior is incorrect or inappropriate and/or why; statements which reject student ideas or behaviors without reference to clearly identifiable authority, external of teacher opinion
4. Cognitive memory questions: questions requiring the reproduction of facts and other aspects of remembered content, through use of such processes as recognition, rote memory, and selective recall
5. Broad questions: includes three categories of questions:

   a. Convergent questions: questions requiring analysis and integration of given or remembered data through use of such processes as translation, association, explanation, and conclusion
   b. Evaluative questions: questions requiring a judgment, rating, or choice; these involve matters of judgment rather than matters of fact
   c. Divergent questions: questions requiring independent generation of ideas, of taking a new perspective or direction through use of such processes as elaboration, divergent association, and implication

6. Narrow questions: questions to which the specific nature of the response can be predicted (e.g., "yes or no" answers without clarification)
7. Accepts or uses ideas of students: statements clarifying, building, repeating, answering, or developing ideas and questions elicited by a student
8. Praise or encouragement: complimenting statements, telling students why what they have said or done is valued, encouraging students to continue, trying to give them confidence in themselves

STUDENT BEHAVIOR

9. Student response: response by student to teacher's question or the question of another student, five-second period of completion (e.g., silence following questions); student comments about either an activity which asks for information and/or procedure, or about the teacher's opinion or that of another student
10. Oral reading: instances when oral reading is done by one or more students in response to a teacher's request, directions, or command

11. Silent reading: instances when students are reading silently in response to teacher's request, suggestions, directions, or commands
12. Directed activity: other instructional activities requested or suggested by teacher

NONFUNCTIONAL BEHAVIOR

13. Confusing and irrelevant behavior: any behavior which is not related to instructional purposes (e.g., small talk, interruptions, routine)

Pattern, Activities, and Materials of Reading Instruction

Throughout the observational period, the observer also categorizes the general organizational pattern existing in the classroom, the type of activity and material being used, and the number of groups and students with which the teacher works.

Organizational Pattern

Three organizational patterns are commonly used by teachers. They include whole-class, group, and individualized formats. To assess the teacher's use of these patterns, two alternatives are suggested.

1. If an intensive analysis of the teacher's organizational pattern is sought, each category of teacher behavior can be tabulated in accordance with whether the teacher's behavior is intended for the class, for a group, or for an individual. To this end, the numbers 1, 2, and 3 replace the check marks (√) used to tally teacher and student behavior on the checksheet grid. The number 1 is used whenever the teacher engages in individualized instruction, the numbers 2 and 3 are used for group and whole-class instruction, respectively. If information is desired on the number of students a teacher contacts, tabulation based on a seating plan might be used. The seating plan would enable the observer to check either the number of students, or the number of students and the number of times the teacher interacts with individuals.

2. If a less intensive analysis of the classroom organization pattern is desired, the observer may wish merely to estimate and to note the organizational pattern used throughout the observed time period. The observer might just specify the approximate time the teacher spent in whole-class, group, and individualized instruction and the number of groups and individuals with which the teacher actually had contact. The top section of the Reading Instruction Observation Scale checksheet can be used for this purpose.

Activities and Materials

To assess the activities and materials used during reading instruction requires noting the type and amount the teacher uses. For example, to assess the nature of the activities a teacher has used, five minutes at the end of the observational period can be spent estimating the percentage of times that students under teacher direction were involved in the following: word-attack skills, vocabulary activities, comprehension skills, listening skills, oral reading, silent rereading, free reading, study skills, or other activities. A few minutes at the end of the observational period can also be spent estimating the extent to which the teacher used different material. Teachers might, for example, have used books from a basic series, workbooks, worksheets, supplementary series, audio-visual equipment, and other material.

ILLUSTRATION

To illustrate the use of the scale, this section compares the results derived from its use with the following two second-grade teachers. These teachers teach heterogeneous classes within the same school. Without trying to evaluate the worth of one over the other, what suggestions might you make to each teacher?

	TEACHER A	TEACHER B
Teacher Behaviors		
Directions	14.23%	19.80%
Initiates information	.37%	16.83%
Correction	13.87%	2.97%
Cognitive questioning	5.47%	5.94%
Broad questioning	1.83%	.99%
Narrow questioning	2.92%	3.63%
Acceptance	2.19%	5.61%
Praise	1.46%	.66%
Student Behaviors		
Responsiveness	11.68%	13.20%
Oral reading	0	14.19%
Silent reading	15.33%	0
Directed activity	0	12.21%
Nonfunctional behavior	30.66%	3.96%
Pattern		
Whole-class	50.00%	20.00%
Group time	40.00%	50.00%
Number of groups	3	4
Number of groups teacher works with	1	3
Individualized time	10.00%	30.00%
Number of individuals teacher contacts	8	25
Number of students involved in individualized activities	0	0

Activity		Activity	
Word attack skills	0%	Word attack skills	20%
Comprehension skills	30	Comprehension skills	30
Vocabulary activities	10	Vocabulary activities	10
Study skills	0	Study skills	0
Oral reading skills	0	Oral reading skills	15
Directed silent reading	15	Directed silent reading	0
Free reading	10	Free reading	20
Other (discipline)	35	Other (discipline)	5
Materials	**Use**	**Materials**	**Use**
Basic series	extensive	Basic series	extensive
Supplementary series	none	Supplementary series	none
Workbook	some	Workbook	extensive
Worksheets	extensive	Worksheets	none
Newspapers	some	Newspapers	none

Cautions and Comments

There are a number of limitations to the use of this and other scales. For example, the scale restricts its analysis to teacher-student interactions. To this end, the observer follows only teacher-directed activities and may exclude from analysis the activities of other students working independently. Second, neither this scale nor any combination of scales can analyze nuances of instruction including such things as rapport. These scales afford neither a tabulation of a teacher's sensitivity to pupils, noting some of the discrete differences that occur within categories of behavior, nor adequately define the behaviors in terms of all aspects of the classroom setting and population. Third, the classification of behaviors is done quite arbitrarily. It assumes the observer knows that intent of a teacher's questions and often their response. Finally, scales such as these provide an overview of teacher-pupil interactions. Obviously, more discrete analyses of the chain of events within a classroom need to be conducted concurrent with the intentions and interpretations of both pupils and teachers.

REFERENCES

Durkin, D. "What Classroom Observations Reveal about Reading Comprehension Instruction." *Reading Research Quarterly*, 14 (1979): 481–533.

Flanders, N. A. *Analyzing Teaching Behavior.* Reading, Mass. Addison-Wesley, 1970.

Medley, D. M., and Mitzel, H. E. "A Technique for Measuring Classroom Behavior." *Educational Psychology* 48, no. 2 (1948): 86–92.

Simon, A., and Boyer, E. G., eds., *Mirrors for Behavior: An Anthology of Observation Instruments.* Philadelphia: Classroom Interaction Newsletter, 1970.

Tierney, R. J. "A Comparison of Australian and American Reading Teachers." In J. E. Merrit, ed., *New Horizons in Reading.* Newark: International Reading Association, 1976, pp. 537–549.

Withall, J. "Development of a Technique for the Measurement of Socio-Emotional Climate in Classrooms." *Journal of Experimental Education* 57, no. 3 (1949): 347-361.

SELF-APPRAISAL SCALES FOR EXAMINING TEACHER MANAGEMENT AND INSTRUCTION

Basic to improved instruction and classroom management is teachers' self-appraisal of what they are, could, or should be doing. Toward meeting this need, various self-appraisal devices have been developed for both general and specific uses. For general use, self-appraisal scales have been developed for use across a variety of situations. For specific use, self-appraisal scales have been developed for assessing instruction and management within different and specific teaching situations. For example, Allen (1976) has developed a scale, which can be adapted for self-appraisal use, to assess the learning environment of language experience classrooms. Dishner and Searfoss (1974) have developed a scale for evaluating the use of the ReQuest procedure. This can be adapted for self-appraisal use. In Part Three a number of scales suitable for adapted self-appraisal use are included in the section entitled "Needs Assessment." Here we will describe a single scale, "Self-Appraisal Scale for Reading Teachers," which is suited to both general and specific use by teachers.

Self-Appraisal Scale for Reading Teachers

The scale serves two major purposes:

1. It affords a personal, but general, evaluation of a teacher's instructional practices
2. It provides guidelines for improving instruction, based upon personal needs within the context of specific teaching situations

To these ends, the scale provides a list of objectives against which teachers rate themselves. In rating themselves, teachers guide their own instructional improvement by a two-step process. First, teachers select from the listed objectives those they wish to concentrate upon in their teaching. Secondly, teachers consider and generate suggestions for accomplishing these objectives. The objectives are intended to be generic to most teaching situations; the situations are intended to be personal and specific to different teaching situations.

Two sections of the scale afford this two-step process. The first section lists several objectives against which teachers rank themselves. Teachers might be encouraged to differentiate between objectives by a forced ranking method. A forced ranking method would have teachers rank only a certain number of objectives: 1, 2, 3, and 4. For example, teachers might be allowed only four 1s, six 2s, six 3s, and four 4s. The second section of the scale requires teachers to select from among the objectives those needing or desiring concentration. Once selected the objectives are amplified. Amplification is accomplished by the suggestion of strategies that might be used to accomplish selected objectives.

A copy of the Self-Appraisal Scale for Reading Teachers follows:

Self-Appraisal Scale for Reading Teachers

The following objectives represent instructional skills essential to effective reading instruction. However, we often either disregard them, assume them, or fail to systematically develop and implement them. To facilitate your own refinement of these skills, complete the two sections of this scale.

SECTION ONE

Directions: Please indicate, by drawing a circle around the appropriate number, the extent to which you rate yourself on each characteristic.

1. Always
2. Most of the time
3. Sometimes
4. Seldom
5. Never

When you have finished your ranking period, proceed to Section Two.

1.	Clear explicit directions are given to students.	1 2 3 4 5
2.	Objectives and purpose of activities are made known to students as an aid to understanding.	1 2 3 4 5
3.	Student attention is maintained through a variety of activities.	1 2 3 4 5
4.	Activities facilitate the participation of all students.	1 2 3 4 5
5.	The various activities are coordinated, and there is sequential development across activities.	1 2 3 4 5
6.	A definite structure of activities is planned, but students are given some choice in selecting among appropriate activities.	1 2 3 4 5
7.	New tasks are related to familiar experiences, to previously learned tasks, and to the steps toward goals.	1 2 3 4 5
8.	Student recall is facilitated through removal of interferences.	1 2 3 4 5

9.	Student success is given immediate feedback through the activity and from the teacher	1 2 3 4 5
10.	Learning involves open communication between student and teacher	1 2 3 4 5
11.	Reinforcement is task-oriented and not student-oriented.	1 2 3 4 5
12.	Appropriate behaviors are shaped through frequent reinforcement.	1 2 3 4 5
13.	Inappropriate behavior is interpreted and extinguished through appropriate techniques.	1 2 3 4 5
14.	Questions of various types are asked.	1 2 3 4 5
15.	Students are encouraged to build upon responses.	1 2 3 4 5
16.	Techniques which match purposes for reading/task and techniques apart from teacher questioning are used to facilitate comprehension.	1 2 3 4 5
17.	Student responses are probed by various means.	1 2 3 4 5
18.	The effectiveness of the lesson is continually being evaluated (in terms of student understanding, interest, and attitude) and, when necessary, modified and restructured.	1 2 3 4 5
19.	Students are kept informed about their progress.	1 2 3 4 5
20.	Physical arrangements are adapted to the learning task at hand.	1 2 3 4 5

SECTION TWO

Indicate with a check those objectives you would like to focus on during your daily instruction for the next few weeks. Use the next part of Section Two to: (1) study some suggestions, and (2) list your own suggestions for carrying out each objective in your own situation.

1. Clear, explicit directions are given to students

   a. Think the task through before giving directions
   b. Use terms that are easily understood
   c. Speak clearly and slowly
   d. Use point form to describe what to do
   e. Have a student suggest or explain the directions
   f. (List your own)
   g.

2. Objectives and purposes of activities are made known

   a. Conduct a class discussion on the objectives
   b. Make a chart showing course objectives
   c. Briefly state the objectives at the beginning of each class period or activity
   d. Include the objective at the top of each activity sheet or assignment
   e. (List your own)
   f.

3. Student attention is maintained through a variety of activities

   a. Vary activities within class period every few minutes
   b. Vary teaching methods within period: demonstration, independent work, brain storming, research, etc.
   c. Vary group membership
   d. Rotate groups to different activities
   e. (List your own)
   f.

4. Activities facilitate the participation of all students

   a. Use multiple-response cards
   b. Pair or team students for response
   c. Use total-group response
   d. Give every student an opportunity to think about a response before selecting a student to respond
   e. (List your own)
   f.

5. The various activities are coordinated and there is sequential development across activities

   a. Give different students or groups different tasks related to a theme
   b. Build upon students' experiences
   c. Plan activities systematically, one step at a time
   d. (List your own)
   e.

6. A definite structure of activities is planned, but students are given some choice in selecting among appropriate activities

   a. Have students discuss different means to an end
   b. Have students select from prepared contracts
   c. Have students plan and organize their own learning within a framework of responsibility
   d. (List your own)
   e.

7. New tasks are related to familiar experiences, previously learned tasks, and steps toward a goal
   a. Provide opportunities for concrete experiences
   b. Provide opportunities for simulated experiences
   c. Use student discovery and discussion rather than teacher direction
   d. Pose the students problems drawn from their own realm of experience
   e. Let students look for analogous relationships between now and past learnings
   f. (List your own)
   g.

8. Student recall is facilitated through removal of interferences.
   a. Provide opportunities for students' own interpretations
   b. Keep the task within manageable limits
   c. Make practice and application meaningful
   d. Give the students an understanding of why they are doing what they are doing
   e. (List your own)
   f.

9. Student success is given immediate feedback through the activity and from the teacher
   a. Use self-checking materials
   b. Pair students for checking or monitoring
   c. Comment on material immediately in presence of students
   d. Explain to students regularly how you see they are progressing
   e. (List your own)
   f.

10. Learning involves open communication between student and teacher
   a. Establish procedures by which students can openly discuss the proposed learning activities
   b. Establish procedures by which students can express their academic and personal concerns
   c. Encourage students to establish ground rules for themselves and the class operation
   d. Give students an opportunity to respond to a questionnaire about their likes and dislikes concerning the reading program
   e. Share with students the reading you do for recreation
   f. (List your own)
   g.

11. Reinforcement is task-oriented and not student-oriented
   a. Compliment the student for the work completed
   b. Make praise and encouragement specific and not general

c. Explain to the class the work a student has accomplished
d. (List your own)
e.

12. Appropriate behaviors are shaped through frequent and varied reinforcement

a. Avoid repeating the same phrases
b. Use verbal and physical reinforcement
c. Look for things worthy of positive reinforcement, e.g., improvement, effort
d. (List your own)
e.

13. Inappropriate behavior is interpreted and extinguished through appropriate techniques

a. Understand the purpose of the student's behavior
b. Explain to the student reasonable choices from which to select
c. Disengage from reinforcing inappropriate behavior by nagging or reminding, and engage in positive reinforcement for appropriate behavior
d. (List your own)
e.

14. Questions of various types are asked

a. Avoid asking questions dealing with irrelevant information
b. Ask open-ended questions
c. Avoid questions that call for just a "yes" or "no" response
d. Ask questions that encourage the application of understanding
e. (List your own)
f.

15. Students are encouraged to build upon responses

a. Have students clarify responses
b. Have students extend responses
c. Have students examine each other's responses
d. Have students extend each other's responses
e. (List your own)
f.

16. Techniques that match purposes for reading/task and techniques apart from teacher questioning are used to facilitate comprehension

a. Have students do free recall and then probe
b. Have students question each other
c. If appropriate, have students outline
d. If appropriate, use radio plays, dramatizations, interviews, and other activities

e. Have students read different sections and explain them to each other
f. (List your own)
g.

17. Student responses are probed by various means

a. Use further questioning to clarify responses
b. Have students synthesize each other's responses
c. Have students compare and classify responses
d. (List your own)
e.

18. The effectiveness of a lesson is continuously evaluated (in terms of student acquisition of skills, interest, and attitude) and, when necessary, modified and restructured

a. Have alternative strategies in order to shift gears whenever necessary
b. Provide for differentiation of instruction
c. Provide for periodic evaluation and checks on understanding
d. (List your own)
e.

19. Students are kept informed of their progress

a. Have students keep their own records
b. Hold regular conferences with each student
c. Recap what you have done at the end of the day and what has been accomplished
d. Have the students describe their class, group, or individual progress
e. (List your own)
f.

20. Physical arrangements are adapted to the learning task at hand

a. Establish an area for learning centers and individual work
b. Reorganize the class for research work
c. Give groups the opportunity to establish their own work areas
d. Make the classroom dynamic
e. Establish a class committee for this purpose
f. (List your own)
g.

Cautions and Comments

Every reading program should have, as one of its goals, ongoing evaluation directed toward the question: Are we progressing toward our goals? Self-appraisal scales for reading teachers provide a means toward this end. In particular, they afford an examination of what exists and what might exist. They have one major advantage over the various forms of external evaluation by either supervisors or "experts." Namely, self-appraisal affords an evaluation which is non-threatening. It is non-threatening because it originates from within the program. In all, self-appraisal scales for reading teachers afford an evaluation of self, by self, for self without forfeiting the suggestion of alternatives for change. The disadvantage of self-appraisal scales is obvious—possible lack of objectivity.

REFERENCES

Allen, R. V. *Language Experiences in Communication.* Boston: Houghton Mifflin, 1976.

Dishner, E. K., and Searfoss, L. W. Request Evaluation Form. Unpublished paper, Arizona State University, 1974.

NEEDS ASSESSMENT

Needs assessment addresses the formal and informal evaluation of programs. It can be done within classrooms and across school reading programs at all levels. On a formal basis, it can be planned and periodical. Informally, it can be done on a daily basis as the needs of programs arise and are met. Regardless of the level of formality, needs assessment provides ongoing monitoring of the progress being made with a specific population at a specific time.

To provide for an understanding of needs assessment methods, the following example of a formal needs assessment conducted for a junior high school reading program is given. The illustration includes:

1. A description of the steps involved in a formal needs assessment
2. Examples of selected questionnaires used in the needs assessment
3. The report generated by the needs assessment

This example is not intended to be definitive, but suggests the scope of needs assessment both formally and informally.

Steps Involved in Formal Needs Assessment of Progress—Junior High

The steps used to conduct the needs assessment were as follows:

a. The dimensions of the needs assessment were discussed with the school staff; it was suggested that the needs assessment was to be comprehensive and a team effort and that it was intended to address the needs of the reading program and to establish ongoing needs assessment practices

b. The potential sources and methods of the needs assessment were established
c. Data using systematic and nonsystematic needs assessment methods were collected; systematic observational methods, interviews, self-appraisal methods, questionnaires, and attitude scales were used
d. The data were organized and a synthesis presented to the faculty
e. The comments of the faculty were used to formulate recommendations, to develop ongoing needs assessment methods, and to develop a report

Examples of Selected Questionnaires[1]

Among the data collection tools used in the formal needs assessment were various questionnaires, self-appraisal scales, and attitude questions. Here are some selected examples of the questionnaires used.

a. Needs assessment questionnaire for teachers, aides, and the program coordinator
b. A subject area teacher's questionnaire
c. A questionnaire for administrators and supervisors
d. A student's questionnaire

NEEDS ASSESSMENT QUESTIONNAIRE FOR TEACHERS, AIDES, AND COORDINATORS

Current Assignment (e.g., teacher; aide) ______ Number of College Courses or Workshops (credit) in Reading ______

The following scale is meant to provide a framework for evaluating the reading program and to suggest possible areas which might be examined in assessing the needs of the reading program. The use and completion of this scale should be approached with the following understandings:

1. Needs assessment is meant to be supportive
2. The information will be examined objectively, keeping in mind that reading programs are expected to differ since they attempt to serve the needs of learners in a specific place at a specific time

Please respond to this as completely as you can.
A thoughtful response is desirable.

1. Define the program objectives as you see them.

1. Selected forms and the evaluation report are based on those prepared by Robert J. Tierney and Joseph L. Vaughan in a collaborative effort for Tucson School District No. 1.

2. Describe the nature of each of the following people's input into the program's goals.

   Rank: 1–much input
   2–some input
   3–little input
   4–no input

Teachers	1 2 3 4	Librarian	1 2 3 4
Aides	1 2 3 4	Students	1 2 3 4
Coordinator	1 2 3 4	Content area	
Principal	1 2 3 4	teacher	1 2 3 4
Parents	1 2 3 4	Other (specify)	1 2 3 4
School-district administrator	1 2 3 4		

3. What diagnostic devices do you use in your reading program? Check the appropriate ones and describe how you use the information you obtain from each device.

_____Informal reading inventories. Specify use.

_____Published reading tests. Specify test(s).

Specify use.

_____Records from other teachers. Specify use.

_____Teacher-made tests. Specify test(s).

Specify use.

_____Other. Describe.

Specify use.

4. a. Specify the reading materials that you use.

Items	*Publisher*	*Difficulty Level*	*Use Made of Material*

b. Which of the above do you find most helpful? Indicate by placing an asterisk to the left of the most helpful item(s).

5. a. Specify the percentage of time that you spend on each of the following activities over the school week.

   b. Describe your activities.

%	*Type of activities*
_____	Administrative duties:
_____	Testing students:
_____	Teaching students:
_____	Conducting individual student conferences:
_____	Organizing for instruction:
_____	Other:

6. When appropriate, indicate by circling the appropriate number.

   a. Specific practices in reading to be followed by the reading program are specified by:

1. Program director	4. Principal
2. Title I evaluators	5. Teacher
3. Title I coordinators	6. Other; please specify.

   b. Reading material used in the reading program is specified by:

1. Program director	4. Principal
2. Title I evaluator	5. Teacher
3. Title I coordinator	6. Other; please specify

7. a. Personnel providing for supervision of reading program include:

1. Principal	4. Title I coordinator
2. Program director	5. Teacher
3. Title I evaluator	6. Other; please specify.

   b. List personnel providing pertinent suggestions relative to improving your reading program. List:

c. On the average, how long is the reading period for a reading class? Specify:

d. How much time during the school week does a single reader have for free reading? Specify:

e. For how much time during the school week does a single reading class receive study skills instruction? Specify:

f. Describe how the students are grouped in a single reading class. Specify:

g. Give the number of reading groups in a single reading class. Specify:

h. Give the number of students shifted to different groups since school started. Specify:

8. Evaluation of Program, Materials, Equipment, and Practices

Directions: Evaluate your reading program on each item listed below by circling the appropriate number on the four-point rating scale.

1—I am satisfied with this
2—This needs some improvement
3—This needs much improvement
4—This is nonexistent, or nearly so

1. Pattern of organizing within the classroom for reading instruction	1	2	3	4
2. Materials available for use in the program	1	2	3	4
3. Library books and other supplementary materials available	1	2	3	4
4. Teacher knowledge of how to teach reading effectively	1	2	3	4
5. Time available for reading instruction	1	2	3	4

6. Extent to which students enjoy reading	1	2	3	4
7. Extent to which testing program assists in reading instruction	1	2	3	4
8. Extent to which parents are interested in reading program	1	2	3	4
9. Extent to which parents are involved in program	1	2	3	4
10. Extent to which supervisors are involved and provide support	1	2	3	4
11. Extent to which aides provide support	1	2	3	4
12. Extent to which principal provides support	1	2	3	4
13. Extent to which supervisor provides support	1	2	3	4
14. Extent to which content-area teachers are involved in program	1	2	3	4
15. Extent to which content-area teachers are interested in program	1	2	3	4
16. Extent to which evaluators assist program	1	2	3	4
17. Extent to which staff has input on use of finances	1	2	3	4
18. Extent to which program is related to specific needs of all the individuals within program	1	2	3	4
19. Extent to which you are familiar with goals of program	1	2	3	4
20. Overall evaluation of program	1	2	3	4

9. In order to improve the reading program, what changes would you make to the following:

Goals of the Reading Program

Testing Procedures

Teaching Procedures

Materials and Facilities

Supervision

Support Personnel

Staff Development

Content Teachers' Involvement in Program

Community Involvement

Parent Involvement

Needs Assessment

Any other reactions to the reading program would be appreciated.

RATING SCALE FOR EVALUATING RESPONSIBILITIES IN READING INSTRUCTION[2]
(Based on Scale Developed by Ira E. Aaron)

Directions: Selected responsibilities of teacher, principal, librarian, superintendent, supervisor, and parents are listed below. Indicate by circling the appropriate number the extent to which a given person reflects each characteristic or meets each responsibility.

Use the following ratings:

1—Almost always
2—Most of the time
3—Sometimes
4—Seldom or never
5—Undecided
6—Not applicable in program

2. I. E. Aaron, "Evaluation and Accountability." In J. E. Merritt, ed., *New Horizons in Reading.* (Newark, Del.: International Reading Association, 1976) pp. 558–564. Reprinted with permission of the International Reading Association.

Teacher's Responsibilities: The teacher . . .

1. Aims reading instruction toward achievement of specific goals	1	2	3	4	5	6
2. Adapts reading instruction to the individual levels, abilities, and needs of all students	1	2	3	4	5	6
3. Uses diagnostic-perscriptive approach in reading instruction	1	2	3	4	5	6
4. Establishes a good working relationship with students	1	2	3	4	5	6
5. Merges materials and equipment into a total program	1	2	3	4	5	6
6. Understands the nature of the reading process	1	2	3	4	5	6
7. Leads students toward enjoyment in reading	1	2	3	4	5	6
8. Evaluates progress in reading in terms of instructional goals	1	2	3	4	5	6
9. Organizes the classroom for effective management of reading instruction	1	2	3	4	5	6
10. Informs parents about the reading program and about the individual progress of their children	1	2	3	4	5	6

Principal's Responsibilities: The principal . . .

11. Leads in developing and conducting of needs assessment of school reading program	1	2	3	4	5	6
12. Leads in directing changes in reading program based on needs assessment	1	2	3	4	5	6
13. Converses knowledgeably with teachers and parents about the school's reading program and practices	1	2	3	4	5	6
14. Assists teachers in obtaining needed teaching materials	1	2	3	4	5	6
15. Leads in planning necessary staff development for teachers	1	2	3	4	5	6
16. Taps all available resources for assistance for teachers	1	2	3	4	5	6
17. Encourages teachers to move toward excellence in reading instruction	1	2	3	4	5	6
18. Observes classroom teaching for instructional effectiveness	1	2	3	4	5	6

19. Creates an atmosphere that encourages teachers to seek help when help is needed	1	2	3	4	5	6
20. Identifies leaders among the teachers who will assist in coordinating efforts in reading	1	2	3	4	5	6

Librarian's Responsibilities: The librarian . . .

21. Plans with teachers for reading support programs and for gathering materials (media) to support these programs	1	2	3	4	5	6
22. Assists teachers in knowing what materials are in the library and in making requests for purchasing materials	1	2	3	4	5	6
23. Confers with teachers on reading abilities of individual students and assists students with reading guidance	1	2	3	4	5	6
24. Works out with teachers an efficient system for a constant flow of materials to and from the classroom	1	2	3	4	5	6
25. Teams with teachers to introduce, teach, or reinforce certain skills according to individual or group needs	1	2	3	4	5	6
26. Cooperates with principal in suggesting and obtaining professional materials	1	2	3	4	5	6
27. Aids in staff development programs for teachers by providing materials and information on use of materials	1	2	3	4	5	6

Content-Area Teacher's Responsibilities: The content-area teacher . . .

28. Understands the demands of text within specific subject area	1	2	3	4	5	6
29. Provides students aids for dealing with content	1	2	3	4	5	6
30. Continues to work toward the development of each student's reading-study skills	1	2	3	4	5	6

Supervisor's Responsibilities: The reading supervisor . . .

31. Assists in keeping teachers and principals abreast of new materials and developments in the area of reading	1	2	3	4	5	6

32. Assists principals in planning and conducting staff development in the area of reading for teachers and aides	1	2	3	4	5	6
33. Prepares and works with leaders in each school who will in turn work with teachers	1	2	3	4	5	6
34. Assists the superintendent in motivating principals and teachers to move toward excellence in reading instruction	1	2	3	4	5	6
35. Assists the superintendent in motivating principals and teachers to try out new or different practices if they offer promise for improvement	1	2	3	4	5	6
36. Creates an atmosphere that encourages teachers and principals to request help when help is needed	1	2	3	4	5	6
37. Observes instruction to locate "promising practices" and to assist in improving reading instruction	1	2	3	4	5	6
38. Provides leadership in evaluating the total reading program of the school system	1	2	3	4	5	6

Superintendent's Responsibilities: The superintendent . . .

39. Sees that adequate staff development for reading instruction is planned for system schools	1	2	3	4	5	6
40. Sees that all school personnel are motivated to move toward excellence in teaching reading	1	2	3	4	5	6
41. Sees that adequate personnel and materials for teaching reading effectively are available	1	2	3	4	5	6
42. Sees that persons making system-wide decisions about reading are representative of groups affected and are well qualified	1	2	3	4	5	6

Parents' Responsibilities: The parents . . .

43. Work toward building concept backgrounds in their children	1	2	3	4	5	6
44. Encourage their children to read	1	2	3	4	5	6
45. Read to their children and let children see them reading	1	2	3	4	5	6
46. Learn about the reading programs of their children	1	2	3	4	5	6

SUBJECT AREA TEACHER'S QUESTIONNAIRE

1. What subject area do you teach?

2. When you are in your own classroom, do you make efforts to teach reading as well as your subject area?

   Circle One: YES (go to question 3)
   NO (go to question 4)

3. Briefly describe what you do.

4. Briefly explain why you do not.

5. How would you rate this reading program in terms of its effectiveness?

   Circle One: a–excellent b–good c–average d–fair e–poor

6. On what do you base this evaluation? (Be specific.)

7. What improvements do you think can be made in this reading program?

8. How can you help implement these improvements?

9. In what other ways can you help improve this program?

10. How do you perceive your role relative to this reading program?

QUESTIONNAIRE FOR ADMINISTRATORS AND SUPERVISORS

Name:

1. What is your position?

2. How would you rate this reading program in terms of its effectiveness?

   Circle One: a–excellent b–good c–average d–fair e–poor

3. On what do you base this evaluation? (Be specific.)

4. What improvements do you think can be made in this reading program?

5. How can you help implement these improvements?

6. In what other ways can you help improve this program?

7. How do you perceive your role relative to this reading program?

8. In what ways are you specially qualified to supervise, direct, or evaluate this reading program?

STUDENT'S QUESTIONNAIRE

______________	______________	______________	________
(School)	(Grade)	(Period)	(Date)

1. How much has this reading class helped improve your reading ability? Circle the appropriate letter.
   a. A great deal
   b. Somewhat
   c. A little
   d. Not at all

2. How long have you been in this reading program?

3. List those things you *like most* about this reading class.

4. List those things you *dislike* about this reading class.

5. Describe the three activities you do most often in this reading class:
   a.
   b.
   c.

6. What suggestions could you make to your teacher that would improve this class?

Report Based upon a Needs Assessment

The following needs assessment report of the Junior High Reading Program was developed by synthesizing observational data and recommendations collected from:

1. Persons directly involved with the program
2. Persons indirectly involved with the program
3. Persons acting as outside observers

....

NEEDS ASSESSMENT REPORT
PROGRESS JUNIOR HIGH READING PROGRAM

The observations, evaluation, and recommendations collated in this report are intended as supportive information to direct improvements in the existing program.

Observation by Categories

The following observations are based upon a synthesis of the data derived from teacher and aide questionnaires, student questionnaires, interviews, and both systematic and nonsystematic observations of the reading program.

I. *Objectives*

1. The program is directed toward improving the reading ability of students, specifically in terms of those reading skills necessary for reading with understanding, recreational reading, and effective living.
2. The program lacks a comprehensive statement of objectives dealing with the cognitive and affective aspects of reading, reading needs in the content areas, survival reading skills, and study and research skills.
3. Interested teachers, parents, content-area teachers, students, and other resource people have had little input into the goals of the program.
4. There is no mechanism for either formulating program objectives and program plans, or for gathering input from all interested and involved persons.

II. *Materials*

1. Extensive use is made of basals, high-interest and low-vocabulary material, supplementary skills material, reading series and library material. These materials are of various reading and interest levels. The high-interest, low vocabulary material and library material are used extensively for free reading purposes. Basals, kits, and supplementary skills material are used in conjunction with comprehension (DRTA and cloze) and worksheet activities.
2. The teachers utilize a wide variety of these materials in their instructional program. However, there appears to be more material available than is used.

3. There appears to be a limited amount of variations in the actual uses made of instructional material. For example: (1) worksheets appear to be the predominant activity used with much of the material; (2) DRTAs seem to be the predominant activity used with story selections.
4. Magazines and other periodicals are not among the materials available in the reading centers. Newspapers are available and used.
5. Application forms and "everyday" reading matter (e.g., T.V. guides and schedules) also are not among the materials incorporated into the center's instructional program.
6. Staff members appear satisfied with the material that is available. Some suggest the need for more high-interest, low-vocabulary material for lower ability students. Some suggest the need to become more familiar with the material and its uses.
7. There is apparently no use made of audiovisual equipment.

III. *Organization for Instruction*

1. Physical location:
   a. Physical location of the reading center appears ideal in terms of: (1) the library's accessibility and (2) the accessibility of the reading center to the content teachers. Already, the library is an integral part of the reading program. Library and reading center staff have an excellent working relationship.
   b. The furnishings within the center are adequate. There is an abundance of shelf space, chalkboard space, and display areas and an ample number of carrels, magazine racks and tables and chairs which can be easily rearranged. Unfortunately, this equipment and these areas are not used to their full extent. Indeed, the center appears rather static.
2. Students are organized in groups for instructional purposes. These groups are determined by reading levels and by student personality. Those students involved in the upper and middle group are divided into smaller groups for instructional purposes. The lowest group remains largely intact for these purposes.
3. There appears to be a genuine desire for individualization. However, most assignments do not vary within the group situations (except in the area of free reading).
4. The three aides provide assistance to all three of the reading center teachers. One aide spends most of the time completing administrative chores and undertaking home visitations.
5. Teachers spend only 40–50% of their available time actually teaching the students. Two of the aides spend approximately 50% of their time teaching students. The teachers spend approximately 20–35% of their time involved in administrative activities. Those aides who are involved mainly in teaching spend 5–10% of their time in administrative activities.
6. Student records are considered up-to-date. However, they are not used as a guide for daily teaching. On a day-to-day basis, the student's work-

sheets are filed in individual student folders, but there appears to be a great deal of variation in the amount of material in the different folders.

7. There is no involvement of the content teachers in the reading program.
8. Parent involvement is restricted to monitoring of homework, a home visitation program, and a rather ineffectual parent advisory committee.

IV. *Diagnosis*

1. The staff members vary in the extent to which they consider the testing program of assistance to the reading program.
2. Extensive testing of the students' reading ability is undertaken at the commencement and at the completion of the school year via informal devices (IRI), standardized tests, and a teacher-made test. This consumes 9–12 weeks of school time at the beginning of the year.
3. Interest and student-attitude inventories and parent questionnaires are not included as diagnostic strategies.
4. Within the instructional setting, minimal use is made of the individually derived data obtained at the commencement of the school year. Rather, these data are used in terms of prescribing the program for group instruction.
5. Teaching is not done in terms of constant diagnosis. Up-to-date diagnostic information derived from instruction is lacking.
6. Likewise, specific skills and abilities needing diagnosis do not appear to be specified.
7. Student progress as it relates to free reading is recorded on a regular basis by both student and teacher.

V. *Instruction*

1. Skill instruction was apparent, but did not appear to be either systematic or sequential (especially in terms of an individual student's skill needs).
2. Skills that were taught did not appear to include sufficient study skills and content-area reading skills.
3. The major instructional activity appears to revolve around the use of the DRTA with basal type stories and worksheets involving cloze, vocabulary, word-recognition, and miscellaneous acitivities.
4. The DRTA appears to be used very effectively in terms of improving pupil reading comprehension abilities.
5. Instructional activities are interesting, somewhat effective, and appropriate in terms of the level of difficulty. However, these activities do not appear to be greatly challenging, varied, or related to the experiences of the students.
6. During selected instructional activities (mainly worksheet-type activities), teachers appear to be grading student performance rather than guiding learning in terms of the students' out-of-school experiences.
7. Free reading is an integral part of the instructional program.

8. A star chart, parent monitoring of students' "home reading," and teacher-student conferences are integral to the free reading program. Unfortunately, teacher-student conferences do not appear to be greatly varied and students are not given sufficient nor varied opportunity to share their book with their peers (either orally or by poster display or other means).
9. The librarian plans and assists the teachers in gathering and suggesting materials.
10. In terms of specific teaching behaviors, on the one hand teachers are accepting of student responses and involve the student in purposeful reading activities. On the other hand, students' responses are not extended. Praise, though it is present, is not extensive.
11. Teachers have good rapport with their students.
12. Interaction between students, either within or across instructional groups, is rare.
13. Students appear to lack self-direction. They enter the reading clinic not knowing what to do and wait till the roll check is completed before they become involved in meaningful activity.
14. Students do not appear to be given many opportunities for input into the program.

In summary, the reading program appears to be reading-based, but the activities are not varied in terms of student interests, skill needs, or potential.

VI. *Attitudes*

1. As revealed by the Estes Attitude Scale (Reading Subtest), the majority of students enrolled in the reading program have an above-average attitude toward reading
2. As revealed by the student questionnaire, the majority of students consider the reading program either "somewhat" helpful or greatly helpful.
3. The attitude of the students toward benefits derived from the reading program did not vary according to the number of years the students had been enrolled in the program. The proportion of students who responded positively remained relatively the same for students who had been enrolled in the program for either one or two years.
4. As indicated by the subject-area teachers' questionnaire and attitude scale, twelve of the fourteen content-area teachers responded that they made an effort to teach reading in their subject area and indicated that they had a positive attitude toward this. Their responses indicated that these persons are sensitive to the reading difficulties incurred by their students, and use a number of instructional strategies as an aid to reading in their subject areas. In the main, these strategies were restricted to vocabulary activities, cloze, and guided reading.
5. As indicated by their questionnaires, the principal, vice principal, and two counselors have very positive attitudes toward the reading program and would like to contribute in either an administrative or supervisory capacity to the program. They made a number of suggestions relative to improvements to the reading program. These included: (1) giving the faculty more

opportunity for input relative to direction of the reading program; (2) spending less time testing pupils; (3) providing inservice training for aides; and (4) involving the content-area teachers in the reading program.

RECOMMENDATIONS BY GROUP

I. Reading Center Staff Recommendations:

The following specific suggestions and strong recommendations were compiled from the questionnaire completed by the staff of the reading center.

Suggestions:

1. Better prescription in terms of what teachers can and cannot do
2. More efficient use of the staff and aides' time
3. Clearer delineation of the directions of the program
4. Improvement in the pattern of organizing classes
5. Smaller classes or more staff to facilitate more concentrated work
6. Improvement of staff's knowledge of remediation strategies, materials available, and methods of using material

Strong Recommendations:

1. Provision of more supervisory feedback
2. Provision of more time for inservice education and planning
3. Provision of more high-interest material to students of lower reading abilities
4. Extending the involvement of parents in the reading program
5. Involving the content-area teachers in the reading program
6. Streamlining initial diagnostic procedures and reducing initial testing time

II. Students' Recommendations:

The following information was derived from the questionnaire completed by the students.

Likes:

1. Free reading was cited consistently as being liked
2. Several other instructional activities were favored by students, including DRTA, cloze, language experience, study skills
3. Other likes cited included: the library and quiet

Dislikes:

1. Worksheets were cited consistently as being disliked
2. Selected students suggested they disliked having to request their parent to monitor their home reading

Suggestions:

1. More library, more fun activities, more reading, and new books
2. Fewer worksheets and new worksheets
3. Less DRTA (it should be noted that this is inconsistent with "Likes," no. 2)

4. More opportunity for free talk
5. Being placed in smaller groups to work together

III. Recommendations from the Evaluation Team:

The four members of the evaluation team concurred on the following recommendations. These recommendations represent a synthesis of the findings: (1) derived from the various questionnaires and scales completed by persons directly and indirectly involved in the reading program; and (2) the subjective and systematic observation by the evaluation team.

1. Extend the program to involve the content-area teachers. Not only should the content-area teachers become involved in the reading center, but also the reading center personnel should become involved in the content-area classes. One should consider such involvement "a two-way street."
2. Increase the continuity of instruction via the integration of diagnoses and instruction.
3. Make instructional activities more functional, challenging, and student-centered.
4. Continue the emphasis upon free reading, but vary the format of the student-teacher conferences. Provide the students opportunities to share books with their peers and develop motivational strategies to further their reading.
5. Provide subject-area teachers, parents, and reading-center faculty opportunities for input into the program's directions.
6. Vary instructional strategies, and make fuller use of the potential of the center and pupils. For example, pupils might be encouraged to develop posters, newspapers, etc. A reading area might be added to the center. This area might include beanbag-type furniture, an old lounge, etc. Greater use could be made of display areas, carrels, and chalkboards.
7. The excellent relationship with and use made of the library should continue to be fostered.
8. Identify procedures for ongoing evaluation of the reading program, and supervisory procedures by which promising instructional practices can be introduced, encouraged, and implemented.

Cautions and Comments

Needs assessment should be viewed within the framework of the ongoing evaluation of a reading program. To this end, needs assessment should meet the requirements for evaluation:

1. Needs assessment should address the needs of a specific program at a specific time in a specific situation
2. If it is to be effective as a catalyst for change, needs assessment must afford a knowledge of the program as well as a knowledge of alternatives
3. If suggestions for change are to be meaningful, they should be in harmony with the goals and values of a program

4. Finally, evaluation should be an ongoing procedure, originating from within a program

Given these assumptions, the needs assessment procedure and report described in the present unit should be viewed as an example, rather than as an exemplar of procedures to be used by school personnel.

APPENDIX

Examples and Activities to Accompany Selected Strategies and Practices

Examples of Study Guides

STUDY GUIDE

"New Frontiers—The Kennedy Years"

SECTION I

Match the strategy in Column B with the appropriate heading in Column A.

A. *Topic*	B. *Strategy*
_____1. Neutralist Laos	a. The CIA believed that a landing of a Cuban exile force would touch off an uprising against Castro.
_____2. Alliance for Progress	b. In foreign affairs, Kennedy continued to follow the policy of "containment" and a cautious continuation of the New Deal and the Fair Deal.
_____3. The New Frontier	c. They did work as varied as laying out sewage systems in Bolivia . . . Above all, they were teachers of English and practical skills.
_____4. The Berlin Wall	
_____5. The Peace Corps	
_____6. The First Cuban Crisis	

B. *Strategy* (continued)

d. The willingness to accept a neutralist regime.

e. Over a ten-year period, the United States proposed to help themselves by improving their schools, housing, and other areas.

f. In mid-October the President received aerial photographs that showed the Russians were building missile bases in the Western Hemisphere.

SECTION II

Below is a list of legislative successes and failures. Identify those that President Kennedy was successful in getting Congress to pass (P) and those that were not passed (NP). You will find useful information in the page(s) noted after each item.

_______ Large subsidies to public schools in 1961 and 1962. (750)

_______ Medicare bill to provide hospital services for the aged to be paid for by Social Security taxes. (750)

_______ Funds for slum clearance and aid to distressed areas. (750)

_______ Increase the minimum wage level from $1.00 to $1.25 per hour. (750)

_______ Funds for the Peace Corps. (750–752)

_______ Increased appropriations for defense and the accelerated missile program. (750, 769–770)

SECTION III

Questions for Group Discussion

After everyone has completed Sections I and II above, you will be assigned to a group for the purpose of discussing the following items. Insights gleaned from your outside readings may be needed, along with the material in your text, in order to answer these questions.

1. Why did Kennedy resort to a naval quarantine of Cuban waters instead of an air strike?
2. Why do you think the Organization of American States (OAS) endorsed Kennedy's action in the second Cuban crisis?
3. Can you provide at least three reasons why the Soviets erected the Berlin Wall?
4. What do you think President Johnson meant when he said he thought what was needed was to put America on "the road to the Great Society"?

5. During the Kennedy administration, a form of military doctrine evolved called the Graduated, Flexible Response Doctrine; can you identify a situation in which it was applied and suggest other ways in which it can be applied?

Why does Nathaniel Hawthorne use a pattern of contrast in the opening chapters of *The Scarlet Letter?* (pgs. 34–42)

ORGANIZATIONAL PATTERN: CONTRAST

Society	*Word of Contrast*	*Individual*
"the black flower of civilized society, a prison" p. 35		p. 35
"The grim rigidity of the faces of the on-lookers indicated an execution." p. 35		p. 35
p. 36		". . . a penalty which, in our day, would infer a degree of mocking infamy and ridicule." p. 36
p. 38		"It was artistically done, and with so much fertility and gorgeous luxuriance of fancy . . . had the effect of a last and fitting decoration . . ." p. 38
p. 39		"Her attire . . . seemed to express the attitude of her spirit . . ." p. 39
". . . she perchance underwent an agony from every footstep of those that thronged to see her." p. 40		p. 40
p. 41		"Had a roar of laughter burst from the multitude . . . Hester Prynne might have repaid them all with a bitter and disdainful smile." p. 41

Examples of Structured Overviews

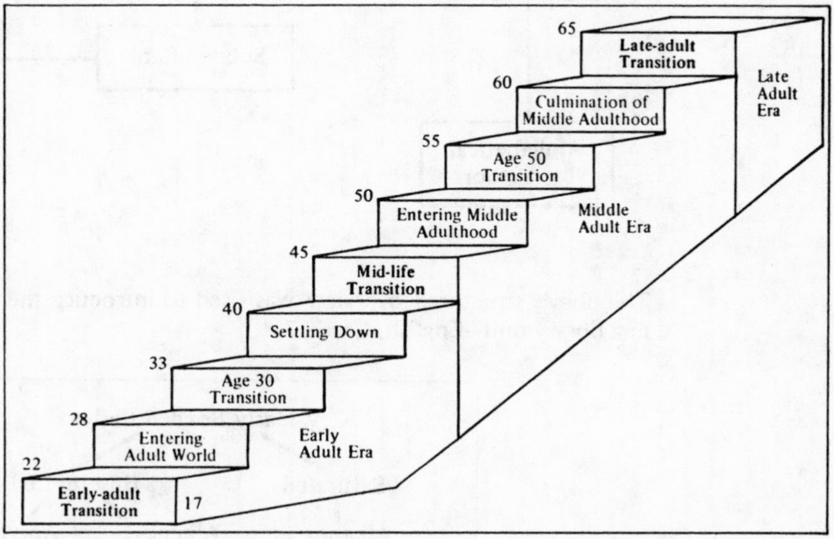

The above structured overview was developed following the reading of *The Seasons of Man's Life*, D. J. Levinson, C. N. Dawson, E. B. Klein, M. H. Levinson, and B. McKee. New York: Alfred A. Knopf, 1978.

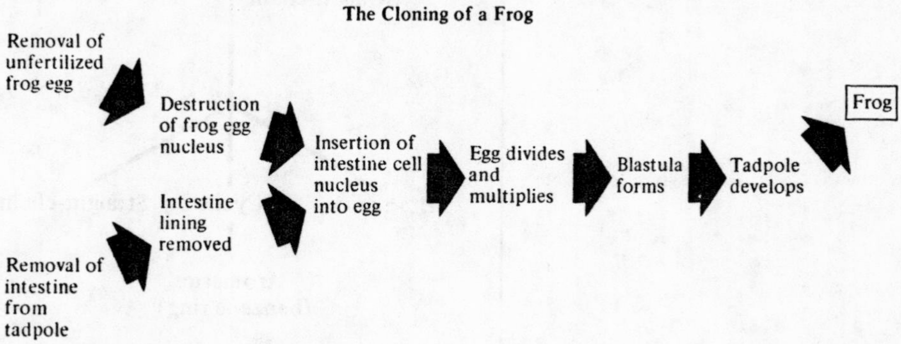

The above structured overview was developed following research on cloning.

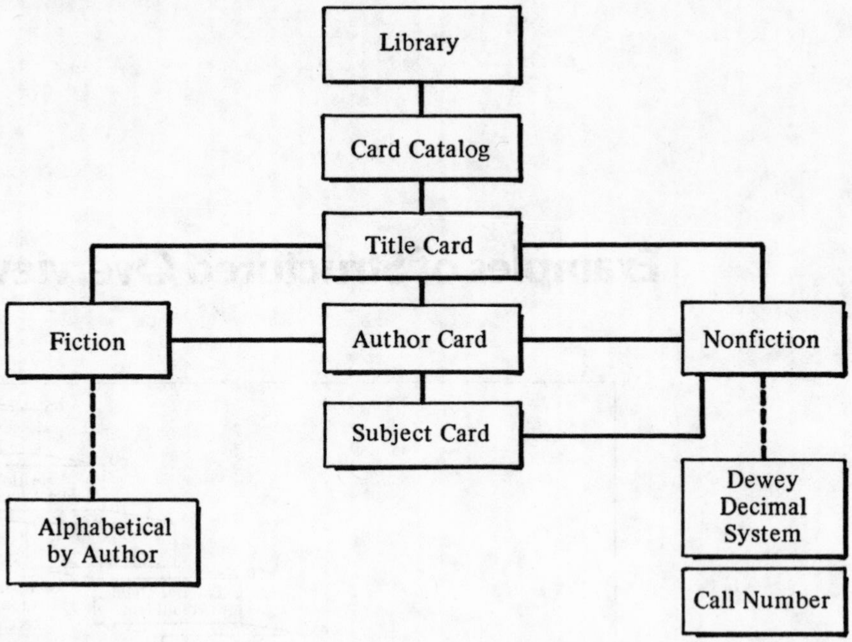

The above structured overview was used to introduce the use of the card catalog in a library unit—English, Grade 7.

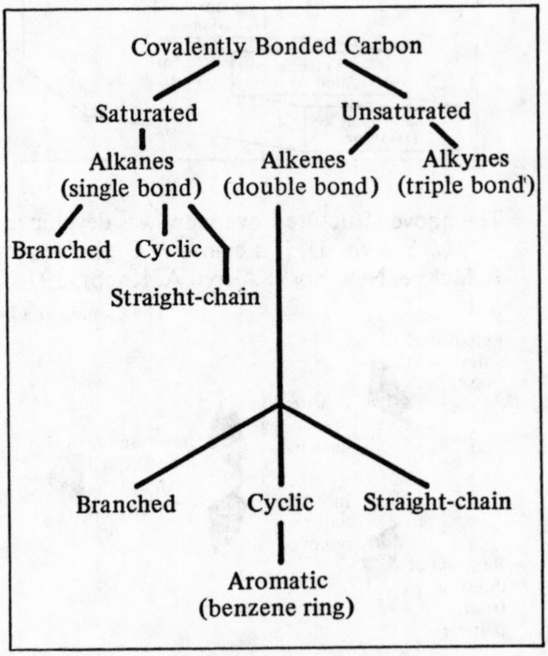

The above structured overview was used as part of an introduction to a chapter on "Hydrocarbons" in a chemistry class.

Example of Guide-O-Rama

GUIDE-O-RAMA

Chapter 3: "How the Romans Gave Us Government: Respect for Law and Justice," pp. 51-60.[1]

Pages 51-53.
Look at the picture on page 51 and then read this section quickly to get a feel of Roman life. Pay special attention to the following terms: toga (page 51), Forum (page 52), Senator (page 52), Law Court (page 53), and Law (page 53).

Page 54.
Look at the map on this page and find the city of Rome, the island of Sicily, and the Apennine Mountains.

Pages 54-55.
Read the section entitled "Who were the Romans?" to see how the country was settled.

Page 54, par. 1.
Pay particular attention to the word "peninsula."

Pages 55-56.
Just read the sentences that are in boldfaced print on these pages. I will discuss the other information on these pages in class.

Page 58, col. 2.
Read the first two paragraphs carefully. You will need to know the two classes of citizens in Rome. Read the remainder of this page for a detailed description of the two classes.

1. McClellan, Jack. *Your World and Mine.* (Boston: Ginn, 1965).

Page 59, col. 2, par. 1.
Read this carefully to discover what the "Laws of the Twelve Tables" were.

Page 59, col. 2, par. 2.
Read this paragraph to find out what the term "veto" means.

Suggestions for Setting Purposes for Reading

The method you select should be based upon your analysis of a story's characteristics, student needs, and student capabilities.

1. Present students with a story or selection title and have them predict what the story will tell.
2. Present students with a few key words from the story and have them predict what the story will be.
3. Present students with a few key sentences from the story and have them predict the context and what the story will tell.
4. Present students with a few key but incomplete sentences, and have them predict the completion and what the story will tell.
5. Present students with setting, place, time, and characters and have them predict events of the story, or vice-versa.
6. Present students in random order either pictures depicting the events, sentences describing the events, or a combination of the two. Have students predict the order of events.
7. Present students a list of causes and a list of effects and have them suggest the right sequence.
8. Have students read varying portions of the text material and predict outcomes.
9. Have students read either the introductory paragraph, the middle section, the last paragraph, or a combination and predict the story context.
10. Have students study picture(s) and predict story content.
11. Present students with an incomplete picture and have them predict either its completion or the story that accompanies it.
12. Have students predict as many different events as they can which may precede, occur simultaneously, or follow the action depicted in either a picture or a paragraph.

13. Present the students a picture, title, or segment of a text, or a combination of these, and have the students generate as many different questions as possible that have not yet been answered in the text.
14. Present the students a story depicted in cartoon frames and have the students complete the captions.
15. Present cartoon frame captions to the students and have them predict the cartoon frames.
16. Present the students a story and have them predict the pictures that accompany it.
17. Delete the middle, the introduction, or the ending of a story and have students predict or write a replacement.
18. Delete the middle, introduction, or ending of the story and present students with several options as replacements. Have students predict the most likely option or have them arrange the options in order of predictability.
19. Have a student or a group of students read the selection. Present a title picture or portion of the story to other students, allowing them to question the first students on what the story might tell. Establish rules by which only a certain number of questions are asked and allow students responding to questions to give either a "yes" or "no" response.
20. Present the students various descriptive words, phrases, and sentences, and have them categorize by prediction the characters, the events, or the setting. Have students read the selection to compare their categories.

Suggestions for Word Box Use

1. Alphabetize words in word banks.
2. Match the word with the same word as it occurs in newpapers, magazines, etc.
3. Make a poster of the words known. A profile of the student can be drawn from the known words.
4. Complete sentences using word banks. Provide students with a stem or incomplete sentences and have students fill slot with as many different words as possible. Example:
   He ran to the _____. The _____and _____ran into the park.
5. Find or categorize words in word banks:

   naming words
   action words
   descriptive words
   words with more than one meaning
   words with the same meaning
   opposites
   everyday words
   people words
   science words
   color words
   animal words
   names of people
   Interesting words
   funny words
   happy words
   exciting words

6. Organize words into small books or posters. Have pupils make a dictionary, picture dictionary, or books for certain categories of words.
7. Locate words beginning the same, ending the same, or meaning the same.
8. Locate words with various endings.

9. Complete sentences using different-category words. Example: Today I am _______ (feeling word). Juan _______ (action word).

10. Match sentences in stories with words from word bank.

11. Make punctuation cards. Locate and match punctuation in stories.

12. Describe cartoon captions with words from word banks.

    Where are you _____?

    I am leaving for the _____

    I wonder what they _____

13. Organize captions and titles for pictures and cartoon frames, using words from word banks.

14. Organize words from word banks into complete sentences.

We	drove	to	the	farm	.

15. Organize words into sentences, commands, and questions.

We	went	to	the	farm	.
Where	are	we	going	?	
Go	to	the	farm	!	

16. Have students describe someone or something, using words from the word banks separately or organized into sentences. Have other students guess the person or thing.

17. Have students select a word from their word bank and use it in as many different sentences as possible.

18. Have students play dominoes with each other's words.

pot	Tom	mother

19. Use word bank cards for matching-card games, such as grab and bingo.

20. Form phrases using words from different categories. For example, select a color word and have students find as many words as they can which match.

21. Organize words into a story. Students might need to borrow words for this use and may wish to illustrate or make a permanent record of it.

22. Delete words from a story. Have other students use words from their word banks to complete the story.

23. Scramble the sentences in the story and have students rearrange them in an appropriate order.

24. Scramble the words in a student's sentence and have other students unscramble them.

25. Illustrate different stories and have students describe a story with their word cards. Have students match the illustration with the word cards.

26. Complete stories with sentences formed by the word cards.

27. Create a silent movie with word cards for captions.

28. Create advertisements with word cards.

29. Organize words or sentences into a "Top 40" list based upon popularity. Students can vote which of the sentences used in class seemed the most interesting. This can be done with words, phrases, or imaginary book and song titles.

30. Establish class word banks for different classroom centers, such as science words, number words, weather words, house words, family words.

Suggestions for Stimulating Creative Writing

1. Use magazine pictures to stimulate the imagination. What do you think is happening in this picture?

2. Here are comic strips with the print removed from them. Write your own story about your favorite comic.

3. Here are some newspaper headlines. Pick one and create a story about it.

4. Write about people prominent in the news. An imaginary interview might be appropriate.

5. Look at a mirror and describe what you see.

6. The person I'd like to be. Write about an imaginary person and what he thinks about.

7. Describe yourself. Write about your likes and dislikes. Let other students guess who you are during the sharing period.

8. Write about your latest dream.

9. When I grow up, I'm going to be a ______. Write about the job you'd like to have and why.

10. Describe your favorite animal, either real or imaginary.

11. Make up a tall tale or silly story, one that could not possibly happen.

12. Make up a story about your favorite storybook character or TV personality.

13. Write down your favorite joke. See if other students laugh about it.

14. What would happen if:
    a. The lights went out for a whole day?
    b. Water stopped coming out of the faucet?
    c. No food was available to eat?

15. What would it be like to live in another country? As an Eskimo? In the jungle?

16. What would you do if you were:
    a. Shipwrecked on a deserted island?
    b. In an earthquake?
    c. Caught in a burning building?

17. You are a salesperson. Write about what you would sell to the class.

18. What would it be like to be president?

19. What would it be like to live as a cave man? As a knight? As a spaceman in the future?

20. What would it be like to live on the moon? The sun? Another planet?

21. Write about a time when giraffes had short necks, camels had no humps, elephants had short noses, fish had no fins. What happened to change them?

22. Write a short play that can be acted out by the class. It can be funny, sad, or scary!

23. What would it be like to meet your favorite movie star? Sports hero? The governor of your state?

24. If you had a million dollars, what would you do with it?

25. Write a story about a person who turned out to be different than you thought he or she would be.

26. What is your favorite day? Why?

27. You are going to have a party for your best friend. Write about what you will do.

28. You are going to be a teacher for a day. What will you do?

29. You are traveling in a time machine. Where did you end up in time? The past or future? What are the people like there?

30. Make up your own title for a story and write about it. Make it silly like:
    a. The Green Gorilla
    b. The Singing Dog

c. The Runaway Orange Juice
d. Fun on a Sponge
e. The Day the Socks Became Angry
f. The Frightened Hamburger

31. You are the oldest person on earth. Write about your life.

32. Write about your favorite place. A vacation spot? A day at the beach?

33. Write about your dream house.

34. You have just created a new invention. What is it? Tell how it will help people.

35. Take your favorite story and write a new ending.

36. Write a story about your favorite movie or TV show.

37. Make up an imaginary word and write a definition for it.

38. You have just written a new book. What is it about?

39. What would it be like if:

    a. Trees could talk?
    b. All people turned orange?
    c. The sky became green?
    d. The sun went out?

40. A Martian lands in your backyard. What will you do? What is the Martian like?

41. Write to friends in another country, telling them about this country.

42. You are a fork (chair; magazine; flower). Tell me about a day in your life.

43. What would it be like without a mother or father? Without any brothers or sisters?

44. What would it be like if you met God?

45. You have a chance to spend a day with your favorite historical character. Who will it be? Write a story about your adventures.

46. What is your favorite smell? Why? Write a story telling others why they would like it, too.

47. What would it be like to visit the Empire State Building? The Grand Canyon? The Eiffel Tower?

48. What would it be like to be the only boy or girl in the whole world?

49. You are stuck in an elevator (lost in a cave; lost in the jungle). What will you do?

50. The world will blow up in one week. How are you going to prepare for it? What will you do during this week?

Suggestions for Book Making

There are four phases to book making:

I. Proofreading
II. Preparation for publication
III. Constructing the book
IV. Distributing the book

I. Proofreading
Before material is ready for publication, it needs proofreading by the author(s) and other students. The following steps are suggested.

1. Author proofs own material.
2. Author checks material with another student.
3. Author presents proofed draft to either a designated editor or editorial committee.
4. Editors proof material by reading it several times. They assess the following:
   a. Complete and meaningful sentences
   b. Organization across sentences
   c. Paragraphs
   d. Punctuation
   e. Spelling
   f. Format
5. Editors suggest revisions. If revisions are minor, the material is forwarded for preparation for publication. If several revisions are suggested, the editors return the manuscript to the author for further development.

II. Preparation for Publication

Before the material is bound, it is prepared for publication. This involves the following:

1. The manuscript is checked for a title page and the possible addition of a table of contents and illustrations.
2. A manuscript has chapters or various sections, and these may be marked; a table of contents may be used. When illustrations are to be added, events, moods, and characters are selected for illustration.
3. The number of copies to be made is designated. Certain manuscripts may be released in multiple (duplicated) copies.
4. The manuscript is organized by pages, leaving spaces for illustrations, allowing for a blank page front and back, and allowing for binding of the book.
5. The manuscript is either written or typed in final form and may be duplicated.

III. Constructing the Book

Constructing and binding the book is completed using the following steps:

1. Two pieces of cardboard are cut ¼-inch larger on all sides than the pages of the book.
2. The cardboard is laid side by side on the book cover material. Wallpaper fabric, colored paper, or contact paper can serve as the cover paper.
3. Leave enough space between the cardboard pieces for the manuscript to fit. Cut the cover material one inch larger on all sides than the cardboard laid out. Lightly mark the location of the cardboard on the cover material.
4. Bond the cover material to the cardboard with glue. If desired, press with an iron.
5. Fold over the corners one at a time, glue, and press. Fold top side, glue, and press. Be sure to keep the cardboard and cover material in place.
6. Place book pages in the binding and either sew or tape in the manuscript.
7. Glue and press blank front and back sheets in place on the cardboard.

IV. Distributing the Book

1. Have author catalog the book.
2. Have authors and editors submit a distribution list. This might include the school and class libraries, the teacher, selected other classes, and the principal.
3. Have the authors and editors decide upon publicity. This might involve the preparation of a poster, a review for a class newspaper, or an arranged interview with the author.

Suggestions for Individualized Reading Contracts

Contract

I, ______ agree to read for
30 minutes each day.

	PAGES	*TIME*
M		
T		
W		
Th		
F		

Comments:

Book Contract

Name

Book title and author	*Dates*	*Opinion*

CONTRACT

Checklist	*Indicate Minutes*	*Comments*
Area:	M T W Th F	
Silent reading		
Comprehension		
Vocabulary		
Study skills		
Research		
Listening		
Story writing		
Bookmaking		
Other; specify		

DAILY ASSIGNED ACTIVITIES

Date ____________ Name ____________

Completion of three tasks in each area is required. More can be completed.

	Checked by Teacher
A. Reading	
a. Read silently (book title) ____________	____________
Pages read: ____________	____________
b Book report, poster, review	____________
c. Comprehension activities	____________
Exercise no. ____________	____________
d. Vocabulary activities	____________
Exercise no. ____________	____________
e. Other ____________	____________
B. Writing	____________
a. Write a story.	____________
b. Write a letter to a friend.	____________
c. Write a postcard.	____________
d. Other ____________	____________
C. Research	____________
a. Plan a trip to California.	____________
b. Learn more about California's history.	____________
c. Develop a schedule for preparing and traveling to California.	____________
d. Other ____________	____________

Evaluation:

TIMED AREA CONTRACT

1. Reading: 30 minutes minimum

   Book title:

   Pages read:

   Time ________ to ________ = ________

2. Social Studies: 45 minutes minimum

   Research area:

   Work done:

   Time ________ to ________ = ________

3. Math: 20 minutes minimum

   Exercises done:

   Time ________ to ________ = ________

DAILY LOG

Name Date

	Activity	*Evaluation*
9:00–9:30	________	________
9:30–10:00	________	________
10:00–10:30	________	________
Recess		
11:00–11:30	________	________
11:30–12:00	________	________
Lunch		
1:00–1:30	________	________
1:30–1:45	________	________
Recess		
2:00–2:30	________	________
2:30–3:00	________	________

An Example of an Individualized Theme Contract Dealing with Values and Media

Some commercials state that if you use their product, you will be more beautiful, your work will become easier, your life will be more enjoyable, etc.

Watch 10 commercials. List the product being advertised. Check the "benefits" of using each product.

Product	*Increases Beauty*	*Saves Time*	*Helps Make Friends*	*Lessens Work*	*Makes Life More Comfortable*	*Relieves Pain*
1.						
2.						
3.						
4.						
5.						
6.						
7.						
8.						
9.						
10.						

List three "benefits" stated above that are most often mentioned in T.V. commercials.

____

____

____

Can you tell what a person cares about by the bumper sticker on his or her car?

Sticker	*Value*
Save the Whales	______
If you can read this you are too close	______
Back the Farmers	______
Add others.	______
______	______
______	______
______	______
______	______

Design a bumper sticker with an important message. Make the bumper sticker and put it on your car.

Add a newspaper headline, story heading, or picture to the *Good News Collage.* Do the same for the *Bad News Collage.* For which collage was it easier to find pictures?

______

Why do you think newspapers print more bad news than good news?

______

______

______

______

Write a letter to the editor stating why you think the *Star* or *Citizen* should report more *Good News* to the people of Tucson.

Listen to the top tunes on records or radio. Name your favorite song among the top ten hits.

Title: ______________________________

What is the message of the song?

____

____

____

____

Do you agree with the message?______________________________

______ I like the song because of its lyrics (words).

______ I like the song because of its melody (tune).

What are some of the things the following groups choose to do repeatedly and, therefore, seem to value?

1. Teenagers: ______________________________

____

2. Elderly People: ______________________________

____

3. Teachers: ______________________________

____

4. Musicians: ______________________________

____

5. Hippies: ______________________________

____

Some people use billboards to advertise their message.
Does Kino have a message worth advertising? ______________________________

Investigate the possibility or renting billboard space for one month to advertise our message. Where should our billboard be located?______________________________

(Maybe we should ask a business with a similar message to sponsor this project.)

Graduation Requirements

110. State why you like or dislike a specific sculpture, painting, architecture, etc.

105. Write critiques on several T.V., radio, billboard, newspaper, or magazine advertisements.

114. Find three examples of recorded music that generate three different feelings or emotions. Describe your feelings.

115. Create something of personal value in at least one of the following:
    - photography
    - music
    - art
    - dance

126. Find an object that represents these values: beauty, love, friendship, truth, peace, and equality. State your reasons for choosing each object.

113. Produce and present a multimedia prayer experience for
142. the Kino Community.

Index